ELEVENTH HOUR

Joseph V. Hughes Jr. and Holly O. Hughes
Series on the Presidency and Leadership

James P. Pfiffner, General Editor

A list of titles in this series is available at the end of the book.

Eleventh Hour

THE POLITICS OF POLICY INITIATIVES IN PRESIDENTIAL TRANSITIONS

David M. Shafie

Texas A&M University Press | College Station

First edition
This paper meets the requirements of ANSI/NISO Z39.48–1992 (Permanence of Paper).
Binding materials have been chosen for durability.
♾ ♻

LIBRARY OF CONGRESS CATALOGING-IN-PUBLICATION DATA

Shafie, David M.
Eleventh hour : the politics of policy initiatives in presidential transitions / David M. Shafie. — 1st ed.
pages cm. — (Joseph V. Hughes Jr. and Holly O. Hughes series on the presidency and leadership)
Includes bibliographical references and index.
ISBN 978-1-60344-954-0 (cloth : alk. paper) —
ISBN 978-1-62349-004-1 (e-book)
1. Executive power—United States—Case studies. 2. Administrative procedure—United States. 3. Presidents—United States—Transition periods. 4. United States—Politics and government—1981–1989. 5. United States—Politics and government—1989– I. Title.
JK516.S42 2013
320.60973—dc23
2013008852

This book is dedicated to Carol Shafie

& the memory of Parviz Shafie.

Contents

Abbreviations

APA	Administrative Procedure Act
ANPRM	advance notice of proposed rulemaking
CERCLA	Comprehensive Environmental Response, Compensation, and Liability Act
CRA	Congressional Review Act
DPC	Domestic Policy Council
DQA	Data Quality Act
ESA	Endangered Species Act
FLPMA	Federal Land Policy and Management Act
FMLA	Family and Medical Leave Act
MSHA	Mine Safety and Health Administration
NEPA	Environmental Policy Act
NHTSA	National Highway Traffic Safety Administration
NIOSH	National Institute for Occupational Safety and Health
OIRA	Office of Information and Regulatory Affairs
OMB	Office of Management and Budget
OPM	Office of Personnel Management
OPS	Office of Pipeline Safety
OSHA	Occupational Safety and Health Administration
OSMRE	Office of Surface Mining, Reclamation and Enforcement
RARG	Regulatory Analysis and Review Group
RCRA	Resource Conservation and Recovery Act
SMCRA	Surface Mining Control and Reclamation Act
TSCA	Toxic Substances Control Act

Figures

Table

Acknowledgments

This book would not have been possible without the help of a number of people. Lori Cox Han showed her enthusiasm for this project when it was just the seed of an idea and continued to be an instrumental source of support as it developed. I also wish to thank my research assistants in the Henley Social Science Research Lab at Chapman University: Cassidy Gayner, Sara Juarez, Lauren Pont, and Nicole Tellier.

The librarians and staff of the National Archives at the Jimmy Carter, Ronald Reagan, George H. W. Bush, and William Clinton presidential libraries helped me locate documentary materials and provided other valuable assistance. Portions of this research were supported by a Peter and Edith O'Donnell Grant from the Brent Scowcroft Foundation at Texas A&M University and a pair of institutional grants from Chapman University.

I wish to thank Mary Lenn Dixon, Katie Cowart, Sally Antrobus, and the staff of TAMU Press as well as series editor James Pfiffner for guiding me through the process. I am also grateful for the contributions of anonymous reviewers who provided so much constructive feedback on the draft.

I would like to thank the current and former officials of various federal agencies who took interest in my research and were kind enough to take the time to share their insights and experiences with me.

Ann and Sarah Gordon have my sincere gratitude for reading versions of this manuscript and for their invaluable criticism. Finally, I want to thank Tara for accepting and understanding why her dad was preoccupied for so many months. You're a great kid!

ELEVENTH HOUR

Introduction

On a chilly January morning in 2001, Bill Clinton was outside the National Arboretum near the Capitol Building, publicly reflecting on the environmental legacy of his presidency. The soon-to-be ex-president made few specific references to past accomplishments, focusing instead on what his administration was still doing. Clinton took the opportunity to announce newly adopted EPA rules for diesel engine emissions and boasted about the twelve national monuments he had recently created or expanded: "We have saved and restored some of our most glorious natural wonders, from Florida's Everglades to Hawaii's coral reefs, from the redwoods of California to the red rock canyons of Utah."[1] He had no intention of slowing down during his two remaining weeks in office. There would be eight more national monuments and new proposed rules for food safety, energy conservation, and drinking water contamination.[2]

The centerpiece of Clinton's speech was his announcement of a ban on building new roads in roadless areas of national forests. Acting under a presidential directive, the US Forest Service had spent the previous year conducting a review that produced a plan to preserve nearly 60 million acres. "Today we free the lands so that they will remain unspoiled by bulldozers, undisturbed by chainsaws, and untouched for our children," he told the audience.[3] As expected, oil, gas, and timber interests fumed at what a typical news report called Clinton's "aggressive campaign during his final weeks in office to hamstring President-elect George W. Bush as an environmental policy-maker before the Texas governor takes power."[4] Republicans were powerless to stop the frenetic lame duck activism, even though they had just retained control of Congress in the November election, and their party was preparing to occupy the White House again after an eight-year hiatus.

The timing became a rallying point for critics of the rule's opponents. The chair of the House Natural Resources Committee called the roadless policy "last-minute manipulation and grandstanding by a man desperate for a legacy."[5] Focusing on the "last-minute" nature of the final rules and proposals, critics suggested that they were pushed through because they lacked popular support. In his speech at the National Arboretum, Clinton already had an answer to this objection. He defended the roadless rule by pointing to the 1.5 million comments in support of the proposal, arguing that "more Americans were involved in shaping this policy than any land preservation initiative in the history of the republic."[6] From Clinton's perspective, executive action was justified because of congressional inaction.

This book explores the strategic considerations behind rulemaking as a form of policy entrenchment by lame duck presidents. A feature of transitions since 1980, eleventh-hour rulemaking is a consequence of increased policy activism by presidents, who have strong incentives to centralize and expand their control over the executive branch.[7] Because of deadlocked politics over social regulation (such as health, safety, and environmental protection) significant policy change is more often the result of presidential leadership and bureaucratic discretion than of legislation. In certain policy areas, such as natural resources, rulemaking has become the dominant form of conflict resolution.[8] In the case of forest management, a policy stalemate persisted for decades. After passing the Wilderness Act of 1964, Congress resisted demands to protect additional land by declaring wilderness areas. All the while, it imposed high timber quotas on the US Forest Service without increasing its budget for road maintenance. Under pressure from all sides, the Forest Service was in an economically and environmentally unsustainable situation.[9] In the absence of reform, which only Congress can deliver, Clinton exploited a window of opportunity at the end of his second term to break the stalemate.

Clinton used the rulemaking process to enact a significant number of policy changes that his successor opposed, from pollution standards to regulations protecting the confidentiality of patient medical records and rules requiring government contractors to disclose violations of employment laws. Since regulations are not laws, these would appear to be fleeting accomplishments, because the next president could try to rescind or modify them. However, these end-of-term initiatives are more than just a nuisance for the incoming administration. As I argue in this book, executive policymaking during transitions has lasting consequences. The popular notion of a "midnight regulation" refers to any rule completed near the end of a president's term. The phrase is a misnomer, however, inasmuch as it implies a hasty and capricious decision, more likely motivated by political factors as opposed to measured scientific or legal judgments. Any rule created with such disregard for procedure is unlikely to withstand the scrutiny of regulatory review, let alone judicial review.

There are strategic considerations behind successful eleventh-hour rulemaking. Planning must begin well in advance of the president's final year in office. The stages of the rulemaking process, as required by the Administrative Procedure Act, must be satisfied in order for the rule to withstand legal challenges.

And eleventh-hour rulemaking requires careful consideration of the political environment. If rules are popular with the public or influential interest groups, the incoming administration will have a more difficult time reversing them. Likewise, if Congress perceives the rules as popular, this can also be a deterrent for rescission. In this sense a true "midnight" rule is unlikely because it might not withstand reversal by the incoming president, Congress, or the courts.

To explain the evolution of the eleventh-hour strategy better, this volume features five cases representing the most recent examples of presidential transitions; and most relevant to today's political climate. These particular cases also offer variance on key independent variables: the two Democrats used the interregnum period as an opportunity to initiate new regulations, whereas the three Republicans mainly used last-minute rules for deregulation. Three of the outgoing presidents had served two full terms, whereas one-term presidents Carter and George H. W. Bush faced the pressures of unfulfilled demands and unfinished agendas after losing their reelection bids. Finally, one case represents a transition between two presidents of the same party, although it was a conservative Republican (Reagan) who was succeeded by a more moderate Republican (George H. W. Bush).

Plan of the Book

The first chapter discusses the politics of executive policymaking. Even though the executive branch is granted a limited policy role under the Constitution, that role is expanding as presidents have exercised their influence over the executive bureaucracy. This section considers the incentives for outgoing presidents to turn to rulemaking as a method of policy entrenchment as well as the options for incoming presidents seeking to reverse the late-term policy initiatives of their predecessors. Due to the constraints they face, late-term policy initiatives are remarkably durable.

The institutionalization of the domestic presidency is discussed in chapter 2. The chapter reviews the history of presidential domestic policy leadership, with particular attention to the Nixon Administration's centralization of policy within the White House staff. This represented a sharp break with the Johnson Administration's approach of coordinating with the heads of executive departments. The section proceeds to describe the evolution of domestic policy management in the Ford and Carter administrations. I argue that the regulatory policies of the 1970s contributed to deadlocked politics, which elevated the importance of presidential administration. Because of the cyclical pattern of the presidency, there are regular and predictable opportunities to influence policy at the end of the term as well as in the first hundred days.

The discussion of presidential administration is followed by an overview of late-term rulemaking since the Carter-Reagan transition. Over time, departing presidents have expanded their use of rulemaking, executive orders, and proclamations to entrench their domestic policies. As the chapter illustrates, there has been a sharp increase in the use of end-of-term rulemaking, especially from Bill Clinton and George W. Bush.

Chapter 3 provides the first of five case studies of administrative policymaking that accompanied the most recent White House transitions. The weeks in between the 1980 election of President Reagan and his inauguration in January 1981 are significant because the defeated incumbent party used the opportunity to enact a broad policy agenda that the winning party opposed. Democrats passed major legislation on energy, pollution, and public land conservation following their loss of the White House and the Senate. The regulatory actions at the end of Carter's term also had lasting implications. Federal agencies had been working to implement policies regarding the environment, energy, consumer protection, health, and safety, which the Reagan team opposed. Working overtime, the Carter Administration in its last three months added more than twelve thousand pages to the *Federal Register*. From Reagan's perspective, every rule adopted before the transition limited his discretion to shape policy in his own way. Even worse, they were adopted in defiance of the Reagan agenda that the voters had endorsed in the election.

Chapter 4 considers the lone example of an intraparty transition. Even though his designated successor Vice President George H. W. Bush won the election, several administrative actions were used prior to the transition to retrench the Reagan Administration's policy preferences on the environment, health, and safety. The Reagan-Bush transition differs in one other important way. Each of the interparty transitions in this study featured a surge in the quantity of final rules during the departing president's last quarter. There was no increase in the volume of economically significant rules at the end of Reagan's term; however, several controversial rule changes were proposed. The administration attempted to loosen restrictions on meat inspection and strip mining as well as to grant licenses to nuclear power plants immediately after the 1988 election took place.

Chapter 5 examines the policy initiatives at the end of George H. W. Bush's single term. Not only was there a sharp increase in new rules during the ninety days before Bush was succeeded by Bill Clinton, but economically significant rules were finalized in greater numbers than during the last quarter of any recent president. Paradoxically, deregulation was a consistent theme throughout Bush's presidency, and many of his midnight rules were used to relax and weaken existing regulations. After campaigning on a platform of continuing

Reagan's policies, Bush had established the Council on Competitiveness, chaired by Vice President Quayle, to promote regulatory relief. The final weeks of the Bush Administration featured a last-ditch effort to act upon some of the council's recommendations. More economically significant regulations were issued by federal agencies at the end than during any three-month period in his entire term.

Chapter 6 details the prolific rulemaking by the outgoing Clinton Administration. Clinton took the initiative on a handful of high-profile issues and used the administrative process to make lasting policy changes, sometimes in open defiance of Congress. His willingness to be identified with these policy initiatives stands in contrast to the subtle, under-the-radar initiatives of his predecessor and successor. Like the ban on road building in roadless areas of national forests, many of these initiatives were cheered by environmentalists and bitterly opposed by industry, including new restrictions on hardrock mining on public lands and snowmobiles in Yellowstone National Park.

The final case study, of the transition from Bush to Obama, shows how the evolving eleventh-hour rulemaking strategy came to fruition. As chapter 7 explains, Bush made extensive use of the administrative process to advance domestic policy goals throughout his presidency, despite the presence of Republican majorities in both houses of Congress for most of those years. However, agencies completed more rulemaking at the end of 2008 than at any other time during his presidency. These included rules to waive some requirements of the Endangered Species Act and to relax restrictions on mountaintop removal mining in Appalachian valleys, which took effect in time to preclude the successor administration from overturning them. Nearly as many economically significant rules were promulgated at the end of the Bush presidency as in the final months of Clinton's term. Bush largely avoided the charge of "midnight" rules by letting more of them take effect before November.

The concluding chapter discusses the evolution of eleventh-hour rulemaking as a strategy for policy entrenchment. The five transitions document its development into a sophisticated process of advancing domestic policy priorities by promulgating rules resistant to reversal. Finally, I explain why the continued use of this strategy should be expected, given the paradox that modern presidents face.[10] They have limited means to deliver upon their promises amid deadlocked domestic policies. Therefore, looking forward to the future, it is likely that presidents will continue to rely on unilateral instruments when legislative options are unavailable or politically infeasible. From mining regulation to public land conservation to workplace safety and beyond, in most cases, these policies were resistant to reversal by the incoming administration. There are reasons to expect late rulemaking to occur with greater frequency in the future.

1 | Political Cycles and the President's Agenda

The days that followed the historic election of Barack Obama in 2008 as the forty-fourth president were filled with heady celebration as well as uncertainty. From the election until Inauguration Day, the national imagination was focused on the president-elect and his ideas to rescue the economy and end two wars, even though another ten weeks remained in the presidency of George W. Bush. Scarcely noticed were more than thirty major last-minute policy changes that were moving through the regulatory process. The outgoing administration was extremely busy during those weeks, and much of this activity had nothing to do with national security or the unfolding financial crisis.

Prior to handing the executive branch over to the Democrats, the Bush Administration followed through with policy initiatives that had been in the works since it had come into office eight years earlier. In 2001 Vice President Richard Cheney convened an advisory committee to develop an energy policy agenda for the new administration. White House officials received input from a number of advisory panels as they settled in and established their priorities, but the energy task force was noteworthy for its degree of influence and the breadth of its recommendations.[1] In response, the White House supported legislation to encourage natural gas drilling and oil exploration in the Arctic National Wildlife Refuge, among other proposals. A top priority of the coal industry was to repeal regulations prohibiting deposits of mine waste within one hundred feet of rivers and streams, which restricted how and where mountaintop removal mining could be conducted. Rather than pursue the difficult task of changing the two-decade-old surface mining law to expand mountaintop removal mining, the administration opted for a less conspicuous strategy. The policy was addressed through the administrative process.

In April 2001, the very same month that the task force was formulating the National Energy Strategy, heavy spring rains began to fall in West Virginia. Before long the southern part of the state experienced a series of devastating floods. Hillsides denuded of trees and topsoil easily gave way, sending torrents of water and mud through small communities along the Upper Big Coal River, the New River, and their tributaries. "Streams normally only inches deep became torrents 20 to 25 feet high," the *Charleston Gazette* reported. "A propane tank from a store in Fayetteville near the New River was pushed 60 miles downstream into a floating pile of debris at the London Locks and Dams. Homes, cars, buses, even caskets, were floating. Highways and hollows became whitewater rivers."[2] Flash flooding continued intermittently for ten weeks. When the worst was over in July, five people had been killed, more than fifteen hundred homes had been destroyed, and residents of the devastated communities focused their rage upon the two companies that were engaged in mountaintop removal mining upstream, Arch Coal and AEI.[3] Angry residents also demanded answers from state regulators who approved the mining permits but failed to cite the operators for violations of waste containment rules until after the floods.

Mountaintop removal mining was already unpopular in the region, and rolling back regulations on the practice after the catastrophe should have been unthinkable. However, this is just what the Bush Administration was planning. The coal industry used its access to press for rule changes that would further relax restrictions on mountaintop removal mining. Coal operators finally got what they wanted after the election of 2008, in the form of a new Department of Interior rule that exempted valley fills from the hundred-foot buffer requirement. Other initiatives taken by the outgoing administration exempted entire industries from the Clean Water Act and rolled back requirements of the Endangered Species Act. By listing the final rule before the end of December 2008, the Bush Administration avoided the mistakes of the Clinton Administration, as well as that of Bush's father, and made the rule extremely difficult for the incoming administration to reverse. The rules were delayed until very late in Bush's second term, but they took effect in time to prevent the Obama Administration from overturning them unilaterally.

Late-term rulemaking became routine and predictable because of the cyclical nature of presidential politics. In contrast with the beginning of a president's term, when there are few incentives for unilateral policymaking, the costs are considerably lower in the final months. Consequently, presidential transitions are preceded by surges in rulemaking, as outgoing administrations initiate last-minute policy changes. As was the case with the mountaintop removal mining controversy, much of this late-term activity affects policy on the environment, occupational health, and safety, areas in which entrenched interests, public opinion, and ideological divisions along partisan lines would require presidents to spend considerable political capital.

"Midnight" Regulation and Executive Power

Mountaintop removal mining is just one example of the evolving strategy of entrenching policy through administrative rulemaking. Congress was reluctant to clarify problems with the Surface Mining Control and Reclamation Act of 1977, giving the executive branch the opportunity to solidify its own interpretation. "That's the nature of legislation," said an official responsible for implementing the law. "In order to get it passed, you have to include a lot of ambiguous language."[4] In the absence of reform, which only Congress can deliver, lingering issues with the law were left to the executive branch to settle in the form of rulemaking.[5] Consequently, surface mining policy reverses direction like a political football when control of the White House changes.

The largest number of rules finalized in the concluding weeks of the Bush Administration concerned environmental, health, and safety policy. A prime example, surface mining deregulation had been sought by the coal industry as early as the 2000 campaign, and it was part of the president's agenda as soon as Vice President Cheney's energy task force convened in 2001. A president's preference for unilateral action over the more traditional approach of working with Congress is not so puzzling when one considers the advantages of interregnum rulemaking as an instrument of presidential power.

Recent research has confirmed the pattern of regular increases in policymaking activity during the final weeks of recent presidential administrations.[6] Rulemaking, in particular, has emerged as an important way presidents continue to deliver on their campaign promises before leaving office, even in the absence of a supportive Congress. The phenomenon originated in the weeks that followed the 1980 election, when agencies rushed to finalize regulations before the inauguration of Ronald Reagan. These were labeled "midnight" regulations by Bush's father, then Vice President George H. W. Bush, acting as Reagan's point man on regulatory relief. It was an allusion to the "midnight judges" appointed by outgoing President John Adams, in a bid to discredit the rules and ultimately overturn them. Invoking that episode raised the specter of the abuse of unaccountable executive power, much like the modern phenomenon of agency burrowing.[7] Twelve years after criticizing Carter's last-minute regulatory activity, the senior Bush and his administration issued their own flood of final rules after losing the election to Bill Clinton. That transition also featured the famous "midnight pardons" that Bush issued to members of his administration who were implicated in the Iran-Contra Scandal.[8]

A conventional way to conceive of presidential power has long been the "power to persuade," since Richard Neustadt first posited the presidency as essentially weak and exercising policy leadership by influencing the other branches of government.[9] This perspective underestimates the value of prerogative powers, which presidents can use to enact policy independently. Rather than merely being an alternative to presidential bargaining, unilateral action is often a more attractive strategy for presidents to assert leadership and enact their policy preferences. A substantial literature has emerged to explain when and why presidents prefer to bypass legislation in favor of executive policymaking.[10] Persuasive presidents are effective, but persuasion is not necessary when presidents use the resources of the executive branch to make policy unilaterally.

The strategic use of unilateral action became an important instrument of the modern presidency when President Carter issued last-minute rules that frustrated the incoming Reagan Administration in 1980. As the example of the surface mining rule shows, presidents are able to bypass Congress and—often quietly and under the radar—initiate significant policy changes unilaterally by using the authority delegated to the executive branch via existing statutes. Agencies may be better situated to use their discretion to make decisions by applying their expertise to particular circumstances and to respond quickly to crises. Congress cannot act as quickly, particularly in the areas of environmental policy, health, and safety regulations, because of the gridlock that is often the consequence of partisan divisions and interest group influence. The executive branch has an advantage over Congress in its ability to take unilateral action to change policy quickly, and this has become an increasingly popular strategy for outgoing administrations to entrench their policy preferences and limit the prerogatives of their successors.

The cyclical nature of the presidency and shifting political forces impede as well as facilitate domestic policy leadership. The determination of presidents to show accomplishments in their first hundred days is well established. Enacting a legislative agenda early is critical because presidential influence declines as the political cycle progresses, and there is no guarantee that Congress will ever be as willing to cooperate. The end of the term is one other predictable point in the political cycle where presidents have an opportunity to affect policy. Lame duck presidents use this window to make significant changes while avoiding the scrutiny they would otherwise face.

Two changes in the institution have augmented the policymaking capacity of the White House. One is the institutionalization of the domestic presidency in the Nixon years. The second is the centralized system of executive policymaking that began when the Reagan Administration consolidated its leadership of the bureaucracy. These innovations contribute to the frequency of eleventh-hour policymaking because modern presidents have greater means to pursue policy goals independent of legislative branch.

Domestic Policy Leadership

An elaborate structure has evolved within the executive branch for the purpose of managing the president's policy agenda. The entities that comprise the White House policy establishment routinely develop policy proposals and advocate for each president's priorities.[11] The Office of Management and Budget (OMB), established during the Nixon years to replace the Bureau of the Budget, would later become a central policy actor during the Reagan years. Concerned that the civil service employees of the federal bureaucracy might undermine his plans, Nixon created his own parallel policy structure in the form of the cabinet-level Office of Policy Development (OPD) and the Office of Assistant to the President for Domestic Policy. Nixon was able to exploit this permanent domestic policy presence in the White House to centralize agency activities for the benefit of his administrative presidency.[12]

Carter expanded presidential control over administration, even though his own presidency began with a well-intended return to cabinet government. Taking office with fresh memories of the Nixon White House, Carter was eager to build trust by reassuring the public that the White House staff would not be allowed to usurp the authority of cabinet officers.[13] At first, cabinet secretaries were empowered to set the agendas and fill subcabinet leadership posts, but Carter's enthusiasm for cabinet government cooled.[14] By the end of his term, the White House increased coordination over such critical areas as energy, conservation, and economic policy; ordered agencies to perform regulatory analyses of their proposed rules; and established the Regulatory Analysis and Review Group to oversee the agency reviews. Furthermore, Carter supported government reform legislation that hastened the demise of cabinet government by expanding the number of political appointees serving in the bureaucracy, rendering policymaking much easier for those staff departments with managers whose loyalties are with the president as opposed to the cabinet secretary. This midterm about-face and subsequent weakening of cabinet government began a recentralization of policymaking completely in the White House, although the man who defeated him in his bid for reelection became the first to enjoy the advantages of this enhanced appointment power.

Domestic policymaking was further centralized when Reagan assumed the presidency in 1981. The OMB was given the responsibility for guiding agency initiatives and ensuring that they were consistent with the administration's priorities. However, the Reagan White House was less willing than its predecessor to trust agencies to conduct their economic analysis. Rather, a system of regulatory review was created within the Executive Office of the President to reflect the preferences of the president.[15] Under Reagan, the OPD assumed greater responsibility for coordinating agency activities and agendas. None of Reagan's successors reversed this centralization. The one significant change to this structure was a 1993 Clinton Administration reorganization that split OPD into the Domestic Policy Council (DPC) and the National Economic Council, which inherited the office's economic policy responsibilities.[16] In subsequent administrations the DPC continued to be the principal organization that communicates the president's domestic priorities to Congress and coordinates policy across federal agencies.

Newly elected presidents are expected to propose a policy agenda without delay. There is always pressure to deliver on major promises during the first year, if not in the intensive dealings with Congress during the crucial first hundred days, because deferred agenda items are more likely to stall. Typically, presidents assume office with a domestic agenda outlined during the campaign, and the White House policy establishment develops proposals and communicates the president's priorities to Congress.[17] Since the window of opportunity may close before the administration is fully staffed, it is essential to have the leadership of these policy, support, and political offices in place in order to "hit the ground running."[18] The success of the president's legislative agenda depends largely upon how quickly these critical tasks are accomplished, because the likelihood of cooperation decreases as the political cycle progresses.

These initial staffing choices are also essential for the president in order to take control of the bureaucracy and the budget.[19] Prompt action on the budget is essential because the new president has only about sixty days to propose changes to the outgoing administration's lame duck budget, which takes effect in October. Of the 14 million employees of the federal bureaucracy, only about five hundred top agency officials are nominated by the president and subject to Senate confirmation. Even those at other levels of the bureaucracy have significant power to integrate the president's priorities into their agency plans—as well as having leverage to undermine them. In addition, the president depends upon agencies to coordinate with one another, since fragmentation is a feature of many domestic policy areas. That is, responsibility is shared between several different agencies and departments. The experience of recent presidencies has shown that the bureaucracy can be enlisted to affect policy change if leadership is established early and accommodates the career civil service, whereas ambitious reorganization attempts can delay the implementation of the president's agenda.

New presidents enjoy a honeymoon period of approximately one hundred days, in which they typically enjoy high popularity ratings and good relations with Congress (as was the case from the coining of the phrase with the

Roosevelt Administration on). Therefore presidents have a strong incentive to develop and advance a policy agenda before an inevitable decline in influence over Congress. As Bill Clinton discovered in 1993, post-inaugural popularity may not translate into leverage with Congress. Chapter 6 details the setback Clinton encountered with mining reform, which prompted his attempt to change policy through the administrative process after legislation stalled in the Senate. Moreover, a president cannot expect that a string of legislative victories out of the starting gate will lead to future successes.[20] The typical pattern is a "cycle of decreasing influence," marked by a several-month-long decline in popularity and by losses for the president's party in the following midterm elections.[21]

There is risk in using the administrative process to advance policy priorities too early. Presidents are constrained by the need to sustain majority coalitions in Congress and the electorate, avoiding decisions that could potentially alienate the median voter. This creates an incentive to downplay and delay divisive unilateral actions until these no longer jeopardize their own reelection or their party's prospects. At the beginning of the cycle and prior to midterm elections, the cautious approach to controversial rules cultivates a good relationship with members of Congress and voters. These factors help explain why there are fewer rules beginning the notice-and-comment process during a president's first year than in later years.[22] Furthermore, unilateral policy action that defies the will of Congress at the beginning of the term jeopardizes future cooperation on legislation. It may even provoke Congress into enacting legislation to overturn the president's order, as President George W. Bush experienced in 2001 when the EPA pulled back standards for arsenic in drinking water promulgated by the Clinton Administration. At the end of a president's term, this line may be crossed with fewer repercussions.

Another constraint that limits unilateral action on the domestic agenda throughout the political cycle is finite agenda space. As new priorities inevitably crowd the institutional domestic agenda, presidents are more likely to react to issues that emerge from external sources.[23] Presidents become preoccupied with foreign and economic policy, further restricting the resources the White House can devote to its initial domestic policy agenda. As the term progresses, new issues are forced onto the agenda by circumstances often beyond the president's control. The public and the election cycle largely determine which emerging problems will receive the president's attention.[24] Institutional sources, such as the White House policy establishment and the congressional agenda, have little influence by comparison.

Ensuring a Policy Legacy

Democrats and Republicans alike have used last-minute rulemaking to entrench their policy preferences and tie the hands of their successors. The late-term actions by antiregulatory presidents such as George W. Bush show how routine the practice had become. Of the unilateral instruments available to presidents, regulations have the most potential for lasting consequences. Unless Congress intervenes or the courts do so, the only way an incoming administration can reverse a final rule is by beginning anew.[25]

It is unusual to commit agency resources toward a second rulemaking so soon after completing the initial one, and the cost to undertake a new rulemaking can be prohibitive, depending on the rule.[26] Susan Dudley, the director of the Office of Information and Regulatory Affairs in the White House of George W. Bush, believes rules are the most prone to abuse because they are difficult to reverse. "They can't just be reversed by an incoming president like an executive order or a proclamation. You have to go through a whole new rulemaking process."[27] For incoming presidents with policy agendas of their own, the opportunity cost of undoing midnight rules can be unacceptable.

The "worst case" of entrenchment, according to Nina Mendelson, is "one undertaken with an awareness not only that the President just elected would choose to do something different but that the outgoing administration's actions are likely to hinder the President-elect's implementation" of goals.[28] As the following chapters demonstrate, late-term rulemaking as a political strategy has become more powerful but also more problematic over time. Observers have debated whether the phenomenon represents a normal instrument of the policy process or a form of partisan mischief.[29] The latter view frames news media coverage of presidential transitions. One of the headlines that appeared in the weeks between Election Day, 2008, and Inauguration Day, 2009, was "White House Pushes through a Flurry of Rule Changes Sought by Business."[30] Another was "Bush Administration Pushes Their Final Environment and Energy Policies."[31] From this perspective, interregnum rulemaking is a form of scorched-earth policymaking that does more to stymie the incoming president than to advance the policies of the outgoing one. Either way, the constraints of the modern presidency present advantages for presidents who hold certain policy initiatives in reserve until the very end of their time in office.

Interregnum Administration

Lame duck presidents are politically weak, with few opportunities to make decisions of lasting consequence if they lack leverage over Congress. It is safer politically to exercise leadership on foreign policy than to pursue ambitious domestic policy goals. Since presidents normally dominate foreign policy, they are less likely to be challenged by Congress over decisions in the interregnum period. Paradoxically, the interregnum presidency was strengthened with ratification of the Twentieth Amendment, which shortened the period before Inauguration Day. Robert Klotz argues the administration is subject to comparatively little oversight because Congress is out of session for most of the duration.[32] In matters of domestic policy, the incumbent can have the most impact through administrative action because it does not require coalition building. Through the skillful application of administrative action, Presidents Carter and Clinton accomplished at least as much during their last hundred days in office as in their first hundred days.[33]

Many, if not most, of these late-term policy actions are minor, motivated by a desire to finish business that began under their watch.[34] Nonetheless, transitions present optimal circumstances for interest groups with access to the executive leadership to advocate for favorable policy changes. Because the incoming president is the focus of media coverage, the activities of the lame duck administration receive far less scrutiny.[35] Unilateral policy decisions made by outgoing administrations have lasting consequences because changing them would require the incoming president to devote scarce institutional resources and political capital to this.

Thus William Howell and Kenneth Mayer distinguish between late-term actions that are consistent with the president's program and those that deviate from prior actions. If the president's party is defeated in the November election, unilateral policy instruments may be employed to entrench policies without fear of retribution.[36] There are few permanent actions a president can exercise completely within the eleven-week interregnum. Administrative rulemaking is appealing because once in effect, rules are resistant to unilateral reversal. It is also problematic because any significant rulemaking requires more time than the interregnum permits. These actions must be planned well before the president's successor is determined.

The cost of unilateral action at the beginning of a term is prohibitive because it could alienate potential allies in Congress. An incoming president who acts unilaterally to overturn midnight regulations potentially places the agenda at risk. Jason Loring and Liam Roth examined the fate of the multitude of final rules listed during the final weeks before Bill Clinton and his predecessor George H. W. Bush left office, finding that Clinton was more assertive in withdrawing new rules than George W. Bush was in reversing Clinton's own rules.[37] This leads Loring and Roth to conclude that it is easier for incoming presidents to reverse last-minute deregulatory actions than for antiregulatory presidents to reverse regulatory actions. Such was the Reagan Administration's dilemma in 1981, when it was forced to respond to Jimmy Carter's lame duck policy initiatives.

The transition that followed the election of 1980 represented the first time that an outgoing administration had enacted a policy agenda with such a broad scope at the end of its term. After losing his reelection bid to Reagan, President Carter and a lame duck Congress moved quickly to protect the Arctic National Wildlife Reserve and enacted the Superfund law, the last (and most expensive) of the major pollution statutes of the "environmental decade." Out of the spotlight, yet equally significant, was the rush by the Occupational Safety and Health Administration (OSHA) to finalize new regulations on lead exposure and workplace noise and several other rules. The regulations received far less attention, but the combined total of all of the administration's actions in its last three months added more than 12,000 pages to the *Federal Register*, a record that stood until the Clinton Administration added more than 26,500 pages during the equivalent period.[38]

The last-minute rules derided by the incoming Reagan Administration had been under development for some time. Federal agencies had been laboring separately under legislative mandates to implement policies regarding the environment, energy, consumer protection, health, and safety. The regulatory agendas of those agencies had been established much earlier, with minimal White House involvement. Ironically, the one aspect of regulatory policy in which the White House took the strongest interest was regulatory review. Carter used structures within the executive office of the White House to impose discipline on the regulatory process and to scrutinize rulemaking. This had the effect of delaying new regulations at the end of his term, making them vulnerable to reversal by the incoming Reagan Administration.

Reagan's major contribution to the midnight regulation phenomenon is the procedure he established to centralize, monitor, and review regulations. Initially he raised public awareness of the proliferation of regulations through the review he imposed upon Carter's last-minute rules. Furthermore, his directives for cost-benefit analysis and OMB clearance for new rules drastically increased the scrutiny of rulemaking by outgoing administrations, including his own. In the lone example of an intraparty transition, the departing Reagan Administration issued a comparatively small number of rules. Nonetheless, Reagan

Figure 1.1
OIRA Review Counts, by Quarter
Economically Significant Rules, 1982–1992

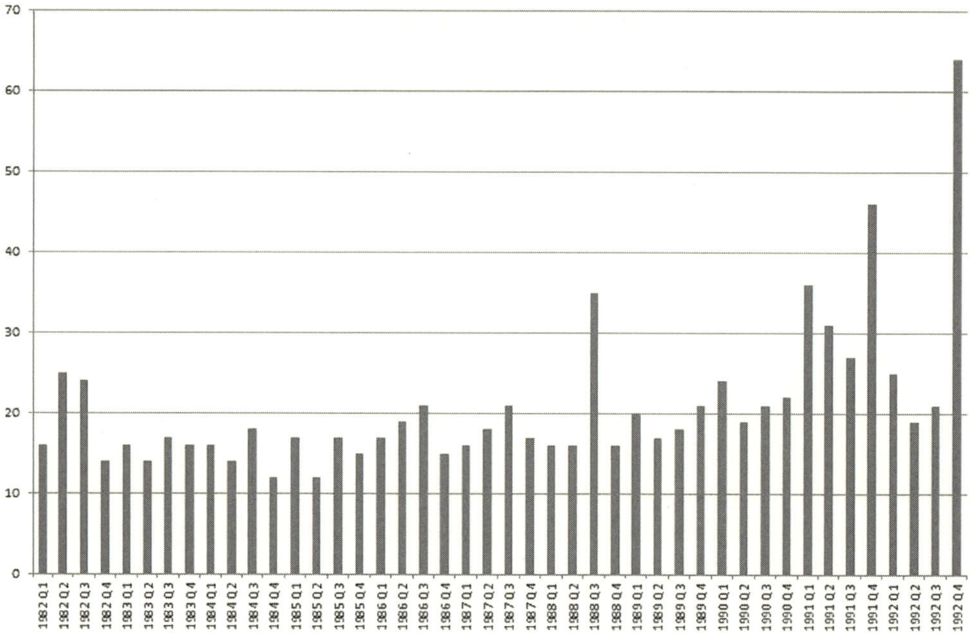

used various last-minute administrative actions to retrench his own policies. Throughout his presidency Reagan used the tools available to him as chief executive to propel his own agenda of deregulation. From his appointments of loyalists to leadership positions in the bureaucracy to the use of OMB to micromanage policy, Reagan came to personify the administrative presidency. Fewer rules were promulgated at the end of Reagan's presidency than during the transition from Bush to Clinton, as illustrated in regulatory review counts in figure 1.1.[39]

Even though most of the Reagan Administration's deregulation agenda was accomplished very early in the presidency, new rules to weaken key environmental, health, and safety laws further were proposed as late as November of 1988. By then it had become clear that Reagan would be succeeded by George H. W. Bush, another Republican and his own vice president. Figure 1.1 shows the frequency with which economically significant rules were under review in each quarter of every year from 1982 until the final quarter of the Bush Administration in 1992.[40] Unlike the interparty transitions that came after the Reagan years, there is no evidence of a surge in the volume of late-term rulemaking in the final quarter of 1988. In contrast, there was a sharp increase in economically significant rules during the ninety days before George H. W. Bush was succeeded by Bill Clinton.

As the single term of George H. W. Bush wound down, there was a steep increase in new rules affecting multiple areas of domestic policy. His administration has the distinction of promulgating forty-one economically significant new rules in its last three months. More economically significant rules were finalized during the last quarter of his final year as president than by any other recent president. This was nearly two-thirds of all the economically significant regulations issued by federal agencies during the entire four-year term. Deregulation was a consistent theme throughout his presidency, and some of the policy initiatives at the end of his term were promoted by the White House Council on Competitiveness, chaired by Vice President Quayle, to promote regulatory relief.

The surge in rulemaking that occurred at the end of Bush's term is distinct from the rest of the cases for another reason. The majority of those rules were promulgated under legislative mandate. Furthermore, they were mandated to implement civil rights, consumer protection, and environmental laws that

Figure 1.2
OIRA Review Counts, by Quarter
Economically Significant Rules, 1993–2000

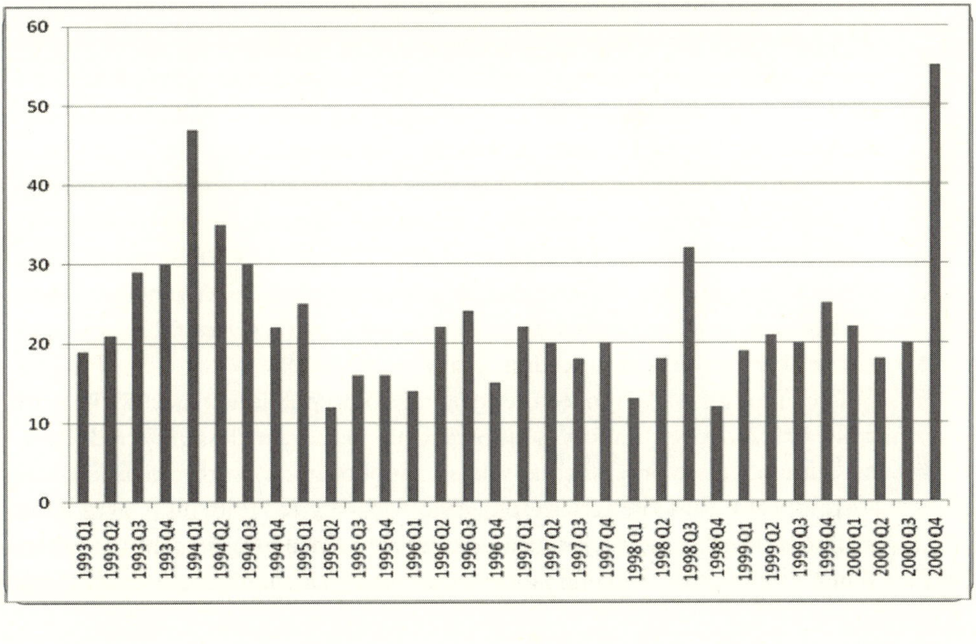

Bush championed earlier in his presidency, including the Clean Air Act Amendments, the Waste Reduction Act, and the Americans with Disabilities Act, all passed in 1990. Not surprisingly, the EPA supplied the plurality of final rules adopted during the administration's final weeks. Due to the requirements of these statutes, the last-minute surge of rules at the end of Bush's term consisted of mandatory rather than discretionary rules.

The final rules at the conclusion of Bill Clinton's presidency represented a more coherent program than that of any of his predecessors. Compared to the mixture of regulatory and deregulatory initiatives of the Bush Administration following the 1992 election, the Clinton Administration used administrative rulemaking to advance liberal policy objectives that congressional Republicans had thwarted for years. Clinton came to rely on unilateral policy instruments to advance his domestic agenda after the defeat of his health care reform proposal and the Democrats' loss of their congressional majority in 1994. To avoid partisan battles with Republicans, Clinton relied on administrative strategies such as executive orders and signing statements.

For much of his presidency, Clinton's policy accomplishments were achieved in an "end run" around Congress, but several of his remaining policy goals were realized in the form of new rules adopted during his final weeks in office. As figure 1.2 shows, more economically significant rules were under review during his last quarter than at any other time of Clinton's presidency. Clinton took a different approach, using the administrative process to make lasting policy changes, sometimes in open defiance of Congress. Certain policy initiatives at the end of Clinton's presidency, including the prohibition on snowmobiles in Yellowstone National Park and a ban on road building in roadless areas of national forests, were suited ideally to build a legacy. His willingness to be identified with these policy initiatives stands in contrast to the quiet, under-the-radar initiatives of his predecessor and successor.

A more sophisticated approach to the eleventh-hour agenda was taken by the Bush-Cheney Administration. Even though there was a sharp increase in the quantity of economically significant rules at the end of 2008 (see fig. 1.3), most of the final rules were completed early enough to take effect at least thirty days prior to Inauguration Day. This ensured that President Obama would not be able to overturn them unilaterally.

Even though Bush enjoyed the advantage of Republican majorities in both houses of Congress for most of his presidency, he nonetheless preferred to use the administrative process to advance his policy goals on the environment, energy, health, and safety, with some priorities deferred until his final months in office. Those agenda items included environmental measures that had been White House priorities originating with Vice President Cheney's energy task

Figure 1.3
OIRA Review Counts, by Quarter
Economically Significant Rules, 2001–2008

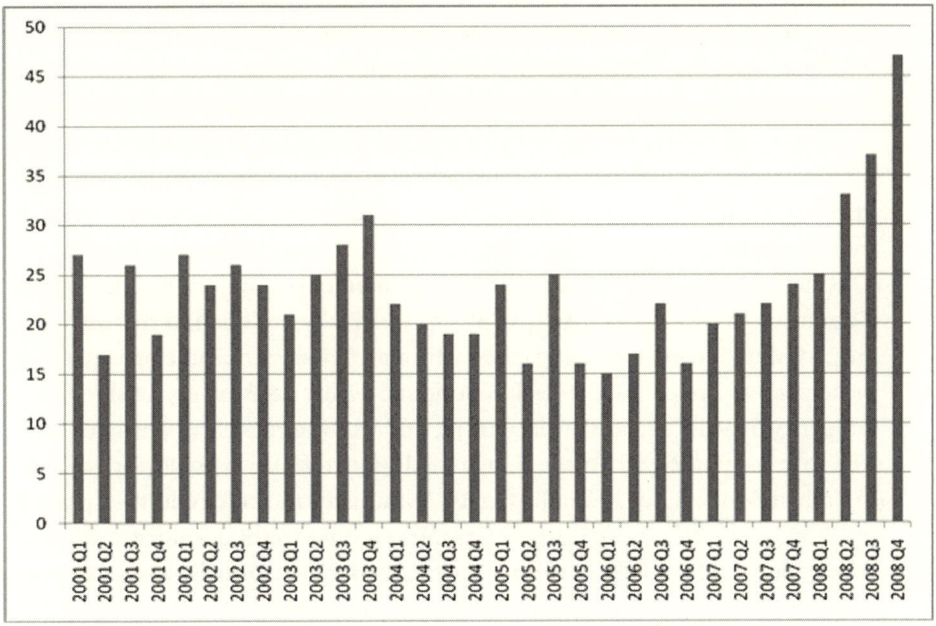

force. This unfinished business resulted in last-minute proposals to deregulate strip mining in Appalachian valleys and to ease restrictions on air pollution in national parks.

The surge of eleventh-hour rulemaking was unlike those of Bush's predecessor and his father. Most rules were finalized very late in 2008 but early enough to take effect and preclude the successor administration from overturning them. In this sense the Bush-Obama transition featured the most cynical use of last-minute rulemaking. Early in 2008 Chief of Staff Joshua Bolten announced a ban on midnight rules, instructing all federal agencies that all rulemaking must be final by November 1.[41] Still, the administration planned ahead. Federal agencies issued one hundred final rules in November, December, and January. This was fewer than the Clinton Administration had during the equivalent time period. However, Bush issued eighty-five in the two months leading up to the election, which was more than his predecessor did in September and October of 2000. Therefore, the Bush Administration avoided the appearance of "midnight" rules by completing more of them at the eleventh hour.

Responding to Last-Minute Maneuvers

Incoming presidents have always been interested in rescinding the commitments of their predecessors in order to maximize their own discretion, but this motivation has intensified in the years since late-term rulemaking became institutionalized. Their options are limited once a final rule takes effect, and for major rules, the effective date is normally sixty days after adoption. If a president takes office after that window, there are legal, institutional, and political constraints if they choose to resist implementing the rules they inherit from predecessors.

Rules are adopted by adhering to the requirements Congress set forth in the Administrative Procedure Act (APA). It is generally understood that agencies are prohibited from modifying rules without following the same process. This principle was upheld in a 1983 US Supreme Court decision establishing that an agency may not reverse a rule without undertaking entirely new rulemaking. The case originated when the Reagan Administration was sued for rescinding a National Highway Traffic Safety Administration rule requiring passive restraints finalized during Carter's term. In a rebuke to the administration, the court ruled in *Motor Vehicle Manufacturers Association v. State Farm* that even in a deregulatory action, an agency must examine the relevant data and provide a satisfactory explanation of its decision.[42]

The decision to modify or rescind a rule depends upon factors other than the administration's legal justification. Institutional constraints also determine whether such interventions are worth considering. The administration should have the capacity to undertake an entirely new rulemaking. The process could potentially divert manpower for years with its requirements for conducting studies to issuing findings and notices, developing draft and proposed rules, and soliciting public participation in the form of comments and hearings, before finally issuing a revised rule. Given that new presidents have scarce resources and favor priorities of their own, they are unlikely to have the interest or the capacity to engage in disputes over completed policy actions. For this reason, Loring and Roth contend that the *State Farm* decision has been a major obstacle for antiregulatory presidents seeking to reverse regulatory actions.[43] Furthermore, initiating a new rulemaking is risky because a president cannot predict how faithfully the revised rule will reflect the new administration's preferences or how successful the process will be. Administrative reforms since the 1970s have expanded presidential influence over the bureaucracy; nonetheless, the White House and Congress are competing principals. Since the bureaucracy is staffed largely by career civil servants and subject to congressional oversight and appropriations, agency independence and congressional rivalry limit the president's control. Since the cooperation of the implementing agency (or agencies) is not always assured, it is often said that the term "chief executive" is misleading.[44]

The president's ability to respond to eleventh-hour rules is further constrained by the political environment. For example, without the antiregulatory national mood in 1981, Ronald Reagan could have faced a more determined resistance from Congress and the public when he rescinded dozens of his predecessor's last-minute rules (see chapter 3). Similarly, the Department of Agriculture proposed to relax meat inspection rules at the end of Reagan's second term. As is explained in chapter 4, public opinion shifted back in favor of stronger consumer protection, and Reagan's successor, George H. W. Bush, withdrew the proposed rule under pressure in 1989. Withdrawing a rule can be disastrous if the issue is salient and public opinion is strongly supportive of the policy. George W. Bush discovered this in 2001, when his administration decided to reverse an arsenic standard for drinking water, issued on Bill Clinton's last day in office, only to reinstate the rule amid a public outcry and a revolt over the issue by some congressional Republicans (see chapter 6).

Other variables in the political environment include interest group activity and partisan composition and control of Congress. When conditions for withdrawing a rule are not favorable, the administration can benefit if actors outside the executive branch take the initiative. The incoming administration of George W. Bush deftly coordinated its response with interest groups and congressional leaders, who lined up to assail the Clinton rules. When OSHA completed a new rule to prevent workplace repetitive-stress injuries, it was sued by the Chamber of Commerce and the National Association of Manufacturers. Ohio representative John Boehner assailed the ergonomics rule as "a haphazard last-minute regulation" and called for legislative repeal.[45]

New regulations are usually subject to legal challenge, and those finalized by the Clinton Administration on its way out were no exception. Courts rarely strike down rules on procedural grounds, as long as they are adopted in accordance with the requirements of the Administrative Procedure Act. Agencies are seldom overruled on substance unless they have exceeded the authority delegated under statute and the statutory language is clear. Otherwise, courts tend to defer to agency interpretation, a principle the Supreme Court upheld in its decision in *Chevron v. Natural Resources Defense Council*.[46] On the occasions when litigation is successful, the incoming administration can use the ruling or court order as a reason to withdraw and replace the rule or to settle. In these instances negotiation results in a modified rule that better reflects the preferences of the interest groups or government entities that were party to the suit as well as the administration. When a federal court struck down a last-minute Clinton Administration rule banning private snowmobiles from Yellowstone National Park in early 2001, the administration of George W. Bush initially issued a replacement rule declaring that snowmobile use was permitted under the National Park Service's doctrine of multiple use. When the Bush Administration's rule was also rejected by the federal court, the administration negotiated a settlement with environmentalists, the snowmobile industry, and state governments, and this became the basis for a new modified rule. Much like a negotiated rulemaking, settlements can produce rules with greater legitimacy through the consent of the parties involved.[47]

The most decisive response is legislative action. Depending on partisan control of the Congress and the leadership's willingness to cooperate, the White House can defer to the legislative branch if leaders support a bill to repeal the rule and are confident of a majority vote in both chambers. This has become more of a challenge since the legislative veto was declared unconstitutional in 1983. Following the Supreme Court's decision in *Immigration and Naturalization Service v. Chadha*, the only way Congress can repeal a rule is by passing a bill through the normal legislative process, which requires the president's signature (or a successful vote to override a veto).[48] In 2001 Congress took the lead in reversing new ergonomic standards from OSHA that took effect in the final days of the Clinton Administration. Industry groups objected that the rules would have been too costly to implement, and Republican lawmakers took up the battle cry of "midnight" regulation. The rules were overturned by invoking a filibuster-proof procedure that the 104th Congress created for just such an event, the Congressional Review Act (CRA).[49] The ergonomics standards were quickly reversed, although this represents the only time the CRA was used to repeal a regulation. The 1996 law permits Congress to repeal regulations by passing a resolution of disapproval with a simple majority vote of both houses, within sixty days of their effective date. That vote would have been subject to a veto if Clinton had been succeeded by Vice President Gore, so realistically, the CRA can only be used when the new president and both houses of Congress are of a different party than the departing president. The adoption of the ergonomics standards so close to the first sixty days of the Bush-Cheney Administration represented the exceptional confluence of circumstances for the CRA to work.[50]

When the options for repealing eleventh-hour rules are unavailable, it may be easier to allow the rule to stand than to expend the political capital necessary to repeal it and start over with a new rulemaking. This alternative, in effect, adds new priorities to an already crowded policy agenda in the president's critical first hundred days. These were the constraints President Obama faced in 2009, when deciding which of Bush's eleventh-hour rules to reverse and which to let stand. Obama decided not to withdraw a rule that took effect in December, 2008, relaxing the requirements for independent scientific reviews under the Endangered Species Act. Rather, he issued a directive to the Department of Interior, instructing its employees to continue the old practices, effectively ignoring the Bush rule. Obama announced the policy in person before a cheering crowd at the department's Washington headquarters, suggesting a strong likelihood that department personnel would observe the directive. However, just as an executive order can be reversed unilaterally, his successor will be able to rescind the directive unless the policy is adopted in a more permanent form.

Summary

Policy entrenchment by rulemaking has become a ritual of the contemporary presidency. The regulatory policies of the 1970s contributed to deadlocked politics, which elevated the importance of presidential administration. Over time, departing presidents have expanded their use of administrative tools, especially rulemaking, to ensure that their domestic policies last in perpetuity. Presidents have strong incentives to use their discretionary powers with restraint until late in the political cycle, when they have little motivation to court Congress and will not face the voters again. Not only do departing administrations have more freedom to act unilaterally without fear of retribution from the voters; they are also subject to less oversight because Congress may not reconvene until the New Year.

The expanded policy role of the bureaucracy has created an incentive for presidents to politicize administration in order to ensure that their policy preferences are sustained. In this sense, eleventh-hour policymaking became commonplace after the presidency emerged as the center of domestic policymaking. It is used to shore up and strengthen provisions of regulatory statutes as well as to relax them. Since it can effect significant policy changes outside the legislative process, it enhances the power of the presidency to leave a lasting impact on the environment, health, and safety of citizens. When used for policy entrenchment, rules are fairly resistant to change. Considering the forces that constrain successors, rulemaking is arguably the most durable strategy available for departing presidents to leave their mark on policy.

Unilateral policymaking is discussed in detail in chapter 2, which then investigates the use and implementation of last-minute policy initiatives in various administrations over time. The chapters that follow explore the evolution of the eleventh-hour strategy by outgoing administrations, the reasons for the choice of certain domestic policy initiatives, and how the responses by successor administrations affect the success and failure of these initiatives. Case studies of five transitions are examined, revealing a complex evolution of this use of power—from the origins of the midnight rulemaking phenomenon during the lame duck months of the Carter presidency, to the escalation in use of the strategy during the Reagan, George H. W. Bush, and Clinton presidencies, to its ultimate expression in the record number of intractable rules in the George W. Bush–Obama transition.

Finally, I consider the future of eleventh-hour policy initiatives. There are reasons to expect wider use of this strategy. Gridlock has become a fact of the legislative process, and contemporary presidents are now more likely to defer action on conflictual domestic policy priorities. Unilateral actions are risky because they can provoke opponents into reversing them through legislation or litigation. These case studies show that policy initiatives, enacted administratively and strategically timed, can be surprisingly resilient. They are rarely challenged, even when the president's successor opposes the policy change. The focus on last-minute rulemaking illuminates a little-understood complication of this bureaucratic policymaking. Specifically, it explores the reasons why many recent presidential elections have been followed by bureaucratic policy changes reflecting movements in the opposite direction from that expressed by the will of the voters.

2 | Lame Ducks and Unilateralism

Despite a limited policymaking role granted by the Constitution, recent presidents have expanded the influence of the office over the policy process through its leadership of the executive bureaucracy. Alexander Hamilton expressed the view that effective governance depends upon presidential leadership of the executive branch. The president's role as the leader of the bureaucracy is affirmed in *Federalist 72*: "The administration of government . . . in its most precise signification . . . is limited to executive details and falls peculiarly within the province of the executive department."[1] Of all the elected and nonelected officials in the federal government, the president is uniquely burdened with the responsibility for government performance.[2] This gives presidents a powerful incentive to politicize the bureaucracy. In that way, loyal political appointees are entrusted to shepherd White House policy proposals from their formulation all the way to the end of implementation.

This chapter maps the growth and development of unilateral action by outgoing presidents over time. Administrative policymaking has become an attractive option for modern presidents to deliver on promises to supporters. In contemporary politics, successful presidential candidates campaign and win office by taking policy positions and making promises.[3] Concurrently, modern presidents have a diminished capacity to make significant policy changes because lawmakers are usually deadlocked over contentious issues of social regulation, such as health, safety, and the environment. Agency rulemaking, in particular, is an effective tool of presidential power because it can be wielded strategically to minimize electoral consequences and congressional oversight.

Going It Alone

Recent experience has shown that presidents have the means and incentives to engage in policymaking when they lack congressional majorities or after the presidential honeymoon has ended. Using administrative policy tools differs from a conventional bargaining strategy because these tools allow presidents to show leadership by acting fast and acting alone.[4] By acting fast, presidents are spared the trouble of coalition building and can be decisive without having to negotiate with interest groups and lawmakers. Acting alone means Congress has the burden of responding to the president's initiative. When Congress makes the next move, it does so in an altered terrain. If the administration's initiative has popular support, then the opposition may find it too costly to overcome gridlock, muster a majority, and rescind it through the legislative process.

The most direct method to circumvent Congress is the executive order, which guides and restricts government agencies. Other unilateral tools with the longest history are budgeting, executive agreements, and commitment of troops.[5] Each involves the exercise of authority delegated by Congress to the executive branch. As such, these actions with wide-ranging impacts are potentially subject to oversight and unilateral reversal by the president's successor, although incoming presidents generally honor the commitments of the previous administration. Mayer's study of executive orders over time shows that they are rarely overturned in this manner.[6]

Presidents have a handful of other tools that can be used for discretionary policymaking, including proclamations, foreign policy directives, and signing statements. These allow presidents to influence policy by affecting the implementation of statutory law. For example, proclamations are used to trigger programs and policies predetermined by Congress. They are similar to executive orders, except that they are directed outside government rather than toward government agencies and personnel.[7] As with proclamations and executive orders, rulemaking has become an important instrument to advance presidential priorities because rules carry the force of law and are not reversed easily. Rulemaking it is not a unilateral power, strictly speaking, because the process takes place almost wholly within the bureaucracy.[8] However, the president's disproportionate influence over the bureaucracy empowers the policymaking role of the executive branch as a whole. Ever since the Civil Service Reform Act of 1978, presidents have taken advantage of its provisions to expand the number of patronage positions and staff the bureaucracy with loyalists.[9]

The majority of administrative rules are developed at the direction of Congress, often under deadline. In her authoritative work on executive leadership, Elena Kagan argued that comparatively few rules are initiated at the discretion of appointed agency heads.[10] Administrators seldom get to choose which regulations are promulgated; instead they use their discretion to affect the process and substance of final rules. Other research on the executive bureaucracy supports a more active policymaking role for White House loyalists. David Lewis found that when the White House enacts policy unilaterally through discretionary rulemaking, the initiatives are driven by political appointees.[11]

Steering the Administration

The bureaucracy's central role in US domestic policymaking is well established. With the growth in the number and scope of federal programs after the 1960s, agencies expanded their role in the policy process, due to their resources, expertise, and the discretion delegated by Congress in the Administrative Procedure Act. Consequently, more policymaking occurs within the permanent government, without the accountability and opportunities for democratic deliberation characteristic of the legislative process. The independence of the bureaucracy makes it resistant to direct control by either the legislative or executive branch, and rules are more likely to reflect the expertise of the regulators. Presidents must use the resources of the White House to press for their policy preferences in order to prevent their decisions from becoming stalled or diluted in the bureaucracy in the implementation stage.[12]

Presidents since Nixon have increased their reliance on administrative tools to affect policy change unilaterally rather than rely on their own power of persuasion and the acquiescence of Congress, particularly in the case of controversial or politically divisive regulations. The tools of the "administrative presidency" include rulemaking, appointment and budgeting powers, signing statements, and executive orders, all of which are justified under the implied powers doctrine.[13] In domestic policy areas such as the environment, recent presidents have been more willing to use these administrative tools, as well as communication and diplomacy, as opposed to legislation.[14]

To some extent, the reliance upon unilateral policy instruments is encouraged by divided government. Presidents facing a Congress of the opposition party are more likely to use executive orders and other administrative tools to advance their agendas.[15]

The threat of unilateral action can also serve as a bargaining chip in debates over legislation. It can prod Congress to act on those priorities, especially for a president facing a Congress of the opposition party. Bill Clinton, who governed with an opposition Congress for most of his time in office, issued executive orders more than 364 times.[16] In comparison, George W. Bush, who enjoyed Republican congressional majorities for most of his presidency, issued 291. Executive orders are more often used for domestic policy than foreign policy, although this focus varies by party. Democratic presidents since World War II have been more likely to use executive orders to advance domestic policy goals, while Republicans use them more often for foreign policy.[17]

The Symbolic Uses of Regulatory Review

The Office of Information and Regulatory Affairs (OIRA) is the unit within OMB that oversees the regulatory process to resolve interagency conflicts, conducts economic analyses on administrative rules, and ensures that those rules are consistent with the president's priorities. This has given contemporary presidents a powerful instrument to advance their policy agendas. Regulatory review is more reactive and conservative than the other administrative tools described. However, tools such as appointments and directives are "inputs" that influence the general direction of bureaucratic policy, whereas regulatory review focuses on the individual rules that ultimately put policies into practice.[18] Presidents do not personally approve (or "sign off" on) rules the way they choose to sign or veto legislation; however, the centralized process Reagan established with Executive Order 12291 after his first month in office tipped the balance of control over agency direction toward the executive branch.

Reagan's directive was in part an ad hoc response to the deluge of new regulations left behind by the Carter Administration, as the following chapter illustrates. Despite some modifications to suit changing circumstances, regulatory review became institutionalized over successive administrations.[19] For example, when Congress moved to curb OIRA for what many saw as interference during the Reagan years, George H. W. Bush transferred its oversight role to the newly established Council on Competitiveness. In 2007, after Republicans lost their majorities in Congress, George W. Bush asserted greater control of the bureaucracy through E.O. 13422, which required one political appointee at every agency to monitor the agency's rulemaking actions and report to OIRA.[20] Over time, these changes have continued the trend toward centralization and consolidation of the executive bureaucracy.

Even though the regulatory agendas of independent agencies like the EPA are largely determined by Congress and the courts, administrators have wide latitude to formulate the details. This discretion was delegated by Congress, the deliberative and representative body that was assigned the responsibility to make policy under the Constitution. Regulatory review injects additional delay and analysis into the rulemaking process, but for some this is justified as making up for the deliberation that Congress deferred by delegating its rulemaking authority to the bureaucracy.[21] In this sense regulatory review is an attempt to restore a measure of accountability in policymaking by giving the executive branch a check on Congress and the bureaucracy.

Regulatory review not only ensures that final regulations reflect the president's views, but the prolonged process creates delays that increase the likelihood of "midnight" regulations. It is also blamed for undermining congressional intent by allowing OIRA to overrule regulatory agencies and by creating a procedural back door for interest groups with access to the White House, sometimes with the help of other entities, such as President George H. W. Bush's Council on Competitiveness.[22] The first of these objections was addressed when Clinton replaced Reagan's directive with E.O. 12886, which imposes a time limit to complete reviews. To a lesser extent, Clinton's order also addressed the latter concern by abolishing the Council on Competitiveness.[23]

The potential to abuse regulatory review by weakening or undermining the goals of a statute persists. This procedural manipulation can be considered a form of symbolic politics because it allows policymakers to claim credit for strong regulatory policies, even if the review process delays their implementation and results in weaker rules.[24] For example, the administration of President George H. W. Bush was criticized for intervening in the regulatory process at the request of the auto and ethanol industries after the Clean Air Act of 1990 was signed into law. Bush was therefore able to appeal to the voters by boasting about his role in formulating the legislation, and then appeal to business groups by weakening specific provisions during implementation of the act, as discussed further in chapter 5.

Limitations

Although unilateral action is less risky at the end of a president's term in office than at other times, the capacity to act alone is still limited by the normal checks and balances of the political system. The temptation to pursue ambitious policy initiatives is tempered by the reality that other political institutions may challenge them after the president's departure. The first and most obvious of these actors is the president's successor. As discussed in chapter 1, incoming presidents are focused on their own priorities and do not usually invest the resources to reverse the policies of their predecessors by engaging in a new rulemaking process or pursuing additional legislation. However, they have reason to be cautious because all recent presidents have been willing to use these channels to undo policy changes they opposed.

Since agency rulemaking is a delegated power under congressional authority, and executive orders are implied powers, both could be reversed by an act of Congress.[25] This assumes the president's action is opposed by a substantial congressional majority; such a response would be unlikely under conditions of legislative gridlock. Presidential decisions are subject to judicial review, and all regulatory agencies face litigation over their rules. Any such action could be challenged in court on substantive or procedural grounds, and the successor administration could simply choose not to defend the policy in court. Public opinion is a limiting factor, not only because an unpopular unilateral action could fail by provoking a groundswell of opposition but also because of the near-universal desire of retiring presidents to leave a positive legacy.

Other limitations affect unilateral strategy, even toward the end of the president's term when the costs are lowest. Implementation depends upon the cooperation of the bureaucracy, and agency officials may not feel obliged to execute last-minute directives that they oppose, that run counter to the agency's mission, or that appear to have little support from the incoming administration or Congress. Even the appointed officials are no longer bound to follow directives faithfully, because they too become lame ducks. As chapter 5 illustrates, EPA administrator William Reilly withdrew proposals favored by the Council on Competitiveness after President George H. W. Bush was defeated for reelection in 1992, and then released a controversial report on secondhand smoke on his final day on the job.

Agencies and Implementation

Although the presidency has the capacity to dominate every stage of the policy process, the recent trend toward politicization of the bureaucracy has created more opportunities for presidents to put their mark on policy during the implementation process. In filling the top administrative posts of federal agencies, presidents are unlikely to select people who do not share their views about the direction of the policies they will carry out. Over time, leadership of the bureaucracy has given the president a wider and wider channel to affect policy outside the formulation and enactment of legislation.

All at once, the bureaucracy is accountable to Congress and the president as well as being an independent entity staffed with civil service employees. Therefore, presidents pursue reforms and seek institutional structures to maximize their influence over the bureaucracy and restrict oversight by Congress. In a study of 182 federal agencies created since World War II, Lewis found that most were established by executive fiat, as opposed to legislation. Furthermore, those agencies formed under statutory mandate had more features designed to insulate them from White House influence and maintain their independence, whereas those agencies created by executive order or administrative reorganization featured leadership and oversight structures that favored presidential control.[26]

Not only does the executive bureaucracy have significant influence over policy implementation because of its rulemaking and enforcement responsibilities, but it is also a major actor throughout the policy process. In the formulation stage, for example, Congress and the president seek input from agencies because of their expertise. Agencies often have the final word when they translate statutory law into administrative rules because of the discretion Congress granted when it passed the Administrative Procedure Act (APA). The 1946 law effectively yielded the implementation decisions for major legislation to the bureaucracy by delegating the responsibility for the details of rules. In creating a procedure for writing regulations, the APA required agencies to create an opportunity for deliberation. Agencies are required to solicit feedback on proposed rules and then consider and respond to the comments. However, the APA does not specify how they should use the information they receive.[27]

Agencies have wide latitude to design rules, because legislation often consists of vaguely worded goals forged by compromise. In order to appeal to a large enough coalition, specific provisions may be eliminated or avoided and left to the administrative agency. Therefore, this ambiguity is by design. Beyond attracting majority support, the challenge for authors of legislation is to craft legislation with the optimal balance between prescription and discretion. Clear directions may help ensure that agencies will comply with congressional intent, but legislators may lack the knowledge and expertise to predict how their policies might apply under specific circumstances. Deborah Stone argues that flexible rules allow agencies to respond creatively to new problems and particular situations.[28] Overly specific policies may prove to become as problematic as ambiguous directives.

Bureaucratic discretion was enhanced with the rise of social regulation, or regulation in the public interest.[29] The language of environmental, health, and safety legislation Congress enacted in the 1970s was marked by ambiguity. Although many of the statutes contained detailed provisions and strict deadlines, goals were defined broadly, and decisions about the means to achieve them were often left up to administrative agencies.[30] Social regulation is distinct from old-style economic regulation in several ways. First, economic regulation is justified by the Interstate Commerce Clause of the Constitution and is concerned with maintaining functioning markets for particular industries. In contrast, social regulation is justified by the constitutional power to promote the general welfare and governs behavior across multiple economic sectors.[31] Second, the general public is indifferent to regulations for specific industries, whereas social regulatory policies are enacted at the urging of public interest groups and enjoy widespread popular support. Thus it is politically risky for policymakers to advocate rolling them back.[32] Finally, agencies within the executive branch are responsible for implementing social regulation. The statutes required the creation of regulatory agencies and commissions such as OSHA and the National Highway Traffic Safety Administration (NHTSA) within cabinet departments. The EPA, an independent regulatory agency, differs little from a cabinet department in terms of its authority. These agencies stand in contrast to the independent regulatory commissions already prevalent before the 1970s, which were largely responsible for enforcing economic regulation.[33]

The new generation of agencies has a more adversarial relationship with regulated interests.[34] Concerning the sphere of economic regulation, some theorized that regulatory policies could be undermined if agencies were "captured" by the interests they regulate.[35] But the size and complexity of issue networks make domination by a single industry unlikely, if not impossible.[36] Rather, the constellation of interests seeking to influence social regulation undermines policy effectiveness by creating a political stalemate. Agencies are under mandate to protect public health and welfare but face backlash and scrutiny for doing so. The onset of legislative gridlock that makes domestic policy resistant to change also empowers the bureaucracy. Administrators have been able to use their discretion to influence policy according to their preferences and to resist reform attempts in Congress. Consequently, the success of a major policy initiative requires the president to assert control over the administration.[37] Regulatory policies are especially prone to manipulation through the administrative process. Once Congress enacted policies in the 1970s addressing the environment, occupational health, and safety, it was not long before a political stalemate developed.[38]

Conflict over social regulation was largely responsible for regulatory policy gridlock. In contrast, the economic regulation predominant in earlier decades was less controversial because the regulated actors usually agreed with the policy goals, and the political environment was generally more stable.[39] Independent agencies such as OSHA and the EPA were relatively new. Their primary purpose is to promulgate rules to implement major statutes enacted by Congress. Their rules fall under the category of social regulation because they tend to have an adversarial relationship with the entities they regulate. Over the course of the 1970s business groups shifted their strategy from containing the regulatory state to a counterattack.[40] Congress was under pressure from business groups to rein in regulatory agencies, and battles over specific regulations were playing out in the courts. For example, virtually every health standard issued by OSHA during the Carter years became the subject of litigation.[41] For example, the textile industry sued OSHA over cotton dust standards designed to protect workers from brown lung disease, automakers sued NHTSA over auto safety standards, and provisions of the Surface Mining Control and Reclamation Act were under challenge from groups representing mining interests, such as the Mountain States Legal Foundation.

The backlash against social regulation helped to fuel the election of Ronald Reagan in 1980. Reagan blamed excessive regulation for slowing the economy, and congressional deadlock became an excuse for unilateral action to delay and reverse regulations. Reagan and his successor, George H. W. Bush, both used administrative actions to entrench their deregulatory agendas at the end of their terms, helping to institutionalize last-minute rulemaking as a conventional instrument of public policy.

Ensuring a Policy Legacy

President Carter made extensive use of executive orders following his defeat by Ronald Reagan in the election of 1980. The forty-one executive orders issued during Carter's last ninety days stand as a record for contemporary presidents. The graph in figure 2.1 shows the frequency of executive orders by quarter from 1980 through the beginning of 2009 as well as the number of economically significant final rules under review from 1982 through the beginning of 2009. Those executive orders represented long-standing priorities that he tried to realize through policy entrenchment at the end of his term, but they lacked the permanence of some of the regulations his administration promulgated before the transition. The most substantial policy legacy from those final weeks consisted of energy and environmental legislation, which he achieved with a lame duck Congress. The range of actions Carter initiated during the interregnum period prior to Reagan's inauguration is detailed in chapter 3.

The frequency of economically significant rules submitted for review after 1981 is displayed alongside the executive orders for the same period. The tendency of administrative agencies to increase their output of final rules during the weeks that preceded recent presidential transitions was well documented before the Bush-Obama transition.[42] The last quarter of 2008 featured the third highest number of economically significant rules for any equivalent time period since OMB review became institutionalized (represented by the spike at the far right side of figure 2.1). The reasons for this sharp increase in regulatory activity during the final weeks of the Bush-Cheney Administration are discussed in chapter 7.

The only two quarters when the bureaucracy completed more significant rules were at the end of the presidency of Bush's father in 1992, followed by the final quarter of Clinton's presidency. The third period when these were most numerous was the last quarter of 1994, when the Clinton Administration finalized a large volume of rules immediately before the impending Republican takeover of Congress. Data in figure 2.1 reveal increases in agency output at regular intervals that correspond to the political cycle. In the transitions that

Figure 2.1
Economically Significant Rules (Review Counts) and Executive Orders, by Quarter

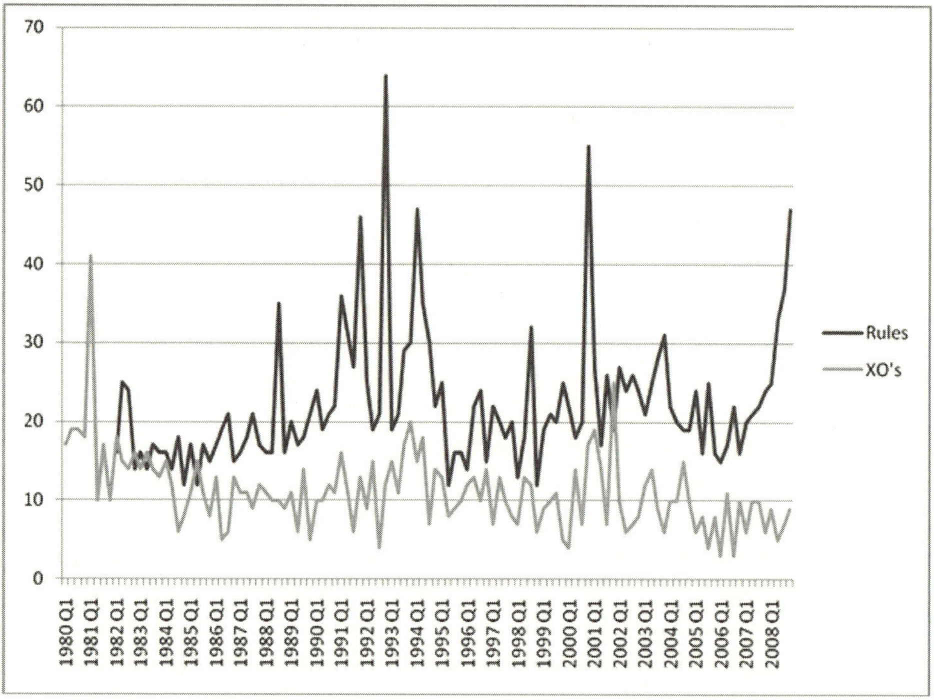

followed the Reagan years, steep increases in numbers of rules were not accompanied by an increased number of executive orders during the same quarter. However, there were modest increases during the quarter that followed each transition from Reagan forward. This can be explained by the penchant for newly inaugurated presidents to use executive orders for "crack-of-dawn" policymaking.[43] An enduring example is Reagan's executive order 12291, which centralized the regulatory review process.

Interest Group Politics

Legislation enacted early in a president's term may still be in implementation stage as the term winds down. As they translate statutory mandates into rules, agencies consult with interest groups, which use the opportunity to seek administrative rule changes for protection, economic benefits, or a favorable regulatory environment. For these reasons, interest groups not only lobby Congress but also devote resources to influencing the rulemaking process.[44] The end of a term presents a final chance for supporters to remind presidents of their promises and to press their demands.

Interest groups try to affect regulations by influencing the provisions developed during implementation with the discretion of agencies. Unlike legislative debates in Congress that routinely fall under the spotlight of mass media, rulemaking is conducted in the relative obscurity of the administrative arena. Those who pay close attention to this stage of the policy process tend to be the interest groups and actors making up the issue network. Since the input from the notice-and-comment period influences regulators to revise provisions of rules, well-organized groups have an incentive to use the implementation process to recoup losses from the legislative debate or to press new claims. Jeffrey Berry calls this "appeals court lobbying," because it can be an effective recourse for those groups to regain what they lost during the formulation of legislation.[45] At this stage of the policy process, business groups have an advantage over public interest or citizen groups because they can sustain their involvement and use their resources to affect the rulemaking process; relevant resources include skilled personnel, technical expertise, and experience with regulators. Cornelius Kerwin found evidence of a strong subjective perception among interest groups that lobbying the executive branch is worthwhile. Surveys of interest groups have found that most consider it to be as important as lobbying Congress.[46]

The executive branch has two major access points for interest groups seeking to influence policy.[47] One is the Executive Office of the President, which houses OIRA, a permanent structure that oversees rulemaking, as well as housing ad hoc groups such as the Council on Competitiveness, which was given oversight authority during the administration of George H. W. Bush (see chapter 5). The point most frequently utilized by interest groups is the notice-and-comment period of the rulemaking process. Empirical research into rulemaking has established that the content of final rules is frequently changed in response to comments.[48] Other studies have confirmed high rates of participation by regulated industries but found little evidence that they swayed outcomes disproportionately.[49]

Analysis

Some empirical research has established that agencies closer to the White House are most active at the end of the president's term. In a multiyear study of proposed rules Anne O'Connell found that cabinet and executive agencies account for the surge in advance notices of proposed rulemaking that occurred in the final year of each presidency, but independent regulatory commissions and agencies were unaffected by the political calendar.[50] Covering the years from 1983 to 2003, the study determined that the administration of George H. W. Bush had by far the most prolific final year. The number of proposed rules in 1992 was 50 percent higher than during the Clinton Administration's last year. Since the repeated surge in rulemaking has been limited to agencies led by presidential appointees, the pattern implies a White House role.

Acts of Congress, and (to a lesser extent) court orders, are the reasons for most of the new rules submitted to OIRA for review annually. Any rulemaking that advances the administration's policy agenda and not mandated by Congress or the courts is considered discretionary. If presidents are using their final months in office as an opportunity to establish a legacy, then this should be reflected in an increase in discretionary rules.

In order to examine this assumption, a dataset of economically significant final rules under review during the final years of the Reagan, Bush, Clinton, and Bush administrations was compiled and coded according to the type of mandate.

Additional evidence of policy entrenchment should be apparent from the incoming administration's response to those last-minute rules. In a transition ritual that has been repeated since 1981, newly elected presidents suspend new rules for review and target many of them for reversal. In her examination of a twenty-year dataset of proposed rules, O'Connell observed an association between withdrawals of uncompleted rules and changes in party control of both the White House and Congress.[51] Recent transitions have featured fewer unfinished rules than the Carter Administration left behind. However, final rules may be suspended or withdrawn before their effective dates pass.[52] Incoming presidents use the moratorium and review to identify rules for repeal, and they should be more likely to target policies that they oppose and that were not mandated by Congress. If outgoing administrations use this window to advance their own policy preferences, then this should be reflected in the discretionary rules they finalize before leaving office. Therefore, discretionary rules should account for a greater share of withdrawn rules than mandatory rules finalized at the end of the predecessor's term.

As predicted, there is an increase in late-term discretionary rulemaking but only for the most recent transitions. Table 2.1 reports the proportion of final rules under OIRA review during the final ninety days of the Reagan presidency and the three successor administrations. A greater proportion of economically significant final rules under review during the final quarters of Presidents Clinton and George W. Bush were discretionary. In contrast, the new rules submitted late by Presidents Reagan and George H. W. Bush were just as likely to be promulgated under a mandate. While the picture is mixed, the trend conforms to the expected pattern. The recent examples suggest there has been an increase in strategic behavior by outgoing administrations.

A second hypothesis was that incoming presidents were more likely to withdraw discretionary rules than mandatory rules. Since discretionary rulemaking accounted for a large amount of the late-term activity in 2000 and 2008, there were good reasons to expect the incoming teams to attempt to reverse them. Both elections were followed by a transition from divided government to unitary control by one party. That is, once it became clear that George W. Bush would occupy the White House, he expected to have the backing of a Republican Congress; the large Democratic majorities elected along with Barack Obama's victory eight years later placed him in a similar position of strength.

The largest number of withdrawals occurred in 1993 and 2001. As table 2.1 shows, most of the withdrawn rules had been promulgated under statutory mandate. Despite the trend of increased discretionary rulemaking in the final year, only the George W. Bush administration successfully targeted a significant number of them for withdrawal. Chapter 6 examines how the Clinton White House used the administrative process to enact a broad domestic policy agenda that was opposed by the Republican Congress as well as the Bush-Cheney

Table 2.1
Economically Significant Final Rules, by Quarter and Year

	1988		*1992*		*2000*		*2008*	
	1st–3rd	4th	1st–3rd	4th	1st–3rd	4th	1st–3rd	4th
Mandate								
Legislative	5	3	10	29	9	15	11	14
Judicial	1	0	0	2	1	1	2	0
None	18	9	22	8	23	27	26	29
(Withdrawn)		(1)	(1)		(1)	(4)		(9)
Total	24	12	32	39	33	43	39	43

Source: OIRA Historical Review Counts

Administration. Under identical circumstances eight years later, the Bush Administration promulgated an even larger volume of economically significant rules that angered a Democratic Congress and the incoming Obama Administration. As I explain in chapter 7, Obama had few alternatives for undoing Bush's eleventh-hour agenda because most of the rules were already in effect well before the transition.

After the Reagan Administration rescinded rules finalized during Carter's term, the Supreme Court ruled in its *State Farm* decision that a rule already in effect could not be withdrawn without initiating an entirely new rulemaking. This forced presidents who followed Reagan to be selective about withdrawing the last-minute rules they were handed. The five recent transitions demonstrate that presidents have been increasingly strategic and effective with their end-of-term policy initiatives.

Summary

Presidents may not make policy by decree, but unilateralism alters the terrain in ways that dampen the checks and balances on the presidency. The skillful use of these tools allows presidents to circumvent the legislative arena and operate in the administrative arena, where they enjoy an advantage. This is particularly important for a lame duck president with little to no leverage. Instead of being forced to bargain with Congress to support the program, the president need only persuade the other actors that it should not be actively opposed.

A consequence of the political cycle is the regular increase in the volume of rulemaking that precedes presidential transitions, especially around interparty transitions. Beginning in 1992, there has been a peak in the number of final rules submitted for review in the last ninety days of every presidency. As noted, more economically significant rules were finalized in the quarter that preceded the Bush-Clinton transition than in any other equivalent time period. The Clinton-Bush transition that followed eight years later was a close second, followed by the Bush-Obama transition.

A significant trend is the increase in discretionary rulemaking by outgoing administrations. The data indicate that the final rules promulgated without a statutory or judicial mandate accounted for a larger portion of the rules issued by the Clinton and Bush-Cheney administrations compared to the administrations of Reagan and George H. W. Bush. Since discretionary rules were expected to reflect the preferences of the outgoing administration as opposed to Congress, incoming presidents should be more likely to withdraw them. Even though Clinton, George W. Bush, and Obama all targeted their predecessors' rules for repeal, few were withdrawn unilaterally. Only the Clinton

Administration finalized a large number of discretionary rules during its final quarter, and as expected, the Bush-Cheney Administration withdrew several of them.

The expansion of the institutional presidency and rising expectations to deliver on campaign promises have coincided with political gridlock. Even if legislation is better suited to reform these policies and to clarify lingering controversies in major statutes, Congress has been unable to act decisively because of the constellation of interests around them. Stalemate in the legislative arena has caused the nexus of activity to shift toward the administrative arena. Despite attempts to roll back major policies protecting health, safety, and the environment, they remain popular with the mass public decades after they were enacted. Vigilant public interest groups are aware of this and have the means to mobilize the public to defend these policies against rearguard assaults. Since it is politically risky for policymakers to advocate repealing these policies, opponents have little hope of building the consensus necessary to weaken any of their provisions through legislation. Therefore it is more expedient for interest groups who oppose those policies to seek administrative rules that modify portions of the law without repealing them. For antiregulatory presidents, it is preferable to do this quietly; during their final weeks the administrations of Reagan, George H. W. Bush, and George W. Bush all promulgated rules to relax restrictions on strip mining. Since lame duck administrations receive comparatively little news coverage during the interregnum period, delaying these actions until the end also reduces media scrutiny.

Late-term rulemaking can be used just as effectively to advance an activist agenda. At the end of his presidency, Bill Clinton used rulemaking to initiate an ambitious domestic agenda that included environmental protection, public land preservation, and occupational health. As chapter 6 explains, his approach was as different from that of his Republican contemporaries as were his policy goals. In the case studies that follow, individual transitions are examined to show how selected policies, caught in the administrative arena, have become recurring themes in narratives about midnight rulemaking. I also trace the evolution of the eleventh-hour strategy, starting with the activities at the end of the Carter Administration. That flurry of last-minute rulemaking was not exactly the coordinated campaign the Reagan White House claimed, although it cast a shadow over all the transitions that followed.

3 | Jimmy Carter's Unfinished Agenda

The weeks following Jimmy Carter's loss in the 1980 election were some of the busiest of his presidency. Working with a lame duck Congress, Carter succeeded in creating the Arctic National Wildlife Refuge and in creating a fund to clean up abandoned toxic waste sites, the last (and largest) program of the "environmental decade." Carter accomplished just as much acting on his own authority as he did with the cooperation of Congress. His last twenty days in office featured a record twenty-six executive orders, ten of which were needed for the deal he negotiated to free the hostages in Iran during his final hours in the Oval Office.[1] Carter issued a record twenty-six executive orders in his last twenty days in office, a veritable frenzy of executive policymaking. These included major policy initiatives, ranging from restrictions on exports of toxic waste to his creation of the Office of Civil Rights within the Department of Labor to enforce antidiscrimination policies.

Carter's activity immediately preceding departure from office represents the first instance of an ambitious regulatory agenda by an outgoing administration. In addition to its novelty, the administration's lame duck agenda was unique among modern transitions because it was less of a concerted effort than the priorities of several different cabinet departments and agencies acting under their own discretion. The cabinet departments and agencies acted independently, operating effectively and quickly under various statutory mandates. The 1980 election was followed by difficult choices. Faced with the prospect of new appointees in the incoming conservative, antiregulatory administration undoing their work, top administrators scrambled to complete new regulations that had been the focus of their work for months or years. Other priorities with little hope of completion before the transition, such as proposed Department of Education Rules on bilingual education, were abandoned entirely.[2] Altogether, more than twelve thousand pages were added to the *Federal Register* during the eleven-week lame duck period.

The Carter Administration's lame duck agenda was on a collision course with that of the president-elect, who had campaigned and won on the theme of regulatory relief. Within days of taking office Reagan made good on this campaign promise of regulatory relief.[3] Incoming OMB Director David Stockman announced a moratorium on all pending regulations, including final rules listed in the *Federal Register* that had yet to take effect. In the first instance of what would become a rite of inauguration, the Reagan Administration froze Carter's late-term rules and called their legitimacy into question by criticizing their timing. "These are 'midnight' regulations," Vice President George H. W. Bush announced when he convened his task force on regulatory relief. "They will not be made final in their current form, but will be reviewed."[4] The regulatory freeze was also the first stage in an effort to roll back regulations and centralize the regulatory process within the White House, building upon the system Reagan inherited from Carter.

Regulatory Review

A deregulatory mood had taken hold in Washington well before Reagan's 1980 presidential campaign. An estimated 150 regulatory reform bills were introduced in congressional committees in 1979 alone.[5] That Carter's administration would be denounced by his successors for reckless regulation is somewhat ironic, considering his own advocacy of deregulation as an instrument to stimulate economic growth. Contrary to the criticisms made by his detractors that he overregulated, among the significant achievements of his presidency was legislation that deregulated key sectors of the economy.[6]

Carter took a harder line on regulation than his predecessors by institutionalizing regulatory review. Building upon structures introduced by the Ford Administration, the White House review of new regulations became a routine feature of agency rulemaking.[7] Agencies conducted their own analyses of proposed regulations, with the awareness that they could be subject to review by the White House Regulatory Analysis and Review Group (RARG). Finally, Carter instructed agencies to use "common sense" and "clear language" in writing regulations. In announcing his regulatory review directive, Carter urged that the federal government should not just "throw another law or another rule at every problem in our society without thinking seriously about the consequences."[8]

Cabinet Government's Last Gasp

Two misleading allegations are implied in Bush's characterization of Carter's "midnight" rules. First, labeling them "midnight" rules implies that they were hastily formed and forced upon the incoming administration for political reasons without regard for the consequences. As the case study in this chapter shows, the rules promulgated during the final weeks of Carter's term were the result of processes that are better characterized by deliberation and delay. The second charge is that they were "Carter's" rules. The administration's decentralized structure made it difficult for the White House to impose a coordinated late-term agenda across its departments. Carter was the last president who seriously attempted to impose "cabinet" government.[9] He began his term by reducing the size of the White House staff and granting considerable autonomy to cabinet officers, who enjoyed the freedom to set their own agendas as well as having direct access to the Oval Office; but his attitude changed, and the Domestic Policy Staff assumed a greater coordinating role. By the summer of 1979 Carter was dissatisfied with the direction some of his subcabinet-level agencies were taking. He sacked most of his cabinet and required that new appointments be cleared by his newly appointed chief of staff, Hamilton Jordan.[10] Carter used his chief of staff to impose a more centralized system of management; however, the regulatory priorities of executive departments and agencies, such as the EPA, were firmly established already.

In order to understand the timing of the so-called midnight rules of this administration, it is useful to take a longer view of the policies that the executive departments of Carter's administration were assigned to implement. Carter assumed office just as an era of government regulation in the public interest began to wane. During the 1960s and early 1970s the federal government responded to public demands by enacting major statutes to preserve natural resources, supersede state laws on environmental protection, regulate highway safety, and protect workers from occupational hazards. In 1970 alone several regulatory agencies were created, including the EPA, OSHA, the Mining Safety Enforcement Administration, and the National Highway Traffic Safety Administration (NHTSA). By the time Carter took office these agencies already had the responsibility of implementing programs enacted by his two predecessors.

The health, safety, and environmental policies Carter inherited were the product of a bygone period of executive-legislative cooperation, which gave way to gridlock in the aftermath of Watergate and the Vietnam War, as presidential power to persuade Congress diminished. Despite large Democratic majorities in Congress, Carter had limited success with his own legislative agenda. He eventually found that administrative action was a useful strategy to advance his own policy priorities, just as Nixon had discovered when his relationship with Congress deteriorated.

A large number of environmental policy initiatives were already in the pipeline when Carter took office. The policy cycle had begun more than a decade earlier, when Rachel Carson's Silent Spring sounded the alarm about the unintended effects of synthetic chemicals in the environment.[11] Carson's book (and preceding *New Yorker* serial) warning of the toxic dangers of agricultural chemicals and pesticides to birds, animals, and humans, and was publicly praised by President Kennedy after a White House Science Advisory Committee study substantiated her claims.[12] Severe pollution events throughout the 1960s and the first Earth Day in 1970 created pressure for Congress and President Nixon to preempt state laws with major federal statutes, including the Clean Air Act and National Environmental Policy Act (1970) and the Clean Water Act (1972).

Public concern for the environment dissipated as federal agencies labored to write and enforce regulations. Their work would continue for years, and during the Carter years the EPA was still in the process of writing rules to implement the first generation of those laws. Harry Caudill's *Night Comes to the Cumberlands*, which appeared the same year as *Silent Spring*, was also lauded by Kennedy, who appointed a commission to study the conditions of rural mining communities in Appalachia.[13] Caudill's book raised awareness of the environmental destruction from unregulated strip mining, establishing it as part of the environmental agenda well before the first Earth Day. Moreover, it helped build a national consensus for action, such as the creation of the Appalachian Regional Commission. In a foreword to the 1963 edition, Interior Secretary Stewart Udall warned of the consequences "when men betray their responsibilities as land stewards. The price we pay for wanton spoliation is sure and certain."[14]

Despite the environmental concerns over coal mining, Congress initially focused on the urgent problem of mine safety. Following the Farmington coal mine explosion in West Virginia that tragically killed seventy-eight miners, Congress passed the Federal Coal Mine Health and Safety Act of 1969. It was not until Carter's first year in office that Congress shifted its attention from safety to ecology and succeeded in passing a law that addressed the environmental damage from strip mining. The Surface Mining Control and Reclamation Act of 1977 (SMCRA) committed the Department of Interior, like other executive departments, to a long and complex rulemaking process needed to implement and enforce this law.

A few years later, another publication served as a catalyst for government regulation on safety. The federal push to improve auto safety followed the 1965 publication of Ralph Nader's *Unsafe at Any Speed*, and congressional hearings forced the public and policymakers to acknowledge the sobering truth about the deaths and injuries from highway accidents. Congress responded in 1966 with a pair of laws, the Highway Safety Act and the National Traffic and Motor Vehicle Safety Act, which would have been the brand new Department of

Transportation's duty to enforce. Subsequently, Congress passed the Highway Safety Act Amendments of 1970, which created NHTSA, the agency charged with the mission of protecting public highway safety. The responsibility for developing national highway safety standards was transferred to this new regulatory agency.

The same year Nader's book was published, the US Public Health Service released the so-called Frye Report, formally titled *Protecting the Health of 80 Million Americans.*[15] The Frye Report contained startling truths about the risks endured by the nation's workforce, including the revelation that a new unregulated synthetic chemical entered the workplace every twenty minutes, which exacerbated fears about the link between chemical exposure and cancer. This fueled a growing movement in Congress for a federal law to protect worker safety. As part of his Great Society Program, President Lyndon Johnson had proposed an office within the Labor Department to enforce worker safety standards, but the legislation he supported was rejected by Congress in 1968. After passage of the Coal Mine Health and Safety Act, a bipartisan group of senators struck a deal that resulted in the Occupational Safety and Health Act, signed by President Nixon in 1970. Courting environmentalists and voters traditionally aligned with labor was part of Nixon's "blue-collar strategy."[16]

When Nixon signed the Occupational Safety and Health Act, he took credit for what was essentially a Democratic, pro-labor bill.[17] The law created OSHA within the Department of Labor, to identify workplace hazards, enforce safety standards, and oversee state programs. The act, along with the pollution control statutes of the 1970s, represented the zenith of a wider liberal mode of government intervention into the economy. According to this definition, a "liberal" policy is:

> an approach to social reform in which state action is strictly limited by the property rights of private firms, and workers do not participate directly in efforts to reconstruct capitalist social relations. Public officials do not exercise significant control over production or investment, and workers do not take an active part in decision making in industry or in the implementation of public policies toward business. While this approach makes political sense in the American context, where the Lockean liberal ideology enshrines private property rights and workers are demobilized as a class, it is an ineffective response to the various ways in which American capitalism discourages social reform in general and workplace safety in particular.[18]

The act was significant because it established for the first time a right to a safe workplace. In practice, this right was difficult to enforce because the authors of the bill used ambiguous language to smooth over sharp political differences and produce legislation with a better chance of passing.

The compromises ensured that policy disputes that might have been settled by lawmakers would linger through implementation. One problem was the concept of "feasibility," which was inserted into the section on health standards prior to the vote. In a 1974 legal challenge to OSHA's asbestos ban, industry plaintiffs argued that the regulation failed a test of the feasibility standard. The court's decision upheld the prohibition on cost consideration, ruling that economically burdensome is not the same as infeasible.[19] Another problem was the law's failure to provide tools for implementation. The Department of Labor wanted clearer language on petitions for new health standards, walkaround pay, and the right to refuse to handle hazardous materials but was unable to obtain stronger language that would force employers to comply with those sections.

Ultimately, the final bill included stronger wording and was more powerful than business wanted. This was largely because of strategic blunders by the Chamber of Commerce, which did a poor job of mobilizing its members to oppose legislation and lost the message war by refusing to admit that there was any problem with health and safety in the workplace, while accusing unions of a power grab.[20] After losing the battle on the Occupational Safety and Health Act, business regrouped. The Business Roundtable was formed in 1972 to launch an ideological counteroffensive that would continue throughout the 1970s. A full-scale drive for deregulation was under way by the end of the Ford years, just as OSHA had an enormous backlog of regulations still under development.

The antiregulatory national mood of the Carter years required regulators to strike a balance. There was indirect and sporadic pressure from White House advisory councils to justify regulations as agencies worked to fulfill statutory obligations in a manner consistent with their agency missions. Many of the unfinished regulations, such as the EPA's hazardous waste disposal requirements and OSHA's occupational noise standards, had been mandated by legislation that predated the Carter Administration, and the regulations were thus long overdue. They were also controversial in the antiregulatory political climate. To the Reagan campaign, OSHA and EPA were the quintessential symbols of government overreach. Reagan pledged to rein in both agencies and pledged regulatory relief for key sectors, including the auto industry. Consequently, the interregnum agendas of these agencies were formed with the knowledge that unfinished initiatives would likely be withdrawn and that even completed rulemaking could be reversed by the next administration.

Environmental Initiatives

Carter weighed several environmental initiatives as he faced uncertain reelection prospects in 1980. Gus Speth, chair of the White House Council on Environmental Quality, warned against pressing forward with legislative proposals that could fail to win congressional approval.[21] Instead, this environmental advisor suggested that Carter act unilaterally to preserve natural resources, such as by designating new marine sanctuaries and scenic rivers in California, which would be popular nationally and would shore up his support with environmentalists before the election.

But such unilateral action would prove to be risky politically. Carter had suffered a backlash when he used an executive order earlier in the year to impose a $0.10 per gallon gasoline tax following the decontrol of gasoline prices. The intent was to promote conservation, fund the administration's synthetic fuels program, and close the budget deficit, while offsetting the windfall profit tax on oil companies.[22] Carter could apply a simple solution to multiple problems with the stroke of a pen. The executive order promised to be a safe strategy, considering the failed attempt by Congress to impose a gasoline tax three years earlier, but circumstances proved otherwise. The unilateral action became a political liability when Republicans accused Carter of abusing executive authority to raise revenue to finance an election-year tax cut, and Democrats deserted him when they saw an opportunity to criticize the gasoline fees as an unfair tax on consumers. Not only did Congress overturn the gasoline fee, but both houses voted in excess of the two-thirds majority needed to override a presidential veto. The rebuke left Carter politically wounded and the Democratic congressional leadership in disarray.[23] Reflecting on the failed gasoline tax, Carter said in a 1980 interview, "As you know, I attempted to impose a conservation fee on gasoline. It should've been done."[24]

A number of unilateral actions were considered following Carter's loss in the November election. The impending takeover by a new president intent on exploiting federal land for energy resources led to some preemptive administrative actions. A final rule from the National Oceanic and Atmospheric Administration designated new marine sanctuaries around the Channel Islands and Barrier Islands, locking up sections of ocean floor and foreclosing the possibility of offshore drilling. He used the same last-minute strategy to protect vast expanses of wilderness from strip mining.

Rulemaking at the End

Much of the rulemaking still under way at the time of the 1980 election was required by statutory mandate. Several of these laws were enacted early in Carter's term, including five major environmental statutes that Congress had recently reauthorized. President Ford had vetoed a prior bill to reauthorize the Clean Air Act as well as vetoing strip mining legislation. Clearing this backlog gave Carter many of his early legislative accomplishments. For regulatory agencies, these mandates added to an agenda already packed with the implementation of policies enacted at the end of the Ford Administration. For example, the EPA and BLM already had crowded agendas after Ford signed the Federal Land Policy and Management Act (FLPMA, or the BLM Organic Act) and the Resource Conservation and Recovery Act into law in 1976. Several rules finalized at the end of 1980 became "midnight regulations" only because of delays imposed by Congress, the White House, and a lack of interagency cooperation.

Natural Resources

Upon taking office in 1977 Carter stepped into a controversy over land management that had been simmering for several years. The FLPMA was intended to consolidate and articulate the BLM's mission and help designate uses for the federal land it managed. The act states that the BLM must manage public land on the basis of "multiple use and sustained yield."[25] Unfortunately, the tension between these competing doctrines and unclear language offered the BLM little guidance in resolving existing claims. Further complicating matters was the growth in the number of acres designated as wilderness. When Congress passed the Wilderness Act of 1964, much of the land designated as wilderness was unsuitable for grazing, and preservation seemed like an appropriate use for economically unproductive land. However, withdrawals of land continued during the following decade as the energy crisis created new demands for mineral resources. By 1980 the number of acres with that designation had grown 779 percent, from 9 million to 80 million acres.[26]

One of Carter's most significant and lasting interregnum acts was to withdraw federal lands in the West from development. It was not his first time taking such an action: two years earlier, he had moved to preserve land in Alaska after Congress failed to reach agreement on legislation to satisfy the requirements of the Alaska Native Claims Settlement Act of 1971. The law imposed a deadline to settle native claims and designate uses for one-third of Alaskan land owned by the federal government. Congress deferred action on this contentious problem and extended the deadline twice. After a House-approved compromise died in the Senate in 1978, Carter could have allowed Congress to extend the deadline again, as his predecessors had done. House Natural Resources Committee chair Morris Udall requested that Carter use executive authority to settle the problem. He withdrew significant amounts of land from development, leaving the rest unprotected until his rediscovery of the Antiquities Act.[27] After the midterm election of 1978 he invoked the Antiquities Act to give much of that land national monument status. It was an unprecedented move that doubled the size of the national park system with the stroke of a pen.

In the fervor of the 1980 lame duck congressional session the House and Senate finally reached an agreement on Alaska lands. Glacier Bay and Katmai were reclassified as national parks in this act. In order to seal Carter's allocation decisions before the transition, Congress passed the Alaska National Interest Lands Conservation Act, which Carter signed into law on December 2.[28] As Udall would later write, "In hindsight, I can only thank God that we passed the bill before Ronald Reagan and Jim Watt took office."[29] Carter's executive actions to protect Alaska lands foreshadowed other land preservation decisions at the end of his term. Having lost the election, and already deeply unpopular in the Mountain West, Carter had little to lose by withdrawing more federal land to expand his legacy. SMCRA contained a never-used provision to declare federal lands unsuitable for mining if there was potential for environmental degradation. For four years, Carter disappointed environmentalists by promoting coal as part of his energy strategy. This became an opportunity to advance instead the cause of conservation over coal development.

In the final month of the administration, Interior Secretary Cecil Andrus issued a decision that protected ninety thousand acres of land around Bryce Canyon from future strip mining. Andrus ruled on a petition to declare the land unsuitable for mining, citing the aesthetic benefits of the landscape and the predicted cost of extracting small amounts of coal from a field with such low reserves. The Environmental Defense Fund, which had filed the petition, was disappointed that the decision did not cover the entire coal field.[30] However, the action's greater significance was the precedent it established and its future potential to limit mining and protect federal lands. On its way out the door, the Carter Administration made the first use of SMCRA's provision that federal land could be withdrawn from leasing for mining purposes.

Surface Mining

This was the first of many presidential transitions that featured last-minute efforts to affect administrative changes to strip mining policy. Carter signed

SMCRA into law during his first year in office, and the Interior Department was still working through the initial implementation decisions at the time of his departure. The law itself had suffered setbacks and delays; major environmental statutes Congress had enacted earlier in the decade addressed more general pollution problems, and early mining legislation was focused on the health and safety of underground mine workers. A bill introduced by West Virginia representative Ken Hechler in 1971 to ban all forms of strip mining attracted more than one hundred cosponsors but never made it out of committee.[31] Events conspired to keep strip mining on the agenda despite the slow progress. In 1972 an impoundment containing mine waste collapsed without warning in Buffalo Creek, West Virginia, killing 125 people and leaving more than 4,000 homeless.[32] Congress passed surface mining bills in both the legislative sessions that followed, and both were vetoed by President Ford.

When Congress took up SMCRA in the spring of 1977, Carter's election and a large Democratic majority gave supporters reason to believe that Congress would finally pass regulatory legislation. Passage still was not assured because of opposition from coal state senators. Then a rainy season in April in Harlan County, Kentucky, caused deadly flooding in several coal-mining communities. Mine operators' silt ponds were overwhelmed as runoff from the denuded hillsides overflowed the banks of rivers and streams, killing four people and causing $175 million in damage.[33] The disaster prompted another round of congressional hearings on the role of strip mining in the flooding, and both the House and Senate passed versions of the bill in May. Compromises were made to reconcile the two versions. The final bill included exemptions for small mine operators, allowed variances for the approximate original contour requirement, and contained fewer restrictions on mountaintop removal mining than the stricter House version. Although Conference Committee chair Morris Udall fought off some of the provisions of the weaker Senate bill, those compromises would become lasting sources of conflict in the program's implementation.[34]

The bill that Carter signed reflected the urgency and frustrations that had accumulated over the previous decade. The act created the Office of Surface Mining, Reclamation and Enforcement (OSMRE) to enforce federal standards and approve state enforcement plans. Even though OSMRE was housed within the Department of Interior, its legislative architects fashioned an agency that would be a strong advocate for the environment and remain independent. By law it was prohibited from employing anyone who had previously worked for any other agency that worked with the mining industry.[35] Nonetheless, many environmentalists urged Carter not to sign the bill, and Hechler warned that it could easily be weakened by those administrating the law in the future.[36] The law was enacted in two phases. First, interim regulations, enforced by the federal government, were intended to serve as a bridge until the states assumed responsibility for surface mining regulation. The interim program left existing permits in effect but imposed federal standards on mining operations. The permanent regulations would be developed by the states, subject to federal approval. The first permanent rules were not proposed until March of 1979, and several states had yet to submit their plans by the end of 1980.

The political conflicts that had stalled the surface mining law for so many years did not subside after its enactment. The mining industry felt it had been unfairly excluded from the process of writing the bill in Congress and attacked the law's implementation on multiple fronts, including lobbying OSMRE and state agencies, litigation, and spending money to influence political campaigns.[37] Opponents seized upon key language and argued for interpretations more favorable to mining interests. For example, the act banned mining within one hundred feet of cemeteries or three hundred feet of homes, and within protected areas such as national parks, but made those restrictions subject to "valid existing rights." Confusion over the meaning of "valid existing right" forced the Interior Department to engage in an additional rulemaking to clarify the definition, but the proposed definition was struck down in 1980 by US District Court Judge Thomas Flannery.[38] The conflict lasted beyond Carter's presidency. The interpretation of this particular phrase would be the subject of last-minute rules by two subsequent administrations, as chapters 4 and 5 illustrate.

The law also required that reclaimed land be restored to its "original contour" and included a provision that "prime farmland" be restored to its "original" condition. If the ambiguity over these definitions served a purpose during the legislative debate, neutralizing opposition and ensuring enactment, it simply delayed inevitable conflicts to the program's implementation. The same ambiguity created openings for interest groups to mount legal challenges. Since the law required farmland to be restored to its original condition, the stakes for the mining industry were high.

The ensuing litigation ensured that there would be delays. These conflicts continued well into the 1980 election season. Even as the Department of Interior continued to grapple with implementation, Republican nominee Ronald Reagan criticized the law, and divided congressional Democrats debated whether to make significant changes. Under pressure to relax the reclamation language, Andrus proposed changing the definition of prime farmland to fields that had been used for farming for five of the last ten years, as opposed to the original definition of five of the last twenty years.[39] For coal operators it was advantageous to delay the permanent regulations until Reagan took office because OSMRE was reorganized after James Watt assumed leadership of the Interior Department. This resulted in a decentralized regulatory structure resembling the patchwork of state regulations that existed before SMCRA.[40] In an elaborate illustration of venue shopping, the industry sought relief from the administration after it was rebuffed by Congress. However, the change to the more business-friendly Reagan Administration offered a better opportunity to lobby for rules that would be more accommodating to the industry.

Pollution Control

The problem of hazardous waste control would come to dominate the EPA agenda during the Carter years. This was the consequence of mandates the agency had inherited from recently enacted legislation as well as growing awareness of the problem and pressure from grassroots environmental groups to respond with policies to address hazards such as Love Canal and other toxic waste sites yet to be discovered.

By 1974 major environmental legislation had been realized to address air and water pollution, and Congress had passed the Federal Insecticide, Fungicide, and Rodenticide Act and the Endangered Species Act. The comparatively unglamorous problem of toxic and hazardous waste was not debated until the 1976 election approached. The debate resulted in a pair of laws, the Toxic Substances Control Act (TSCA) and the Resource Conservation and Recovery Act (RCRA). TSCA regulates only the manufacture and distribution of chemical substances. The EPA is authorized by the statute to regulate substances found to present an "unreasonable" risk to human health, with appropriate remedies from labeling requirements to an outright ban. Chemical producers were required to submit information about their products to the EPA, including records about their health effects. The EPA, in turn, uses the information to maintain a public database of existing chemicals. Producers must notify the EPA ninety days before a new substance goes onto the market to allow for screening, and the agency has the authority to suspend the production and sale of any new substances if the producer fails to submit adequate information. In addition, the law gives the EPA authority to inspect public buildings and schools for asbestos and supervise the removal of asbestos. Despite the safeguards TSCA offered for new toxics entering the marketplace, its provisions do not address their transportation or disposal or the problem of waste.

Following TSCA, deliberations on the nation's first hazardous waste disposal law began in the summer of 1976. Hoping to show results before facing the voters, Congress would pass RCRA with little debate or input from the EPA. The legislation authorized EPA to define wastes as "potentially hazardous" to human health or the environment and to promulgate rules for the transportation and disposal of those wastes. In their haste, RCRA's authors omitted crucial directions and definitions. The ambiguity of the final legislation contained the seeds of conflict that would delay and undermine its implementation. The bill's ambiguity also made compromise possible, allowing Congress and President Ford to take credit for passing RCRA just one week before the November election. Taking effect during a transition, RCRA would consume much of the EPA's energy for the duration of the Carter presidency. EPA administrator Douglas Costle called this the first crisis of his tenure at the agency.[41]

The transportation and disposal standards that took effect after the 1980 election were the first hazardous waste rules promulgated under RCRA. Already two years behind schedule, the regulations would have faced an uncertain fate had they not been finalized before the transition. In December David Stockman authored a scathing critique of the program, but there was little the incoming administration could do to change course.[42] Some of the delay in RCRA's implementation can be attributed to the agency's decision to maximize opportunities for public involvement. The EPA held public meetings across the country to receive input from regulated industries as well as citizens. During the intervening months, the widespread contamination at Love Canal was publicized, generating more interest in the RCRA hearings and causing the positions of supporters and opponents of the regulations to harden.[43]

Many of the problems with implementation were caused by RCRA itself. Since the law was intended to promote conservation, only one of its nine sections addressed hazardous waste. Its legislative authors lacked knowledge of the problem, resulting in a statute with vague instructions and unspecific goals. Even though the average EPA rulemaking took twenty-six months, the RCRA set an eighteen-month timetable for implementation, which had nearly expired by the time Carter's EPA appointees were confirmed. At the agency level, implementation was hindered by a lack of resources, budget and staff reductions, and having too few personnel with expertise on the problem.[44]

Yet another crisis occurred after the 1980 election. With the first disposal regulations due to take effect at the end of November, the media were filled with reports of "midnight dumping." Thousands of tons of toxic and hazardous waste were discovered in municipal sewers, in parking lots, and on vacant property—even spread onto streets and highways by moving tanker trucks.[45] Following the discovery of the abandoned hazardous waste site at Love Canal, there were new concerns about the RCRA approach to hazardous waste management. It had become clear that a new program was needed to deal with existing hazardous waste that threatened soil and water quality as well as with countless undiscovered toxic waste sites. Unfortunately, the EPA lacked authority to address unlicensed sites that predated RCRA. Carter called for the creation of a "Superfund" to finance the sites' cleanup and protect the environment and public health, but little progress was made until the interregnum period. The gap in hazardous waste regulation was finally closed after Democrats lost the White House and the Senate in the 1980 election. Acting with renewed urgency, Congress debated and passed the Comprehensive Environmental Response, Compensation, and Liability Act (CERCLA) of 1980, which Carter signed into law in just days before leaving the White House. In reauthorizing the Clean Air Act, an innovative cap-and-trade market for sulfur dioxide emissions was created to facilitate power plant upgrades and to expand the cleaner use of coal, consistent with Carter's energy strategy. CERCLA, the EPA's largest single program, was thus a last-minute product of a lame duck president and Congress.

Hazardous Waste Exports

With Superfund's enactment and the implementation of RCRA, an elaborate regime of hazardous waste policies was put in place by the end of 1980. However, the laws offered no solution to the growing problem of hazardous substances that the United States shipped overseas. To address this Carter turned to the executive order. He announced his decision to pursue the action on January 7, 1981, and a draft order was on his desk in seven days.[46] After feedback and clearances from OMB and the Department of Justice, Executive Order 12264 was issued on January 15, just five days before Reagan's inauguration.

More of a right-to-know law than a Basel Convention–type prohibition, Carter's order directed the State Department and an interagency task force to develop a list of hazardous substances significantly restricted under US law as well as to institute a procedure for notifying foreign governments about the possible hazards within the contents of shipments abroad.[47] The order was reversed by President Reagan on February 17, 1981, without explanation. A White House news release issued the following day dismissed it as a "cumbersome, duplicative and burdensome regulatory policy" that "would have threatened American workers' jobs."[48] Reagan's CEQ chair A. Alan Hill later wrote that the policy "would have imposed export controls through a cumbersome regulatory program costly to both the public and private sector."[49]

Energy Conservation

Reagan opposed much of Carter's energy plan and acted swiftly to reverse those provisions that could be undone unilaterally. Among withdrawn regulations were Building Efficiency Performance Standards (BEPS) for new residential and commercial units. The standards were mandated by legislation signed by President Ford and delayed because of disagreements within the Carter Administration over their economic impact and ease of implementation.[50] Carter was unable to finalize BEPS before leaving, but during his final week he made one last symbolic gesture in the name of conservation. He extended the Emergency Building Temperature Restrictions he had first imposed in 1979, prolonging his order that the thermostats of public buildings be kept below 65 degrees in winter and at 78 degrees in summer. The proclamation he issued was at once an explanation of his rationale, a defense of his conservationist energy program, and a warning to his successor:

> New worldwide crude oil production is now and is likely to continue to be at least two million barrels a day less than consumption through the first quarter of 1981. This shortage has resulted in increased petroleum prices, and the combined effects of the shortage and present and future price increases resulting from it may have a major adverse impact on the national economy. The war between Iran and Iraq, as well as border tensions between Syria and Jordan and the Soviet actions in Afghanistan, have also greatly increased the threat to other sources of petroleum supplies in the Middle East. Should other disruptions result, they are likely to be of an emergency nature and to further disrupt the Nation's economy.[51]

President Reagan rescinded the order four weeks later, confident that the decontrol of gasoline prices would make conservation unnecessary. In stark contrast to Carter's elaboration, Reagan issued a one-sentence explanation of his reasoning:

> Although restrictions on building temperatures may result in reduced consumption of fuel, I have concluded that the regulatory scheme designed to accomplish that objective imposes an excessive regulatory burden and that voluntary restraint and market incentives will achieve substantially the same benefit without the regulatory cost.[52]

Also withdrawn by proclamation were contingency plans for emergency gasoline rationing and vigorous enforcement of a federal fifty-five-mile-per-hour speed limit.

Two days after reversing the temperature standards, Reagan withdrew efficiency standards for consumer appliances that the Energy Department had proposed four months before the election and that were singled out for criticism by David Stockman of OMB.[53] The Energy Policy Conservation Act of 1975 (amended in 1978) mandated efficiency standards for nine types of consumer appliances by December 1980 and six others the following year. The department calculated that the cost of appliances would increase as much as $10 billion over twenty-five years, but this would be more than offset by $29 billion in savings over the same time. Manufacturers who had been fighting the proposal found ammunition after RARG conducted a review of the department's cost-benefit analysis. The Reagan Administration also took cover from the report, which concluded that the Department of Energy's economic analysis had underestimated the cost of manufacturing the appliances and exaggerated the savings claims. RARG focused on the retooling costs for industry and the disproportionate impact on smaller consumer appliance manufacturers, concluding that "some small firms may be forced to exit."[54] The council recommended that the department conduct further study before proceeding, and the deadline elapsed without a final regulation. Had the proposed rules taken effect, eight kinds of appliances would have been under new efficiency standards by July, with the final standards going into effect in 1986.

Fuel Economy Standards

The Department of Transportation had several major rules under development in 1980, including dozens of safety regulations that the automobile industry opposed fiercely. At the same time, the recession and a backlash against regulation were making some in the administration skittish. One administration official at the center of these pressures was Joan Claybrook, NHTSA administrator. Carter had appointed Claybrook, a consumer activist and ally of Ralph Nader, to lead the agency responsible for auto safety.[55] Under legislative mandate, NHTSA developed safety regulations on everything from child safety seats to air bags. Claybrook was preparing to make the proposals public early in 1980 when Transportation Secretary Neil Goldschmidt requested that she refrain from proposing any new regulations until after the election. "I was flabbergasted," she recalled. "It reflected so little understanding of what an agency does."[56] Responding that she would not interfere with the rules NHTSA already had in progress, Claybrook persisted.

One of the more contentious transportation regulations under consideration at the very end of Carter's term concerned new fuel economy standards for light trucks. As with the efficiency standards for buildings and appliances, the light truck standards were promulgated under mandate of the 1975 Energy Policy and Conservation Act. The Transportation Department had first set standards for light trucks in 1979, establishing an average of eighteen miles per gallon for two-wheel-drive vehicles in the 1982 model year. By 1980 the average fuel economy rate had improved only 0.21 miles per gallon above 1973 levels, in part because rising truck sales offset the reduction in emissions from cars.[57] Not only did trucks account for a greater share of the domestic auto market, but price controls kept gasoline artificially inexpensive for most of the decade. A new round of standards was proposed in March, raising the fleet average by one mile per gallon in each of the 1983, 1984, and 1985 model years. The rule change was expected to save more than 10 million gallons of gasoline over the lifetime of the vehicles, but automakers complained that it would cost the industry tens of millions of dollars.

Following the election the Carter Administration softened the rule in an attempt to save it. On December 9, 1980, the Department of Transportation published a relaxed proposal, allowing automakers to meet a fleet average or separate standards for two-wheel-drive trucks and four-wheel-drive vehicles. Automobile manufacturers were united in their contention that they could accept an increase to twenty miles per gallon no earlier than 1985, and the Reagan Administration then withdrew the rule. Safety regulations still under development had little chance of completion following the transition. Incoming Transportation Secretary Drew Lewis signaled that safety would not be the emphasis of his department, stating in his confirmation hearing that it had reached a "point of diminishing returns."[58] In her final week on the job Claybrook proposed one rule requiring auto dealers to inform customers better and to provide information on crash tests, and a second rule that required manufacturers to redesign the front ends of automobiles to minimize injuries to pedestrians. With some irony, Claybrook later noted that all but one of the regulations that were suspended or withdrawn by her successor eventually became law anyway.[59]

Occupational Safety and Health

In terms of rulemaking, OSHA became the most prolific regulatory agency during those final weeks. A large number of rules were proposed under Carter, only to be frozen by the Reagan Administration. Some had been under development for months, or even years, including safety standards for electrical equipment and requirements for assessing cancer risk and hazard communication. Others, including noise and cotton dust standards, originated during the Nixon and Ford years, but litigation and other delays had prevented final rules until 1980.

Carter chose a respected occupational health researcher, Eula Bingham, to lead the agency. As the first administrator in its history to hold the position for an entire term, Bingham was in a unique position to redirect the agency and shepherd regulations through the entire rulemaking process. She still bristles at the Reagan Administration's "derogatory" attack on OSHA's unfinished rule-making.[60] It is Bingham's view that labeling them "midnight" regulations ignores the fact that they were promulgated under legislative and judicial mandates and that the agency's agenda was firmly in place by the second year of Carter's presidency. "You know, you'll only have fifteen months," was the advice she received from Assistant Secretary of Health, Education and Welfare Julian Richman on the day she was sworn in.[61] "I thought this was a four-year commitment," was her initial reaction, but she soon understood what he meant: "If you want to do things, you have to do them right away." Due to the nature of the political cycle, the chance of completing any new initiatives after the second year was slim. Come summer of 1978, there would be midterm elections followed by a presidential election. Bingham anticipated that she would spend the last two and a half years in a defensive mode, following through on the initial agenda.

Following the 1980 election a number of planned regulations opposed by Reagan were likely to be reversed, and still other projects faced an uncertain fate. Rather than abandon work on the unfinished rules, Bingham chose to publish them as proposed rules. This made the regulations "impossible to ignore," as Bingham recounted. "By putting them out there, [we made sure] the incoming administration would have to react to them. . . . If they were never published as proposals, then they could just be forgotten."[62]

OSHA proposed a rule designed to encourage more thorough workplace inspections and to facilitate worker participation. The walkaround pay rule would have guaranteed workers their normal wages for time spent with an OSHA official on an inspection or jobsite visit. The right to accompany an official during an inspection is guaranteed by law, but in the absence of a compensation guarantee, a worker would endure a financial penalty for exercising that right. The November 1980 proposal was the agency's second attempt to clarify the policy; a similar rule was listed in 1977 but was struck down in US District Court in the District of Columbia because OSHA had failed to solicit public comments. Bingham later explained that the agency did not think the notice-and-comment requirement applied because it was merely a clarification. Following the decision by the D.C. court, there was precious little time to react. OSHA deleted the old walkaround rule on October 31, proposed the new one on November 18, and scheduled a thirty-day comment period. The final rule was published two days before Reagan's inauguration in 1981 and was quickly withdrawn. Furthermore, the number of workplace inspections dropped because of administrative action by the Reagan Labor Department.[63] From October of 1981 until 1988, complete inspections were required only in manufacturing facilities with below-average safety records.[64] Otherwise, a records check was considered sufficient.

In January OSHA also proposed its generic cancer policy after three years of development. The rule would have required OSHA to publish an annual candidates list of suspected carcinogens and to set standards for any suspected carcinogen found to pose a significant risk. The Reagan Labor Department formally withdrew the generic cancer policy after the review as well as withdrawing the recently completed noise and hazard communication standards.[65]

Noise

In the final week of Carter's term OSHA finalized a health standard for occupational noise, originally proposed during the Nixon Administration. Hearing loss in the workplace was considered such a serious problem that in 1974 the agency proposed an ambient noise standard limiting worker exposure to an average of ninety decibels per day. At the time many types of manufacturing facilities routinely exceeded this level, including textile plants, lumber mills, canneries, and printing presses.[66]

OSHA had yet to issue a final hearing conservation rule in 1976, when it succumbed to pressure to delay its work. That September, the Ford Administration's Council on Wage and Price Stability urged OSHA to withdraw its proposal, arguing that an alternative approach that did not specify technologies for compliance would be more acceptable if it was "noninflationary."[67] Concerns about the cost of compliance prompted OSHA to reopen the comment period to receive more feedback on the proposed rule from experts and industry. The noise standard thus became one of many overdue OSHA regulations that emerged as the Carter Administration's responsibility in 1977.

The estimated multibillion-dollar price tag of the proposed noise rule raised concerns within the Carter White House immediately. In the administration's first month, the Council of Economic Advisors inquired about the proposed noise standard and was told by experts that engineering controls to limit ambient noise in the workplace would cost an additional $668,000 per additional worker.[68] This was the estimated cost over the amount to pay for personal protection equipment. Due to the prohibitive cost, an alternative method of compliance based on protecting the individual, rather than providing the engineering controls for the environment, became the basis of the new approach beginning in early 1977.

On April 30, 1980, OSHA proposed a revised standard for workplace noise that was more flexible and cost effective than the 1974 proposal. The revised proposal maintained the ninety-decibel standard while allowing employers to provide personal protective devices, such as ear plugs or earmuffs, if engineering controls were not feasible. The proposal fell short of a strict eighty-five-decibel standard recommended by the National Institute for Occupational Safety and Health, but it required employers to make hearing protectors available to workers if their environment exceeded an eighty-five-decibel daily standard. The protective devices would have been mandatory if workers were subject to ninety decibels or more.

Had it gone into effect as planned in April of 1981, the rule would have prevented 898,000 incidents of occupational hearing impairment (about 85 percent of annual cases). At a fraction of the 1974 proposal's estimated cost, the revised proposal would have cost employers $235 million to comply with noise testing and record-keeping requirements, training employees to use the hearing devices, and posting warning signs. Since five million employees in 300,000 facilities were exposed to such noise levels, it was expected to cost $53 per affected worker.[69] OSHA director Eula Bingham insisted that its costs would be offset by the benefits of reducing the cost of health care related to instances of occupational hearing impairment. The benefits she cited included reduction of absenteeism, medical costs, and worker compensation payments. She also suggested that there could be other benefits, namely "a possible reduction in cardiovascular illness."[70] Those claims were rejected by the US Chamber of Commerce, which threatened litigation. The final rule was issued in the Carter Administration's final week.

After this final noise rule was suspended in Reagan's regulatory freeze, the new administration proposed its own replacement rule in August 1981. OSHA director Thorne Auchter announced a more business-friendly rule, in which compliance would be voluntary and would impose less expenditure upon industry. Since it retained the testing and monitoring requirements, the most costly features of the Carter rule, while eliminating the enforcement provisions, the Reagan rule only brought the cost down to $182 million from $235 million.[71]

Hazard Communication

Bingham's highest priorities during the final months were rules that empowered workers by protecting their right to information about health risks.[72] On January 14, 1981, the same day the final noise rule was listed, OSHA proposed a workplace chemical labeling standard that had been under development since 1974. The long-awaited regulatory proposal resembled a "right-to-know" program for the estimated 20 million workers who spent time in close proximity to hazardous chemicals. Employers were to provide container labels and maintain records of the names and health risks of the hazardous chemicals found on the premises.

The labeling standard was one of the health regulations promulgated after OSHA shifted its direction in the late 1970s. Rising concern over the effects of toxic chemicals led OSHA to begin developing standards to protect worker health after its early rulemaking on basic workplace safety rules ("consensus" standards) was finished in the 1970s. For most of the decade OSHA was preoccupied with generating a large volume of safety standards for specific industries. Many of these regulations, based on voluntary industry guidelines and specified certain engineering controls, were considered misguided. After years of writing and enforcing coercive rules that did little to improve worker safety, the agency developed a reputation for zealous enforcement of trivial regulations and became a symbol of bureaucratic folly to some politicians and the media.

OSHA was an agency in disarray by the time it was inherited by Carter's Labor Secretary, Ray Marshall. No OSHA administrator before Bingham had ever stayed on the job longer than two years. At first, Bingham succeeded in reviewing and eliminating many of the flawed and unnecessary safety standards. In a second initiative, she shifted the agency's agenda from narrow safety standards to wide-ranging health standards. The labeling standard was touted as an improvement over those ineffective safety rules and representative of OSHA's new direction. Rather than impose a ban or set exposure limits, the proposed labeling rule required employers to identify hazardous substances and provide information about their presence to workers. OSHA collaborated with the EPA to classify hazardous substances for the rule, but this prolonged the rulemaking process to drag into 1980. Delaying the proposed chemical labeling standard proved to be costly. "I could have got it into final form if we hadn't worked with the EPA," Bingham says, "but working with another agency—it adds power to your position." The Carter Administration was aware of industry's opposition to the proposal and had good reason to expect Reagan's appointees to withdraw the standard entirely. Chemical industry lobbyists met with White House staff in 1980, seeking to forestall the regulations before they were even proposed. "The industry is principally concerned that the labeling requirements will force the disclosure of confidential ingredient information," wrote Kitty Bernick in a memo to the White House Domestic Policy Staff.[73] The proposal had moderate industry support because many employers preferred a national standard—albeit a weaker one—to a patchwork of state standards. Resistance softened once the proposal, developed with industry input, was finally published.

Considering the incoming administration's stated opposition to OSHA regulations, listing a proposed rule on the way out the door would do little to protect worker health. However, OSHA made sure the labeling standard it developed under Carter would not be ignored. In publishing the proposed rule, OSHA ensured that it would be a starting point for a revised standard, and raised the potential cost to the Reagan Administration, should it decide to abandon the rule entirely. The public comment period had not yet begun when the proposal was frozen following Reagan's inauguration. It was withdrawn the following month, and the new secretary of labor, Raymond Donovan, ordered OSHA to work on a new standard more favorable to industry. Withdrawing the proposal, as opposed to continuing the rulemaking and making changes in response to comments had a strategic advantage. It precluded labor and other groups from contributing supportive comments on the existing proposal. Supporters were denied the opportunity to participate in five public hearings scheduled around the country.

Not everyone who lobbied against the proposal cheered at the withdrawal decision. As many had feared, grassroots activists responded by organizing a right-to-know movement and pressed for standards at the state level. Business interests began to lobby for a new national standard to preempt state regulations. In November 1981, Reagan's Labor Department proposed an alternative labeling standard. This version emphasized communication rather than identification, only requiring employers to make decisions about the risks from hazardous substances and to issue warnings. Since employers retained control of information and decisions about notification, it accommodated industry concerns about revealing trade secrets. By then more than forty state and local governments had enacted their own chemical labeling laws, and many business groups resented the administration for having ordered OSHA to withdraw the rule in the first place. This was apparent to Bingham when she spoke with an executive from a manufacturer of consumer goods during a flight home to Cincinnati from Washington. "We have to get this done. This is costing us money," he said.[74]

Transition

Much of the eleventh-hour activism that followed the 1980 election was at the initiative of subcabinet-level administrators. In addition to the final and proposed rules they added to the *Federal Register*, both Bingham and Claybrook took steps to prepare the occupational safety and consumer protection communities for their impending exile from the federal government. The growing grassroots right-to-know movement, for example, benefited from a controversy over a series of OSHA films that Bingham's successor tried to destroy. Bingham worried that the films, still in production, would never be seen following the election. In the final days of Carter's term, editing was completed on three short films narrated by Studs Terkel: *Can't Take It No More* was a history of worker safety and health; *OSHA*, a film documenting how the Occupational Safety and Health Act has been used by workers; and *Worker to Worker*, which informed employees of their rights in the workplace.

Reagan's appointee to lead OSHA, Thorne Auchter, had not seen the films when he ordered that every copy be recalled.[75] The recalled copies were destroyed, but Bingham had acted unilaterally in the final days of Carter's term to ensure that some would be preserved. She sent copies of all three films to labor unions, universities, and public health activists prior to the Reagan Administration's recall. Some organizations returned the films out of fear of losing federal funding.[76] Others defiantly screened the films. The controversy helped grassroots groups organize better the growing right-to-know movement that pressured states to enact worker protection policies. In Bingham's view, the films reached a much wider audience because organizers enticed people with, "Come and see the 'banned OSHA films.'"[77]

Joan Claybrook was in a similar position to Bingham after the election. In 1979 NHTSA began developing a comprehensive source of data on automobile safety and fuel economy for consumers. Nearly complete and scheduled for publication in January 1981, the *Car Book* was intended to empower consumers to make more informed choices in the marketplace.[78] Since Reagan had promised to reverse the regulatory burdens placed upon the auto industry, the *Car Book* appeared to be headed for oblivion. On her own initiative Claybrook appeared on the *Phil Donahue Show* to promote the book, and her pitch on the popular television daytime talk show resulted in more than 450,000 requests for copies.[79]

The new head of NHTSA, Raymond Peck, took the controversial book out of production after the transition. Its author, Jack Gillis, quietly continued the project, gathering data on new car models and even adding chapters on tires, warranties, and child safety seats. At the end of 1981 Gillis informed his superiors what he was up to, resigned from the agency, and published the second edition privately. An initial investment of $50,000 from the nonprofit Center for Auto Safety financed the first printing of 50,000 copies. When Transportation Secretary Lewis denounced Gills and deemed the book "anti-industry," the publicity stimulated more sales and additional printings.[80] The *Car Book* has been updated and published annually ever since. Whereas their "midnight" regulations had been in the works for years, Claybrook recalls that the *Car Book* is an example of a genuine late-term action with lasting consequences.

Reagan's Regulatory Freeze

When Reagan announced his regulatory freeze on January 29, 1981, the directive was aimed at the 119 midnight rules listed during the final weeks of the Carter Administration. The eleven cabinet secretaries and EPA director were instructed to postpone rules that had not gone into effect and to issue no new regulations for sixty days.[81] The directive, written by Reagan's designee for OMB director, David Stockman, was aimed squarely at regulatory agencies. Stockman carefully worded the directive to exclude rules promulgated under formal rulemaking procedures and all informal rulemaking by independent agencies, the Internal Revenue Service, the Armed Forces, and any others for the purpose of government procurement. "It hardly seems worth complicating the initiative by raising any legal questions concerning the scope of presidential authority with regard to these agencies," Stockman wrote to Reagan, adding that the directive "will prevent last-minute regulatory decisions of the prior Administration from becoming effective without our review and approval."[82] If the purpose was to cause delay, then the moratorium was an unqualified success. Not so if the goal was lasting change. As former NHTSA administrator Joan Claybrook recalled, nearly every one of her agency's proposed safety regulations suspended by the Reagan Administration was adopted in some form within a few years.[83]

Progress on all the standards proposed by NHTSA in December and January was halted as part of the "regulatory relief" that Reagan promised in the campaign. Not every late-term rule from DOT was caught in the regulatory freeze, however. In a clear indication of the incoming administration's priorities, OMB chose not to review a final rule that was published by DOT in January to permit hauling of nuclear waste across state lines over the objections of the state governments.[84] No agency suffered a larger setback than OSHA. On February 12, 1981, Reagan's newly appointed labor secretary, Raymond Donovan, announced that seven OSHA rules finalized under Carter would be suspended for reevaluation. Caught in regulatory freeze were OSHA's generic cancer policy to identify and rate carcinogens; the walkaround pay rule; standards for cotton dust, workplace noise, and chemical labeling; and the rule requiring employers to provide employees access to medical records and data about their own health. Donovan's announcement was made without consulting Bingham and even before her successor had been confirmed. Also suspended was a regulatory decision by OSHA to decertify the Health and Safety plan for the state of Indiana. In April 1980 Bingham had proposed to decertify the program because the state agency lacked the resources and personnel to enforce regulations effectively. Even though the action was not a "new regulation," its postponement shows how the moratorium was an effective instrument to stall regulatory enforcement in other ways.

Suspending those late-term rules was part of a broader regulatory reversal. For example, an OSHA standard for airborne concentration of lead was finalized in 1978 and was no midnight rule, but it had yet to take effect because of a legal challenge filed immediately upon its publication. The standard was upheld by a ruling of the US District Court of Appeals in Washington, DC, on October 15, 1980, but the two-year delay made it vulnerable to reversal. Upon taking office three months later, the Reagan Administration simply initiated a new legal challenge.

Preventing rules from taking effect was only one purpose of Reagan's moratorium. The second goal, according to Stockman, was to delay new rulemaking until the administration had a new regulatory oversight process in place.[85] This was established by Reagan's Executive Order 12291, which required agencies to submit new proposed regulations estimated to cost $100 million or more to the OMB for clearance. The OMB was instructed to conduct a cost-benefit analysis on the regulations, which would receive clearance if it were determined that the benefits of the proposed rule outweighed the costs. The order did not give OMB a veto, but there was a clear implication that new regulatory proposals would need to pass the cost-benefit test in order to receive the blessing of the White House. A third development after the regulatory freeze was a comprehensive review of existing rules by OMB. On March 27 the vice president's task force released a list of twenty-seven regulations the administration planned to reconsider. In a move to gather input from and gain the favor of business and industry, Vice President Bush asked business groups for a list of more existing regulations they would like to see modified and solicited their suggestions for changes.[86]

The Reagan Administration's reaction to the Carter rules is instructive because it shows the limitation on an incoming president's power to reverse regulatory decisions. For example, the NHTSA administrator, Raymond Peck, announced his support for regulatory relief of the automobile industry. After taking office Peck reversed the Carter Administration's passive restraint rule, which required air bags on new vehicles. Insurance companies and consumer groups filed suit, and eventually the Supreme Court ruled that the administration could not withdraw a rule without a finding that supported its withdrawal.[87] Consequently the agency promulgated a new rule requiring air bags unless two thirds of states enacted mandatory seat belt laws by 1987. Even though NHTSA skirted its obligation to reinstate the rule in this case, the court's ruling restricted future administrations to consider strategies other than the arbitrary withdrawal of a rule.

Summary

The end of Carter's term was notable for a large number of policy-entrenching activities, especially in the areas of the environment, energy, and safety policy. Following his election loss Carter experienced significant legislative success with a lame duck Congress and poured his remaining energy into diplomacy and foreign policy. Several of Carter's policy initiatives were unilateral, as demonstrated in the preceding discussion of the January 1981 executive order on export of hazardous materials and directives on energy conservation.

Rulemaking accounted for most of the late-term policy action. The rules promulgated at the end of Carter's term reflect efforts to entrench policies across various federal agencies and executive departments. In stark contrast to its characterization by a defeated president as "midnight" regulation, this activity is better understood as a constellation of agencies acting independently to implement policies mandated by Congress years earlier. They were not necessarily Carter's personal priorities, nor were they imposed by a centralized White House policy apparatus. Agencies were led by political appointees, but because of Carter's system of cabinet government, the appointees at the top levels of leadership operated with considerable autonomy and advised the president on their respective policy areas rather than follow the beat of a single drummer. They were free to make their own staffing decisions for the limited number of subcabinet positions. It was probably the last time decisions were made by professionals known for their dedication to their agency missions rather than for their loyalty to the president.

The Reagan Administration's response established a pattern of policy whiplash that would become a feature of subsequent interparty transitions. Executive orders and directives on energy and the environment were easily rescinded, but the fate of the "midnight" rules was murkier. The administration lacked the legal authority to rescind rules that already had taken effect, and most suspended rules were reinstated or modified. Many of the withdrawn proposals, including energy efficiency and auto safety standards, were revisited by subsequent administrations and revived. Carter's successors would create eleventh-hour rules for some of the same issues, including surface mining and air pollution. Standards for hazardous substances in the workplace would reemerge as the subject of last-minute OSHA rulemaking three more times.

The election of 1980 had immediate and lasting consequences for policy before President Reagan even arrived in the White House. Were it not for the lame duck session at the end of 1980, major legislation on the environment and public lands might never have been realized. Also significant was the unilateral exercise of power by the executive branch. Carter issued a record number of interregnum executive orders and used proclamations for various ends, but these were easily reversed by his successor. The causes and consequences of regulatory decisions at the end of Carter's term are more complicated. As opposed to "midnight" regulation, which implies a politically motivated and capricious abuse of authority by an outgoing president, most of the proposed and final interregnum rules had been mandated by Congress years earlier. Since rulemaking is a long, deliberate process, the end of a four-year term and the anticipated change of an agency's leadership is, of course, a natural deadline. If the timing of late-term rules is determined by the political calendar, as opposed to politics, then we would expect to observe an increase in final rules before a transition to a president of the same party. That is the focus of the following chapter, which examines Ronald Reagan's own exit from the White House.

4 | Ronald Reagan

Policy Retrenchment in a Friendly Takeover

In September 1988, Office of Management and Budget director James Miller III released a report that articulated an agenda for the remainder of President Reagan's second term. The White House that boasted about the easing or repealing of federal regulations now identified 451 significant regulatory changes it hoped to accomplish in its last four months. Eight years earlier the Reagan team had denounced the burst of last-minute rulemaking from the EPA and the Departments of Labor, Interior, and Transportation, among others; the same agencies were now engaged in implementing Reagan's eleventh-hour agenda. Though agencies never matched the output achieved at the end of the Carter years in terms of the volume of new regulations or pages added to the *Federal Register*, this burst of final activity is notable in other ways. Action was highly coordinated because the White House policy institution was centralized, and much of the agenda was antiregulatory. In addition, the increase in rulemaking at the end of 1988 defied expectation because the White House remained within the same party.

The intramural nature of the Reagan-Bush transition is the most distinctive feature of this case study. Knowing the incoming administration would be led by George H. W. Bush meant that both opportunities and constraints arose for Reagan's administrative presidency. The political fortunes of Reagan's vice president and designated successor were aided by unilateral actions during the campaign. More controversial unilateral actions were saved for the post-election period, but some could have become an unwelcome distraction during Bush's transition into the presidency had Reagan not acted quickly in his final days in office.

Since policy continuity would be expected of an intraparty transition, the risk of the incoming administration reversing new rules or halting unfinished work was low. This continuity makes the regulatory surge at the end of the Reagan presidency all the more remarkable. Perhaps unexpectedly, some administrative actions, including new proposed rules, were not received enthusiastically by the Bush team. Other last-minute actions were more benign, including rulemaking that resumed progress on some of the very same regulations that had been halted after the Carter Administration departed.

The number of federal regulations issued was relatively constant for most of Reagan's presidency, after the initial review and revisions of some of Carter's late-term rules. After the first flurry of rulemaking following inauguration, the other exception was a sharp increase in 1988. By year's end there were 9,370 regulations, compared to 8,367 at the beginning of the year, representing a 12 percent jump.[1] For example, during the final weeks agencies proposed new rules setting standards for worker safety and for creating mandatory drug testing programs. Other last-minute rules continued the administration's agenda of regulatory relief. Despite the fact that most of that agenda was accomplished very early in the presidency, new rules, in particular to loosen restrictions on meat inspection and on coal mining in public lands, were proposed as late as November of 1988. The timing of those decisions meant that the Bush Administration would face the early decision of whether to implement or reconsider Reagan's last-minute policies.

Much of this last-minute activity was routine because agencies were under pressure from legislative and judicial deadlines to promulgate rules. In other

Figure 4.1
Review Counts, by Quarter
Economically Significant Rules, 1981–1988

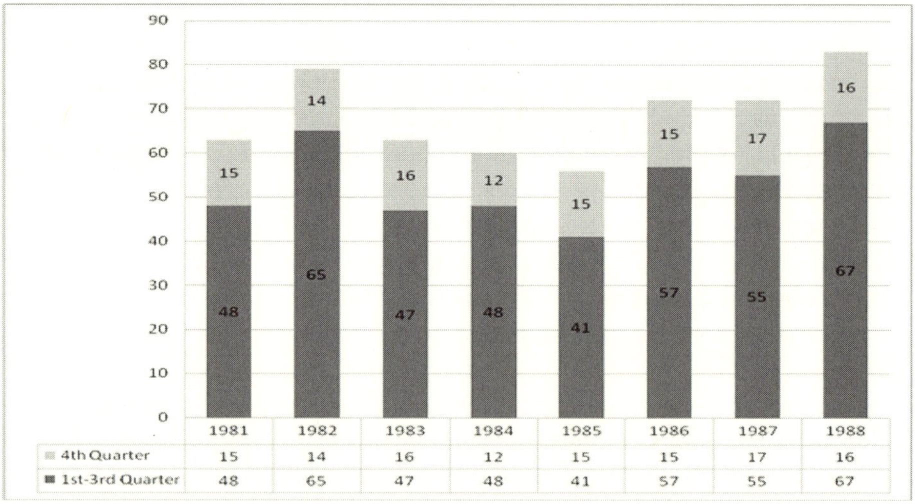

cases, as seen in the previous chapter as well, agencies merely complied with internal deadlines to clean up the docket before the expected change in leadership. However, there were a few uncharacteristic regulatory actions at the end of Reagan's presidency. Prior to the November election, new rules to protect the environment and worker safety were developed by agencies that had suspended or withdrawn similar initiatives eight years earlier. The interregnum period offered a window for some departments to pursue administratively their policy goals in public safety, resource management, and nuclear power, after the administration failed to accomplish them through legislation.

Uncertainty about the 1988 elections prompted various interests to seek favorable policies in the last six months of Reagan's presidency. Significantly, in 1986, California voters overwhelmingly approved Proposition 65, a strict initiative to regulate food safety and toxic substances. Industry fears of a ripple effect, such as other states following California's lead, or Congress responding with a tougher federal Food and Drug Act, created pressure for the Reagan Administration to preempt the law. The Processed Food Association requested that the FDA issue federal regulations, and a task force of the Domestic Policy Council was formed. "As other states follow California's lead, there is a strong likelihood that there will result a crazy-quilt of regulations," the Domestic Policy Council was cautioned.[2] Some members of the council, including Attorney General Ed Meese and Agriculture Secretary Richard Lyng, favored preemption, and the council determined that intervention was allowed by federal law. However, it concluded that such action would not be justified in the absence of an imminent conflict over federalism; without some conflict or thwarting of federal purpose, the federal agency has no implied authority to issue preemptive regulations. One critic of preemption was Health and Human Services Secretary Otis Bowen, who objected that federal action to preempt a state initiative was inconsistent with Reagan's view of states' rights.[3] Ultimately the council decided against intervening to preempt the California law. However, there remained a temptation to use rulemaking for other priorities before the transition. Rulemaking was still available to the Reagan White House as a tool to boost the campaign of his successor and to seal Reagan's policy legacy in the post-election weeks.

The Resurgent Administrative Presidency

Despite howls of protest over the predecessor's late-term regulations, the Reagan Administration found that rulemaking was an effective instrument for its own policy objectives.[4] With a Democratic majority in the House of Representatives, the prospects of enacting a Republican legislative agenda were limited. The administration revived a governing strategy from a previous era of divided government. Like the Nixon White House, Reagan attempted to change federal policies by maximizing control of policy implementation within the executive branch.[5] One difference between Reagan's administrative presidency and the earlier model was the central role of rulemaking to affect policy. Putting the brakes on agency rulemaking, developing new rules, and centralizing control of agency rulemaking within the White House were three of the main strategies that defined Reagan's administrative presidency.

Reagan conserved political capital by promoting much of his domestic agenda within the bureaucracy rather than in Congress. He restricted the activities of regulatory agencies by cutting their budgets as well as by naming political supporters to the highest levels of their leadership. Reagan's own campaign featured relentless criticism of regulation and of government itself.[6] As president, he chose to interpret the election result as a mandate to reverse the growth of government regulation.[7] Continuing his predecessor's efforts to deregulate key economic sectors was just one strategy. The other involved dismantling and transforming the regulatory state. Following the election, Reagan's team arrived in Washington with a list of specific regulations to target for rescission and with recommendations for using the executive branch to enact a policy agenda.[8] In order to make the changes he viewed as necessary, Reagan quickly took control of the budget, made the support of his program a prerequisite for personnel, and asserted administrative control.[9] Key to Reagan's strategy was the selection of subcabinet appointees supportive of his agenda. His success in this area was due to the fact that he was the first president to take advantage of the Civil Service Reform Act of 1978, a reform that his predecessor sought and won from Congress. In order to increase executive accountability, Carter wanted the ability to appoint more of the agency leaders below the rank of cabinet secretary; Reagan was to be the beneficiary of this expanded administrative control.[10] The appointment power became an essential feature of Reagan's management strategy, as Heclo observed:

> Only with the Reagan Administration has there been a more or less coherent philosophy and program against which job applicants' loyalty could be checked. And by the same token, the conservative networks of policy activists that helped generate the administration's program also provided the manpower tool for filling political executive positions. Thus the new political mobilization . . . could be exploited in executive branch management.[11]

Reagan was able to achieve greater consolidation of the executive branch by placing appointees deep inside every executive department, with the expectation that these top and mid-level managers would be more loyal to the president than the career staff were. The increased number of patronage positions also became an invaluable resource because the promise of employment could be used for maintaining party discipline, to attract campaign workers, and as a bargaining chip with Congress.[12]

Administrative tools were used to propel Reagan's antiregulatory agenda toward occupational health and safety. OSHA appointees expanded control over the agency's rulemaking, redirecting its priorities from developing new regulations to revising existing ones.[13] For assistant secretary of labor in charge of OSHA Reagan selected Thorne Auchter, the owner of a Florida construction company, who had supported his campaign. In addition, OSHA's leadership positions were filled with other like-minded deregulators in a conscious effort to prevent the agency's "capture" by career staff.[14]

Natural resource policy, in contrast, was shifted away from preservation and toward serving resource-extractive industries, in part by expediting leases and cutting royalties. Business interests, from large corporations to small employers, as well as the coalition of westerners employed in resource-extractive industries and who constituted the Sagebrush Rebellion, all found common cause with Reagan's agenda.[15] Reagan declared himself a sagebrush rebel and capitalized on western dissatisfaction with Carter's implementation of the Federal Lands Management Policy Act, which mandated multiple use of public lands but offered little guidance on how to weigh competing uses. Rather than pursue reform legislation, Reagan used the administrative tool-kit of appointments, restructuring, and budgeting. Chief among these appointments was his appointment of James Watt, the former legal counsel for the conservative Mountain States Legal Foundation, as his first Secretary of the Interior. Early in Reagan's first term a US Supreme Court ruling on a challenge to the Surface Mining Control and Reclamation Act of 1977 by Indiana and Virginia upheld the constitutionality of the law. In that lawsuit Watt had filed a brief in support of the states and coal mine operators, who prevailed in lower court decisions that were appealed by his predecessor, Cecil Andrus, in the final weeks of the Carter Administration. The high court rejected Watt's argument that the law "usurped state government functions" and represented a "trend toward centralized decision-making that threatens to destroy the Federal structure of government in America." Watt was addressing a gathering of the National Coal Association in St. Louis when he learned about the Supreme Court ruling. According to media reports, Watt's reaction was indignant: "What a shame. I promise you it will be changed." Watt told his audience that the Office of Surface Mining, Reclamation and Enforcement symbolized "every abuse of government."[16]

Watt was more committed ideologically to supply-side policies than to states' rights; his true objective was to expedite the development of energy resources. Therefore he quickly ruled out the wholesale transfer of public lands to the states. Some states, such as California, had strict environmental laws, so avoiding a patchwork of state mining regulations would be best accomplished through administrative restructuring while retaining federal control of public lands.[17] Despite his criticisms of SMCRA and the FLPMA, Watt told a congressional panel that changing the laws would not be necessary. Rather, he preferred to impose changes by reorganizing the Department of the Interior. A new federal agency, the Minerals Management Service, was created in 1982, and several of the department's leasing and enforcement programs were streamlined.[18]

Regulatory Review

Institutionalizing regulatory review was central to Reagan's strategy for governing.[19] There was little chance of enacting regulatory reform through legislation alone. Consequently Reagan built upon the review process that evolved under the previous two administrations and centralized activity within the OMB. His E.O. 12291 in February 1981 formalized the practice of regulatory review that was carried out only on a case-by-case basis under Carter. After Reagan abolished the Regulatory Action Review Group, OMB became the logical location to manage regulatory review. The successor organization to the Bureau of the Budget, the OMB had been created in a Nixon-era reorganization. OMB was given the responsibility for guiding federal agency initiatives and ensuring that they were consistent with administration goals. Created by the Paperwork Reduction Act during the Carter years, the Office of Information and Regulatory Affairs (OIRA) was charged with carrying out the reviews and helping to promote the administration's agenda of deregulation.

Reagan believed that excessive government regulation was responsible for depressing economic growth, and correcting this was one pillar of his economic plan, along with tax cuts, spending cuts, and an active monetary policy. Unlike the latter three goals, regulatory relief had no obvious home base with cabinet-level clout, such as the Treasury Department, OMB, or the Federal Reserve. The administration's solution was to create the Task Force on Regulatory Relief, chaired by Vice President Bush, to coordinate the administration's deregulatory initiatives and elevate the importance of this part of Reagan's plan.

Although Carter's midnight regulations were the original rationale for the Task Force on Regulatory Relief, it soon developed a new mission. After completing its three-month review of the 181 rules suspended in Reagan's first month, the eight-member panel reviewed fifty-four existing regulations, a process that led to the modification or rescission of twelve rules. In the summer of 1981 Bush announced that the panel was reviewing another thirty regulations to determine if they were "burdensome, unnecessary or counterproductive" and to consider repealing them as a means of economic stimulus.[20] The targeted regulations were overwhelmingly geared toward protection of health, safety, and civil rights.[21] Task force member James Miller III stood alongside the vice president and explained that the target regulations were selected based on more than twenty-five-hundred comments, mainly from business, adding that organized labor, consumers, and minority groups had also been invited to comment.[22]

According to Reagan aide Martin Anderson, the task force served its purpose by keeping agencies and interest groups on the defensive: "As Bush's task force began its long overdue pruning work the bureaucracy and special interest groups began to fight the reforms fiercely. Their intense preoccupation with keeping what they had seemed to take up so much of their time that they didn't have any time left over to dream up many new regulations."[23] As such, the panel's greater value was as "a potent policy chokepoint."[24] This furthered the White House agenda by slowing the workings of the machinery of the regulatory state, at least temporarily. The long-term impact of Reagan's regulatory review directive was the institutionalization of a coordinated and centralized rulemaking process. It would prove invaluable as a source of administrative control for future presidents seeking to put their own mark on public policy, pursue change without Congress, and cement their own legacies through rulemaking.

Reagan's deregulation agenda had run its course by the end of his first term. Many of its objectives had been met, but some legislative initiatives stalled without congressional support. Other goals—primarily environmental initiatives—were abandoned due to the public backlash over his early policies and the scandals of his appointees Gorsuch and Watt. Certain priorities, such as titling land for mineral development and licensing nuclear power plants, could be enacted unilaterally and were deferred until the end of Reagan's presidency, when he would be free to make politically risky decisions without fear of retribution from the voters.

Rulemaking at the End

One of the immediate consequences of Vice President Bush's election victory was the move to grant licenses to the Shoreham and Seabrook nuclear power plants. Reagan had pledged eight years earlier that the plants would begin operating when he became president, but progress on both projects stalled in the wake of the Three Mile Island and Chernobyl disasters. Reagan was forced to sideline his advocacy for the industry because of the public's souring attitude toward nuclear power—and because of outright resistance in Congress. The interregnum weeks at the end of his presidency provided the opportunity to revisit the issue. Within days of Bush's election to the presidency, licenses were granted to begin construction on the long-delayed Shoreham and Seabrook nuclear power plants. Delaying the nuclear decisions insulated Bush and other Republican candidates from any political fallout until after the 1988 election.

Other key decisions prior to the election worked in Bush's favor. Following Reagan's last State of the Union address, the White House revisited the theme of regulatory relief, which had been a successful campaign issue eight years earlier. Another regulatory moratorium was announced, and the presidential Task Force on Regulatory Relief was reconstituted during the primary season. In reprising his chairmanship of the council, Bush reminded supporters of the significant part he had played in the early days of the Reagan White House, and he beat back four rival candidates to become his party's standard-bearer.

If Bush's reputation as a regulation fighter enhanced his standing with the Republican base, it was inconsistent with his desire to claiming the middle ground from his Democratic opponent in the general election.[25] Fortunately for his campaign, the latest regulatory freeze had thawed by the summer of 1988. In order to garner public support, Bush was eager to court voters by advocating strong government action in the service of popular policies. Dozens of new regulations were announced in the weeks leading up to the election, including a number of environmental and worker safety rules that appealed to key demographic and interest groups.

Natural Resources

Just four days before the November 1988 election, a federal judge lifted a three-year-old ban on mining, oil, and gas development on federal land in western states. The injunction, covering 170 million acres, was in response to National Wildlife Federation litigation, which claimed that then Interior Secretary Watt failed to comply with the procedural requirements of the FLPMA before reclassifying the land for development. Besides lifting the ban, Judge John H. Pratt dismissed the lawsuit, claiming that the environmental organization lacked standing to sue because it failed to show any material injury from the BLM policy.[26] In December the Department of Interior sprang into action and began to process its backlog of title-transfer applications for $2.50 per acre. More than a quarter of a million acres of federal land were under claim for oil shale development, and the backlog included applications to lease 24,000 acres filed before the 1985 injunction. The department wasted no time in starting to approve title transfers once the ban was lifted, even though the BLM had yet to finish rulemaking to establish criteria for evaluating the applications.[27]

With few options to curtail the title transfers, Democrats could only express their frustration. With Congress still out of session in the first week of January, Representative Nick Rahall of West Virginia responded with a statement: "The President-elect is being ill-served by the activities of these Reagan Administration political appointees who in the 11th hour are creating a lot of baggage that will have to be carried out by Interior in the Bush Administration," Rahall said.[28] He also accused outgoing Interior Secretary Don Hodel of intervening with the OMB to delay a new Forest Service rule implementing the Federal Onshore Oil and Gas Leasing Act of 1987. Between the Forest Service rule, the oil shale applications, and the surface mining claims, Rahall claimed the Reagan Administration had abused its discretion in the lame duck period to undermine Congress, the incoming president, and the will of the people.

Other Interior Department moves occurred literally on the eve of Inauguration Day. On January 19 Hodel cut the leasing rate for coal mining from $3 per acre to $2, at an estimated annual cost to taxpayers of $35 million.[29] On the same day, Hodel proposed a land swap with Native Alaskan corporations for territory in the Arctic National Wildlife Refuge for the purpose of oil exploration. Unlike Hodel's other interregnum initiatives, any land swap for a portion of this refuge would have required congressional approval, so its prospects were slim. As a last-minute trial balloon by a lame duck administration, it was also less likely to undermine Bush than if it was his own initiative.

Surface Mining

On December 28, 1988, only three weeks remained of Reagan's presidency, and Congress was on break before the arrival of its new members. The news from Washington was preoccupied with the upcoming inauguration, but the front page of the *New York Times* carried an ominous headline: "U.S. May Open Some Parklands to Coal Mining."[30] Amid the demands of the transition the Interior Department was planning some consequential actions in the lead-up to Vice President Bush's inauguration. They included decisions to set royalty rates for oil in Alaska, to grant oil shale leases, and to promulgate rules to settle claims for old mining permits on federal land. The administration had good reason to anticipate a backlash in public opinion and would likely have faced negative consequences in the election had the announcements of its land management decisions come prior to the election.

James Watt was long gone, but environmentalists and their congressional allies continued to view Reagan's appointees with suspicion.[31] Secretary Watt had begun his short and controversial term with an ambitious agenda. He embraced the recommendations from a Heritage Foundation report to encourage "timely and orderly minerals development onshore and on the outer continental shelf with fewer regulatory controls" and "major regulatory reform within the department, with particular attention to permanent rules."[32]

Unlike some of Reagan's top appointees, Watt was unafraid to engage in wholesale restructuring of his department. He sought not only to slow down but to redirect his department from what he saw as a preservation mission to one of encouraging development of resources. To facilitate this, Watt intended to use rulemaking to resolve conflicts over the implementation of SMCRA and the FLMPA in favor of development. In his first appearance before Congress following his confirmation, Watt told the House Interior Committee of his plan to review existing surface mining regulations and propose new rules to address the lingering issues rather than seeking changes in the law. Congressional action was unnecessary, Watt explained, but "there will be major amendments to the way the program is administered."

After one year in office, Watt had sensed that Congress was prepared to push back against his agenda. "It is my judgment," Watt warned Reagan, "that legislation will be passed this year, 1982, prohibiting any leasing or mineral entry in the wilderness areas."[33] Seeking to limit damage and disarm the administration's critics, Watt reversed his prior position on land withdrawals and proposed to withdraw wilderness areas from development for ten years:

> The House and Senate Republicans would be relieved, and the liberal Democrats stunned at such a Reagan Administration position. It would take a volatile political issue away from the Democrats. Our business friends would be disappointed, but understanding, that they have not delivered us the votes to do anything other than what I am recommending or some variation thereof.[34]

Watt continued to be a lightning rod for Reagan's policies, and he submitted his resignation after another year. His two successors, Hodel and William Clark, were less controversial, although they were just as committed to Watt's goals and continued to defend his initiatives as these became bogged down in the courts.

The Interior Department stayed out of the spotlight during Reagan's second term. After Watt's resignation, much of his agenda stalled following the countermobilization that he provoked from environmental groups.[35] Environmental groups were reinvigorated during the Reagan years: the Sierra Club expanded from 9.5 million members in 1980 to 40 million in 1990, and the Wilderness Society grew from 1.5 to 17.7 million during the decade.[36] However, there were lingering tensions over the implementation of major natural resource statutes, and the end of Reagan's term presented a chance to revisit some of those issues left on the shelf back in 1981.

When Watt reorganized the Interior Department in 1981, he cut the budget for the OSMRE and reduced enforcement capacity for surface mining. After the restructuring there were fourteen state offices instead of the two regional offices. New surface mining rules proposed early in the year significantly relaxed the requirements for state surface mining plans. Watt tried to relax what termed the "excessive, burdensome and counterproductive" restrictions on strip mining, including the "original contour" standard and rules to protect rivers and streams from mining waste.[37] The proposal was blocked because of a suit by the National Wildlife Federation, which argued that the required environmental impact statements had not been completed. The following November, the Department of the Interior published a final rule to allow states greater flexibility in their enforcement programs. Under the revised permanent regulations, states were required to have surface mining rules as effective as the federal standards, although some specific provisions, such as the requirement that an inspector visit following a violation, were relaxed.

The strip-mining proposal announced in December 1988, would have resolved one of those lingering questions. SMCRA was more than eleven years old, but conflict over its interpretation continued unabated. The last-minute proposal was an attempt to resolve the conflict over the "valid existing right" clause in the way the mining industry preferred.[38] The Office of Surface Mining had proposed a definition eight years earlier, as the agency scrambled to clear its docket before the Carter Administration left office. That proposed definition was struck down by in the US District Court in Washington by Thomas A. Flannery, the same judge who later struck down a broader definition of "valid and existing right" proposed by Reagan's Interior Department in 1985. "Congress didn't give us any direction," one official who served in OSMRE at the end of the Reagan years explained. "They left it completely up to us to decide."[39] Hodel's proposed definition would have allowed state laws to determine the definition of a valid existing right. Coal companies stood to benefit enormously by shifting the debate to state capitals, venues where they wielded greater influence and faced weaker opposition.[40] Moreover, state-level determinations would force the federal government to compensate those companies for the old mining claims they held.

Despite the headline's focus on parks, only a few parks, such as the New

River Gorge in West Virginia, were associated with privately held mining claims. The National Park Service estimated four million acres would have been affected, mostly wildlife refuges, wilderness areas, and historic sites previously off limits to surface mining.[41] Other affected land was inside national forest boundaries. One of these permit holders was Thomas Belville, a supporter of Bush's presidential campaign and the owner of the Belville Coal Company, who had purchased mineral rights for 7,200 acres in the Wayne National Forest in southern Ohio. Belville was gratified when the Interior Department issued the December 1988 proposal but flabbergasted when it was withdrawn after Bush became president the following year. "That was my thank-you for being so loyal to George Bush," he told a reporter.[42] At least one supporter had hoped the election would bring about a favorable resolution to this lingering controversy.

Pollution Control

The EPA was especially active during the final year of the Reagan Administration because of new mandates imposed by Congress. During Reagan's first term, budget cuts and his own appointees slowed the development of new regulations and blocked the implementation of existing programs. After that experience, an impatient Congress reasserted itself when major statutes were reauthorized during the 1980s. Minimizing agency discretion, the new laws were detailed, contained more specific provisions, and set tight deadlines for new standards. As in the final year of the Carter Administration, the EPA was given a host of unrealistic deadlines in 1988, and it missed all of them.

Scientists at the EPA were active during Reagan's first term, even as much of the agency's activity, especially the writing and enforcement of regulations, ground to a halt. Evidence accumulated of the health risks of previously unknown hazards, especially radon gas, while new findings confirmed that known pollutants posed greater health risks than had previously been understood. The mounting evidence convinced many inside and outside the agency that existing regulations were inadequate, a view that Congress validated as it amended the nation's major environmental laws between 1984 and 1990. The legislation finally gave the EPA a mandate to begin developing rules addressing hazards that were well-known to its scientists. The lead and copper rule for drinking water proposed in late 1988 can be attributed to this backlog.[43]

Public concern for the environment had returned to peak levels by Reagan's second term. This was the result of the growing awareness of global hazards, such as climate change and ozone depletion, and was a natural response to a new round of devastating industrial accidents, from the nightmare of Bhopal in 1984 to Chernobyl and the Rhine chemical spill. It was also a reaction to the Reagan Administration, which the public perceived to be on the wrong side of the issue, if not hostile to the environment. In the 1988 campaign Bush took care to distance himself from those policies without criticizing his boss. Seeking to reassure moderate voters after the Reagan experience, Bush invoked his "kinder, gentler" theme by staking out strong pro-environment positions, disarming his Democratic opponent in the process.[44]

The environment was the central theme of an August 31 campaign speech in which Bush pledged support for wetlands protection and a stronger Clean Air Act.[45] He used more than rhetoric to reassure green voters that he had turned over a new, greener leaf. Bush surrounded himself with environmental experts—notably William Reilly, who would become his EPA administrator—to establish his credibility in environmental issues. The balancing act was all the more extraordinary because of his role as chair of the administration's Task Force on Regulatory Relief. After the environment speech, Representative Edward Markey wrote an incredulous letter to the *Washington Post* recapping several of the environmental regulations from the departing Carter Administration, which the group took credit for blocking in 1981. Markey complained that the task force continued to send his office "'progress reports,' summing up further environmental 'accomplishments': withdrawal of a policy to control airborne carcinogens, pulling back a lead phasedown rule designed to protect children's health and changing Clean Air Act regulations to allow increased pollution."[46]

Given insufficient time and resources to promulgate standards on an unrealistic timetable set by Congress, the EPA labored to achieve certain high-priority goals. In the second half of 1988 Administrator Lee Thomas proposed new standards to protect drinking water from lead pollution, municipal landfill seepage, and underground storage tanks. Vice President Bush was positioned to take credit for these policies, through the stringency and timing of some of the standards that were mandated by Congress out of frustration with the administrative obstruction of Reagan appointees.

When many federal environmental statutes were reauthorized between 1984 and 1988, and lawmakers used those opportunities to enact tougher laws and to reduce the administrative discretion that they felt Reagan appointees had abused. For example, after controversial EPA administrator Ann Gorsuch resigned in 1982 following a scandal over a mishandled hazardous waste cleanup, a legislative effort to prod and micromanage EPA began with the Resource Conservation and Recovery Act amendments of 1984.[47] In revising RCRA, Congress strengthened requirements for disposal facilities, placed new recycling requirements on the states, and banned certain liquid wastes from disposal in landfills. In 1986 CERCLA was reauthorized to include timetables for cleanup operations, and the Safe Drinking Water Act amendments imposed additional mandates for the EPA to regulate specific pollutants and strict deadlines for developing standards. The following year, the Clean Water Act was strengthened to expand the EPA's enforcement powers, and it mandated new nonpoint-source pollution management plans. In 1988 the Coastal Protection Act was amended to include stricter ocean dumping regulations, new permit requirements, and civil penalties for violations.

Hazardous Waste Disposal

A 1988 rule limiting the types of waste allowed in municipal landfills was one of regulations EPA finalized near the end of Reagan's presidency. One consequence of the congressional backlash against Reagan's EPA was a tougher hazardous waste disposal law that restricted the agency's discretion. Among its provisions the 1984 RCRA amendments required the EPA to set disposal standards for municipal landfills by March 1988. That deadline was missed because a lengthy regulatory impact analysis required by the Reagan Administration that had not been completed.[48] Consequently, the proposed standards were six months overdue. Eight years earlier, the Carter Administration officials had been criticized as they scrambled to complete the first round of RCRA rules. At the end of 1988 Reagan's own midnight regulations included the next round.

Unlike the drinking water and landfill standards, a controversial toxic cleanup standard that might have undermined Republican support in 1988 was delayed until after the election. The CERCLA reauthorization required EPA to propose a contingency plan for site cleanups and a final rule by April 17, 1988. In September the proposal was sent to OMB, which held it for four months, exceeding the sixty-day time limit for regulatory review. The proposed rule was finally released by the outgoing Reagan Administration in December. In its review OMB objected to a cleanup standard based on EPA's standard cancer risk level, proposing a narrower level instead. The EPA compromised by adding language to the proposed rule inviting comments on alternative risk levels.[49] The timing of EPA's actions allowed Bush to associate himself with popular issue positions in an election that was expected to be decided by centrist voters. As the election approached, EPA officials acknowledged having regular contact with Vice President Bush's campaign.

Occupational Safety and Health

Persistent public concern over hazardous substances also prevented the federal government from ignoring workplace risks. Some of the OSHA regulations that Reagan halted in 1981 were intended to address this problem; however, the demands for stronger workplace health protection continued. For over a decade OSHA had been preoccupied with consensus standards. After those were issued, the problem of hazardous substances in the workplace became its top priority. By the end of 1988 protecting the health and safety of American workers was the subject of renewed interest by the administration. No longer was OSHA the symbol of government failure, as it had been in Reagan's campaign against Carter.[50] There had been a turnaround in the Reagan-Bush Administration's tone toward OSHA, and by the post-election period, new rulemaking to reduce accidents and control hazardous substances in the workplace was under way. Moreover, these were some of the very same detested regulations that had been under development at the end of President Carter's term and that had come under fire when Reagan took office. One regulation initially suspended by the Reagan White House was the Carter Administration's late-term proposal for workplace chemical labels. A year after withdrawing the rule, the Reagan Labor Department reluctantly reintroduced it in the form of OSHA's hazard communication standard, creating a program widely lauded as a success.[51] As Reagan's second term wound down, still more of OSHA's agenda from the 1970s returned in order to address worker health risks at lower cost and greater flexibility to industry.

Lockout/Tagout Standard

Another important suspended Carter-era OSHA regulation that found new life was the lockout/tagout standard to protect 39 million workers at risk of injury from accidents caused by the unexpected startup of machinery or electric equipment. A 1979 petition by United Auto Workers requested that OSHA develop a rule requiring that devices be installed on electric machinery to prevent those devices from being switched on during cleaning or repair. According to a Labor Department estimate, 120 workers were killed annually and as many as sixty thousand a year were injured in such accidents. Initially OSHA denied the petition. In 1980, however, with Senator Edward Kennedy drawing support from organized labor in his challenge to Carter, the petition was reconsidered, and work began on a lockout standard.[52]

Development was still in the pre-rule stage when OSHA suspended activity in Reagan's 1981 regulatory freeze. OSHA pondered voluntary standards, but progress toward a lockout standard of any kind did not resume until the presidential primary season of 1988. Kennedy, now the chair of the Senate Labor Committee, scheduled hearings on worker safety that highlighted the one thousand workplace fatalities that the United Auto Workers estimated could have been prevented if Vice President Bush's Regulatory Review Council had allowed OSHA to complete its work in 1981. The committee heard from families of workers who had died horrible deaths and who blasted the Reagan Administration for "its decision to let workers die while waiting on a standard."[53]

That fall, with the general election approaching, and the perception that many union votes were up for grabs, OSHA proposed a tagout standard that would have required employers to place warning labels on equipment that could cause injuries in such circumstances. After the tagout standard was roundly criticized by unions, OSHA revised the proposal to require lockout devices on most equipment, and warning tags only on equipment where it was impossible to install lockout devices.[54] The final lockout/tagout rule went into effect in 1989. Cass Sunstein, an official in the Reagan OMB, later called it the most expensive safety standard in OSHA's history, at a cost of $98 million per life saved.[55]

Drug Testing

Reagan also used late-term initiatives to address new priorities, and the War on Drugs was among them. The interregnum rule requiring mandatory drug testing for transportation workers was the farthest-reaching advance of Reagan's two-year push for government-wide drug testing. It was finalized after the election and following a setback in Congress. After Reagan took the initiative and called for a mandatory drug testing policy, the Democrat-controlled Congress spent months debating the proposal but could not agree on a testing program. With the 1988 election approaching, unilateral action by the executive branch on the drug issue promised to help Republicans.

Mandatory drug testing for federal employees was first proposed in a 1986 report by the President's Commission on Organized Crime. Despite a rising national sense of urgency about the use of illegal drugs, the idea of testing federal employees was ridiculed in the editorial pages of major newspapers and dismissed by many in Congress. The growing public skepticism was expressed by Representative Patricia Schroeder, chair of the House Subcommittee on Civil Service: "Drug testing is a short-sighted response to our frustration at being unable to get drugs out of our schools, workplaces and homes. As in all controversial issues we have to make sure that the solution is not worse than the problem."[56]

There was renewed interest in the idea, however, as persistent media coverage of the crack epidemic in major cities and the cocaine-induced death of college basketball star Len Bias focused public attention on the drug problem.

Several antidrug bills were introduced in Congress, as Democrats attempted to seize the initiative on the drug war from the administration before the fall midterm election and claim victories for their party. Nonetheless, drug testing of federal employees attracted little congressional support. Only one provision—requiring testing of workers in the intelligence community—found its way into the Omnibus Anti-Drug Bill passed by the House in October, but it was dropped from the Senate version.[57]

A more controversial proposal came from the Office of Personnel Management (OPM) later that summer. It exceeded the alternatives before Congress in calling for widespread testing of federal workers (who at the time could be terminated after two positive tests). Furthermore, OPM urged that this should replace the current policy of taking disciplinary action only if an employee's job performance was impaired by outside drug use. Whereas many Democrats in Congress considered the OPM proposal too intrusive and punitive, it gained support among Republicans as the fall campaign approached. Erasing any doubt over his ownership of the drug issue, Reagan made mandatory testing the core of his own policy solution and an important election issue.

In a September televised appearance Ronald and Nancy Reagan called for a "national crusade against drugs" and committed the federal government to showing leadership with widespread drug testing. The following morning Reagan issued an executive order instructing federal agencies to begin testing employees in "sensitive" positions for illegal drugs.[58]

Over subsequent weeks Congress debated an omnibus drug bill that included criminal penalties and funds for enforcement, but drug testing of federal employees remained controversial. One issue was the constitutionality of random drug testing, but lawmakers were also divided over the wisdom of ceding such sweeping authority to the executive branch, since it was understood that the president planned to act in the absence of congressional action. There was some support in Congress for testing certain types of employees in the name of public safety, but a provision for mandatory testing of railroad workers, for example, stalled in the Senate.

Any hope for a drug testing program defined by statutory law was doomed by bickering in the Senate.[59] A move to broker a deal backfired when the Federal Railroad Administrator was brought in to help senators craft a compromise over testing railroad workers. Instead, he told the panel he would prefer drug testing to be left out of the bill so that he would have more freedom to work with the railroad industry to design the program.[60]

The provision for random testing of transportation workers was dropped before the floor voted on the bill, which the Senate then passed during the session's final hours. The issue proved too volatile for the runup to an election.

Congress adjourned and stood for election one week later without voting on mandatory drug testing. Within two weeks, the Department of Transportation issued its proposed rule for drug testing.

Some skeptics questioned the evidence linking such testing programs to improvements in public safety. If the policy's value was in its symbolism, then this reason was sufficient to inspire broad support from the public. As symbolic policy, drug testing of federal employees was touted as a way to bolster public confidence in the civil service. Potentially, the real and perceived benefits to public safety would be greatest for public employees in the transportation sector, due to the risk of catastrophic accidents.[61]

Progress on a government-wide program over the next two years was halting; agency plans to begin drug testing were challenged in court, and Congress weighed in with objections. The unprecedented nature of a government-wide testing program made it difficult for most agencies to respond promptly. However, the Department of Transportation had a head start because it had already conducted limited, targeted testing for certain occupations prior to Reagan's directive.

Meat Inspection

One of the last-minute attempts to change a regulation enforced in an occupational setting concerned the safety of the nation's food supply. The proposal to modify the US Department of Agriculture's system of meat inspection originated as one of Reagan's first-term priorities. Several food safety rules were targeted for review when he took office, and in Reagan's first term, the USDA proposed rules to repeal the ban on junk food in schools, reclassify ketchup as a vegetable, and relax the requirement that meat labels note the presence of pulverized bone fragments and marrow.[62] After an early effort to roll back meat inspection rules stalled, it became the subject of a final push at the time of the 1988 election.

Though Agriculture Secretary Richard Lyng, a former meat industry lobbyist, proposed the relaxed meat inspection rule during the interregnum period, it was promulgated under a legislative mandate. The meat industry–backed bill was passed two years earlier, during the final hours of the ninety-ninth Congress, after years of political battles and a crisis. In the summer of 1986 the USDA braced for automatic spending cuts that would reduce its capacity to conduct inspections. The Gramm-Rudman-Hollings spending limits required the Agriculture Department to find $15.6 million in savings in 1985, and worker furloughs were part of the department's plan. The meat industry protested, insisting that the planned furloughs would shut them down because federal law required inspectors to be present.

The 1986 law allowed for modernization of meat inspection by encouraging changes to streamline the process.[63] In the proposed rule that appeared following the election, meat producers with a clean record would have been allowed to inspect their own facilities, skipping the longtime requirement that inspectors be present at all times. The proposal was supported by large meat producers but opposed by smaller producers, who complained that they relied on the presence of federal inspectors as a valuable source of information about standards and compliance. Despite the Reagan Administration's timing, announcing the controversial proposal during the lame duck period following the election, the public was nonetheless alarmed about the prospect of relaxing meat inspection rules. A few months after assuming office, President Bush had the proposal withdrawn amid public furor.

Summary

Despite its stated aversion to regulation, the Reagan Administration used the regulatory process at the end of 1988 to enact a number of policies that were consistent with its domestic agenda. A significant regulation finalized two weeks after the election was Reagan's drug testing rule, which affected thousands of private sector workers as well as federal and local government employees. The cost to test so many workers was uncertain, as were the implications for their right to privacy. In this particular case, the timing was due to the administration's desire to act on a stated priority before leaving. After the effort to settle those issues through legislation failed, the administration took it upon itself to create the policy without Congress. Nonetheless, it represented an expansive intrusion of federal power of questionable constitutionality for a lame duck administration.

The administration's own deregulatory tactics were partly to blame for the overall regulatory surge. Using the centralized regulatory clearance structure as a choke point had slowed the rulemaking process. Then, after years of restraining regulatory agencies, there was a backlog of overdue regulations mandated by Congress. The high volume of regulations promulgated by the Reagan EPA at the end of 1988 was the result of Reagan's own aggressive pursuit of regulatory relief at the beginning of his presidency. The administration's feuds with Congress compelled lawmakers to begin writing more detailed legislation that required more specific regulations and stricter deadlines for implementation.[64] In this sense Reagan squandered an opportunity to collaborate with Congress on a program of regulatory reform and undermined his own cause.

Bush may have benefited from some of the regulatory actions initiated before the election. The candidate was able to associate himself with new environmental initiatives that reassured centrist voters after the Reagan years. The administration also assisted Bush by delaying other initiatives until after the election, when Reagan was free to make politically risky decisions without undermining his party with the voters. However, some of the other initiatives during the interregnum became distractions for the incoming president. While formulating his own legislative agenda, selecting nominees for cabinet posts, and facing the unfolding savings and loan crisis were the most urgent priorities, Bush was also forced to respond rapidly to Reagan's last-minute proposals and to make crucial decisions about suspending or reversing them. As contradictory as they may have appeared, the interregnum environmental actions by the Reagan Administration were consistent with the antipollution and pro-development positions that Bush also stressed as president. Bush appeared to make good on campaign promises to fight air and water pollution by nominating William Reilly to lead the EPA, a sharp contrast to Reagan's first nominee. His selection of Manuel Lujan as Interior Secretary signaled continuity with Reagan's land use policies.

Reagan had eight years to complete his limited policy agenda, and he had the successor of his choice. He would appear to have had few reasons to take any last-minute action to retrench his own policies, but his exit from the White House was preceded by an unexpected mix of deregulatory and regulatory actions. As the following chapter shows, Bush's own eleventh-hour agenda would be a similar mixture of deregulatory and regulatory actions, more urgent and under very different circumstances.

5 | George H. W. Bush

Twilight Time for the Deregulation Revolution

President George H. W. Bush began 1992 in a place he should perhaps have avoided: in chilly New Hampshire campaigning to fend off a primary challenge to his own renomination. His popularity had fallen precipitously over the past year, the economy was in recession, and he was facing criticism for breaking his pledge not to raise taxes. In addition to an icy reception from the conservative wing of his party, Bush received a cold critique from former OMB director James Miller III, who dubbed him the "regulatory president" because of the increase in rules promulgated during the first three years of his term.[1]

Deregulation was the issue that built his reputation in the Reagan White House, and Bush made it a theme throughout his presidency. After campaigning on a platform of continuing Reagan's policies, he tangled with congressional Democrats who sought to reverse White House control over agency rulemaking. He pushed back against an assertive Congress by creating the Council on Competitiveness, chaired by Vice President Quayle, and empowered the council to review regulations and to advocate further regulatory relief. Bush had a record of domestic policy achievement that appealed to moderate voters, but hundreds of new regulations were required to implement the centrist legislation he helped enact. For example, the EPA was preparing to write more than 200 new regulations for hazardous air pollutants, as required by Title III of the 1990 Clean Air Act amendments.[2] Thus a major accomplishment now looked like a liability in an election year. After arguing during the Reagan years that regulations suppressed economic growth, Bush found himself in an awkward position.

The Reluctant Regulatory President

Bush had walked a fine line when running to succeed Reagan four years earlier. He made campaign pledges to deliver a stronger Clean Air Act and promised "no net loss" of wetlands. Thus he distanced himself from his predecessor's environmental record without criticizing Reagan directly. Since Bush was elected along with solid Democratic majorities in both houses of Congress, compromise was essential to his governing strategy. There is little doubt that legislative leadership was a priority during the first two years of his presidency, as he actively negotiated with Congress to pass a fiscally responsible budget as well as major legislation on civil rights and the environment. The unilateral actions at the end of his presidency followed a trajectory of diminishing co-operation with an opposition Congress.

Divided government frustrated the Republican agenda, giving the Bush Administration license to take advantage of administrative strategies. This meant preserving and defending as far as possible the framework of the administrative presidency inherited from the Reagan White House. In a 1991 commencement address at Princeton University, Bush offered a candid expression of his theory of separation of powers. The president, he argued, is the sole elected representative of the people and is responsible for the bureaucracy. Congress, on the other hand, has "taken aggressive action against specific Presidential powers, including the power to appoint or remove employees who serve at the President's pleasure. It sometimes tries to manage the executive branch—micromanage the executive branch—by writing too-specific directions for carrying out a particular law."[3] Modern presidents, in particular, must use all the administrative tools at their disposal to reshape legislation and contain congressional and bureaucratic overreach. Bush cast his presidential administration in defensive terms: separation of powers had tilted so far in the direction of the legislative branch that he had an obligation to act as a bulwark against further unchecked accumulation of congressional power.[4] Later, White House Chief of Staff John Sununu put it more bluntly, telling an interviewer, "If Congress wants to meet one more time and adjourn for the rest of the session, then that would be fine with us." In practice, this theory meant finding new ways to influence policy through implementation, such as the assertive use of signing statements.[5] It also meant continuing Reagan's practice of using centralized regulatory review to manage the bureaucracy. Bush left Reagan's executive order intact, in spite of increasing congressional skepticism and mistrust.

Regulatory Review

Shortly after Bush took office, Representative John Dingell criticized the last-minute maneuvering over rulemaking under Superfund by the outgoing Reagan Administration. He called on the new president to begin by sending a strong message to the White House budget office that secrecy, delay, and unwarranted interference would not be tolerated in the review process.[6] To be sure, congressional Democrats cut OIRA's budget in 1989 to curtail what they perceived as the administration's undue power to undermine policy implementation.

The mistrust grew on both ends of Pennsylvania Avenue. When Congress blocked funding for OIRA, the White House responded by moving some of its functions to the president's Council on Competitiveness, a little-known advisory committee chaired by Vice President Quayle. The council consisted of executive director Alan Hubbard and six cabinet-level officials, but not the secretary of labor or EPA administrator. Initially the council was empowered to resolve disputes between agencies without requiring the president's involvement. It also held private meetings where regulated industries appealed for relief from regulatory excess.[7]

The council's role in reviewing agency regulations began in 1991. When the EPA tried to reduce haze in the Grand Canyon by seeking a 90 percent reduction in sulfur dioxide emissions from the nearby Navajo Generating Station, the council intervened. By going to the council, the owners of the plant were able to persuade the EPA to propose an alternative 70 percent reduction as a compromise.[8] The Bush Administration used the council to continue the centralization of the regulatory process, and it also became useful as a point of interest group access.[9]

After OIRA was defunded, congressional Democrats were predictably scornful of the Quayle council, which appeared to wield the same power with even less accountability. Their criticism centered on the panel's preoccupation with health and safety issues, its penchant for secrecy, and the privileges it appeared to offer industry groups.[10] The special access troubled lawmakers because it gave regulated industries another opportunity to win concessions they were unable to obtain through the open deliberations of the legislative process.[11] In a 1992 hearing, House Oversight Committee chair Henry Waxman asserted that the Quayle council tried to insert industry provisions that had been rejected in the congressional debate.[12] Since the council did not publicize its activities or keep records, there were few sources of reliable information on its activities. This was consistent with the council's unofficial motto to "leave no fingerprints," as a *Washington Post* article reported, and even as Bush and Quayle launched their campaign, the council drew up a fresh list of regulatory changes it would seek in 1992.[13]

The 1992 Campaign

Bush largely avoided domestic issues as his reelection campaign began. The persistence of the recession demanded that he pay attention to the economy, but he was cautioned by campaign strategists that if he allowed Democrats to draw him into public debates over domestic policy, it would undercut the magnitude of his foreign policy triumphs.[14] Four years earlier he had pledged to become "the environmental president"; nevertheless, the 1992 State of the Union address contained no mention of environmental issues, even though the historic Earth Summit in Rio was approaching.[15]

Bush's political fortunes changed drastically following the Persian Gulf War in early 1991. With the economy in recession and a revolt brewing in the Republican base, he no longer seemed to be a political juggernaut. Reprising the idea of a regulatory freeze made sense, given the dividends Bush had received from two previous regulatory moratoriums. He had earned his stripes in the Reagan White House by chairing the council that reviewed federal regulations in 1981, and deregulation helped propel him into the presidency when the Bush council was revived for the 1988 campaign. Days after Miller labeled Bush the "regulatory president," Bush used his State of the Union speech to announce a new moratorium on federal regulations, effective on January 28.

Lobbyists for the business community viewed the latest regulatory moratorium with skepticism, but it was well received by other supporters Bush hoped to reassure.[16] In March, Enron Chief Executive Officer Kenneth Lay sent the president a letter that opened with this laudatory note:

> Your commitment to remove unnecessary regulatory burdens on the economy while also striving to achieve important environmental objectives in the most cost effective manner possible is good common sense and as well as sound public policy. The ninety day regulatory moratorium you put into effect following your State of the Union message has already resulted in a number of promising deregulatory initiatives.[17]

Since many of pending rules were required by statutory mandate or court order, the moratorium affected only discretionary rulemaking. Therefore the impact was minimal. Moreover, the freeze was not preceded by any surge of regulatory activity that suggested the necessity of such an action. The number of regulatory actions in the second half of 1991 remained fairly constant; more regulations were actually promulgated after the freeze.[18] In an April 29 Rose Garden ceremony, Bush and Quayle extended the ninety-day moratorium for an additional four months. Nonetheless, Bush was willing to make a number of regulatory decisions during the campaign season to boost his renomination prospects.[19]

As the presidential primary season began, rulemaking was under way to implement Bush's signature environmental accomplishment, the 1990 Clean

Air Act (CAA). One of the first regulations to be promulgated was a requirement for canisters on new automobiles to capture vapors. The law clarified a controversy from the 1977 CAA amendments mandating a reduction in this contributor to urban smog. For over a decade the auto and oil industries fought proposals for canisters on automobiles and devices on gas pumps. The dispute was eventually settled when safety concerns and the expected thirty dollars each canister would add to the price of a new car prompted the administration to suggest an alternative policy of attaching vapor traps to gas pumps in moderately polluted cities.[20] The reversal was made public just four days before the Michigan primary, when the EPA withdrew the unpopular proposed canister rule. Bush easily defeated conservative challenger Patrick Buchanan in that contest, but the sudden reversal on an environmental policy he had previously championed was viewed with suspicion. Environmental groups sued the EPA, but the suit was not decided until after the election. The day after Bush left the White House, US Appeals Court Judge Ruth Bader Ginsburg struck down the EPA's reversal and ordered the rule reinstated, a decision the Clinton Administration decided not to appeal.[21]

Bush used a deregulatory action to his advantage once more before locking up his renomination. Prior to the California Republican primary, he ordered the Interior Department to reverse a newly finalized rule on water pricing and to release billions of gallons of federally controlled water for use by Central Valley farmers, a popular move with a vital constituency.[22] He made deregulation a major theme for the opening of his general election campaign by announcing during his acceptance speech at the Republican National Convention a yearlong extension of his regulatory moratorium. It had been seven months since the first moratorium, so this meant that had he been reelected, no new regulations would have been initiated before August of 1993.

Rulemaking at the End

Bush did not get the chance to see his last moratorium all the way through, because a little more than four months was all that remained of his presidency. Generally speaking, the regulatory output of federal agencies was no different during the moratorium period. As figure 5.1 shows, there was actually a sharp increase in the number of significant regulations under review during the final quarter of his term. The value of the moratorium, then, may have been more for its symbolism than its impact upon regulatory output. Bush was able to increase his standing with supporters (like Ken Lay, as quoted) simply by highlighting the scrutiny of federal regulations that he normally exercised and without declaring a moratorium. Scott Furlong observed that the moratorium provoked Congress to become an unwitting partner. Concern over a possible regulatory slowdown prompted Congress to conduct additional oversight hearings, and the increased scrutiny became an additional distraction that likely slowed the work of agencies even further.[23]

Despite a self-imposed regulatory moratorium, the final months of his term featured a surprisingly large number of regulatory proposals, affecting multiple areas of domestic policy. On its face, there is nothing out of the ordinary about a burst of late-term rulemaking, when compared to similar midnight rulemaking by Carter and Reagan, as seen in the preceding chapters. But one aspect of this activity makes the Bush presidency unique among his contemporaries: almost half of all the economically significant regulations issued by federal agencies during his final year were adopted during his last three months. Comparatively speaking, the surge at the end of the Bush presidency was the largest. With sixty-four new economically significant rules promulgated during his last three months, Bush holds the dubious distinction of issuing the most midnight regulations. One rule proposed by the Department of Transportation removed limits on the number of hours that truck drivers could be required to

Figure 5.1
Review Counts, by Quarter
Economically Significant Rules, 1989–1992

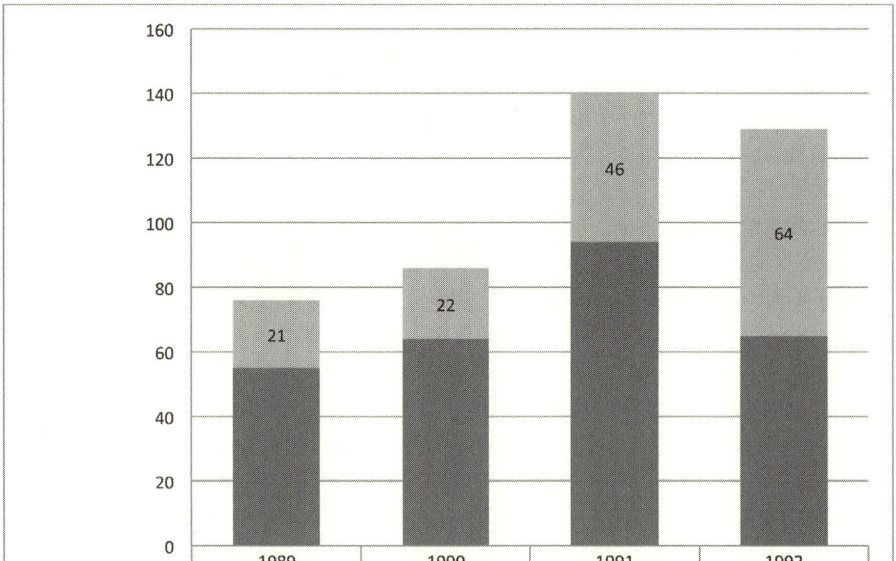

	1989	1990	1991	1992
4th Quarter	21	22	46	64
1st-3rd Quarter	55	64	94	65

drive without rest. The EPA proposed a plurality of the new rules during the administration's final weeks. Among these were a proposal to loosen restrictions on development of wetlands (withdrawn after intense criticism) and another controversial proposal to allow strip mining in national parks, which was blocked by Congress. Ironically, more significant regulations were adopted during those final months than at any comparable time span in his presidency. Many of the regulatory proposals represented policy priorities that had been spurned earlier in Bush's term. These fights would be replayed during his final weeks.

Natural Resources

As the November election approached, Bush had all but given up on his pledge to be the "environmental president." With an economy in recession he was reluctant to embrace the Rio Declaration on sustainability, and his campaign rhetoric had become dismissive of environmental concerns. His appointment of Manuel Lujan as interior secretary signaled a change in direction from the anticonservation Reagan years, but his credibility was soon eroded by a barrage of controversies over protecting wetlands from development and preserving Spotted Owl habitat in Northwest old growth forests from timber harvesting. It was the final month before Election Day when the administration revisited a controversy that had simmered for fifteen years over strip mining on protected public lands.

Strip Mining

In an episode that bore similarities with the end of the Reagan Administration, the Interior Department proposed a rule to facilitate claims for holders of mineral rights on public lands placed off-limits by SMCRA. The 1992 proposed rule would have recognized claims by holders of mineral rights for up to 40 million acres of protected federal land and required the federal government to compensate them for the coal they were not allowed to strip mine. In 1977 SMCRA had banned strip mining in these areas, but the law included an exemption for holders of a "valid and existing right." The Carter and Reagan Administrations attempted to clarify the law, but the rules issued by the Interior Department in 1980 and 1985 were both struck down by the US District Court in Washington, DC. The policy at the time was unchanged after the first of those rulings. In 1980 the court ruled that the definition of a valid and existing right was subject to a good-faith test. That is, the right was considered existing and valid if the party had sought to begin mining operations at any time up to August 3, 1977, the day the law was enacted.

The Reagan Administration proposed giving states the discretion to define valid and existing right following the 1988 election, but a political backlash ensued. President Bush angered supporters in the energy industry when he withdrew the Reagan proposal in 1989 (see chapter 4). The political climate was different in 1992, when the Bush Administration waded back into the controversy by proposing that holders of mineral rights for public land off-limits to strip mining be compensated by the federal government. Unlike the earlier proposals to clarify the policy, this alternative emphasized a taxpayer buyout of mining claims to prevent strip mining. Environmentalists still labeled this a massive giveaway of natural resources.

Had the rule become final according to schedule in November, it would have been in effect for more than sixty days before the winner of the November election took office. In a preemptive move, Congress attempted to resolve the dispute through legislation. In October the House of Representatives passed an energy bill that included an amendment by West Virginia representative Nick Rahall establishing the good-faith test as the legal definition of valid and existing right. That provision would effectively have enshrined a policy based on the 1980 court ruling as law, but it was omitted from the Senate version of the bill.[24] Four weeks before Election Day, a conference committee of the House and Senate added a provision to the energy bill requiring the Interior Department to delay the rule for one year.

Bush did not comment on the preemptive move from Congress, but others did. "Placing a moratorium on rulemaking is a bad precedent," was the response from an Interior Department spokesman.[25] Since the energy bill offered no resolution, the conflict over mining claims remained within the administrative arena. Congressional opponents of the strip mining rule could only delay its implementation long enough to ensure that its fate would be decided by the winner of the November election.

Wetlands

The Council on Competitiveness was especially active during the last eighteen months of Bush's term. A number of its proposals to relax environmental regulations considered too burdensome for business were advanced in the days before the election. EPA administrator William Reilly frequently sparred with the council and found his influence over environmental issues declining during the period of the council's ascendancy, but the loss of the election liberated Reilly to quash certain last-minute proposals that he opposed.

One rule, quietly proposed four days before Election Day, would have exempted Alaska from the ban on wetlands development under the Clean Water Act. Due to the timing, it could have taken effect no matter who won the election. However, it reprised a bitter episode from the previous year, when Bush was accused of violating his own campaign pledge of no net loss of wetlands. The original controversy occurred when the Army Corps of Engineers redefined wetlands in 1991 by reducing the minimum number of days per year that land must be saturated to be eligible for the classification.

Environmentalists were angered after the EPA furnished Congress with an unpublished draft of the delineation manual in August 1991. Bush was seen as breaking his no-net-loss pledge. Bush genuinely seemed to be taken by surprise after an unnamed Army Corps of Engineers source was quoted in a Sarasota, Florida, newspaper, saying that the revised definition could open half of the nation's wetlands to development. "Can this be true what the Corps of Engineers say? I can't believe it," Bush wrote in a note to Dick Cheney after reading the story aboard Air Force One.[26]

A backlash followed the August 1991 release of the revised delineation manual. "We have had several problems with the EPA in connection with the promulgation of regulations," Cabinet Secretary Ede Holiday wrote to Sununu. "After months of difficult negotiations by OIRA and the Quayle Council, Bill Reilly was directly asked not to release the manual to Congress until OIRA and the Council could conclude their review."[27]

The proposed exemption for Alaska could have taken effect on January 20, 1993, had it been finalized by December 21. However, the controversy over the administration's handling of the wetlands delineation manual the previous year was still freshly in mind in the environmental community. The "one percent rule," as it was called, did not mention Alaska specifically. As described in a memo to the president: "The Alaska delegation had also requested issuance of a final rule exempting wetlands in states which have lost less than one percent of their wetlands base (a category which includes only Alaska) from certain wetlands permitting requirements."[28]

In the weeks following Bush's election defeat, the EPA was flooded with more than six thousand comments on the proposed rule. Reilly signaled that the large volume of comments made pushing the rule through before the December 21 deadline untenable. He also deviated slightly from the White House's message by calling it the "Alaska Rule."[29] On December 14 Reilly told reporters that the wetlands exemption would no longer be pursued because of the time required to review the public comments, and because he expected the Clinton Administration to reverse the rule should it be completed by the EPA.[30]

Pollution Control

The council's advocacy continued through the end of 1992, even as the administration's reelection prospects dimmed. The changing political climate caused the administration to reconsider one of the council's priorities as Election Day approached. At the council's urging, a proposed rule governing hazardous waste disposal under RCRA would have allowed manufacturers to dump hazardous waste in ordinary municipal landfills. Reilly opposed the idea, but his protests fell on deaf ears until James Baker III stepped aside as secretary of state to become chief of staff during the reelection campaign. Baker was concerned that the administration's handling of environmental issues had become a political liability and was therefore sympathetic to Reilly's argument. When the White House decided to withdraw the hazardous waste proposal five weeks before Election Day, Baker made the announcement himself.[31]

Air Pollution

The EPA had a crowded agenda following the enactment of the 1990 CAA. Since the statute was detailed and filled with deadlines and hammer clauses, it ensured that hundreds of new rules would be adopted during the next decade. The first were ready to go into effect at the end of 1992. Aside from those implementation decisions, there was little consideration of new air quality legislation during the two years that followed enactment of the 1990 CAA. Several of the air pollution rules promulgated under that law were announced the week before the November election. They included new regulations for ozone, acid rain, and air toxics, which appeared to be timed for maximum impact on the election. At the same time, the administration made last-minute proposals that critics said would undermine the law.[32]

Prior to 1990, the landmark 1970 Clean Air Act amendments had been revised only once, in 1977. This was followed by deadlock during the Reagan years. Bush helped break the logjam by becoming personally involved in the negotiations over the legislation. He was so determined to take credit for the final law that congressional leaders were not invited to stand with him for the signing ceremony.[33] Instead, the authors of the law were seated in the audience as Vice President Quayle and administration officials flanked the president's desk.

Congressional interest in air pollution legislation was spent by 1992. For the better part of the previous decade, lawmakers had battled the Reagan Administration over enforcement and reauthorization of the law, followed by two years of negotiation with the Bush Administration over the 1990 amendments. With the 102nd Congress beset by "policy fatigue" over air pollution, the important policy decisions took place within the Bush Administration and EPA as they implemented the act. Only a handful of the law's provisions were implemented during Bush's term. As Gary Bryner observed, "The disputes that made the passage of the 1990 amendments so contentious resurfaced during implementation," particularly around the way the EPA sets standards and the approval of state implementation plans.[34] Nonetheless, the EPA began a large number of implementation activities centering on standards for airborne toxics, establishing permitting systems for criteria air pollutants and air toxics, regulating motor vehicle emissions, implementing tradable permits for acid rain, and regulating ozone layer–destroying chlorofluorocarbons, or CFCs.

No sooner were the 1990 Clean Air Act amendments enacted than interests on the losing end of the legislative debate sought out a sympathetic audience in the Council on Competitiveness. In an oversight hearing, Representative Henry Waxman charged that the council proposed over one hundred changes to the EPA's proposed permit rule.[35] The council began as an asset for the administration's relationship with the business community, but it soon became the object of unwanted scrutiny.[36]

Despite the negative publicity, the Council on Competitiveness continued to pressure the EPA for regulatory changes in the weeks before the election. One proposal would have degraded air quality in national parks by relaxing standards for emission sources that affect areas with unpolluted air. However, the Clean Air Act stipulates "prevention of significant deterioration" of air quality in Class I areas. In order to maintain that standard, pollution sources affecting these pristine areas have been required to use best available control technologies (BACT) when making upgrades or repairs. Changing the BACT standard was sure to be controversial, given the previous year's clashes between the council and the EPA over the Grand Canyon, source permits, and the canceled recycling program. Moreover, this was a drastic break with past policy and was sure to be opposed by experts within the EPA.

The White House simply left Reilly out of the loop. The proposal was listed following an agreement between Bush campaign chair Robert Teeter and assistant EPA Administrator William Rosenberg, a political appointee and close friend of Teeter's.[37] The prognosis for the Class I air pollution rule was hazy following Bush's defeat, and Reilly was free to speak his mind. He predicted it would die along with another idea backed by the Council on Competitiveness—allowing disposal of hazardous waste in municipal landfills.[38] Before leaving office Reilly sent Rosenberg a parting memo stating, "The current top-down BACT policy is working reasonably well and does not warrant immediate action."[39] Reilly could no longer be undermined by the Council on Competitiveness once Bush was a lame duck president. Since both the president-elect and Congress were opposed to changing the standard, Reilly simply needed to run down the clock.

Stratospheric Ozone

If the election result liberated any individual to act according to conscience, it was William Reilly. Without the political constraints that had limited many of his implementation activities during the second half of Bush's term, the EPA administrator was free to set his own agenda during the final weeks. For example, when the agency prepared regulations for the pesticide methyl bromide, Reilly surprised many by announcing that he supported a complete ban on the ozone-depleting substance.[40] Under pressure from the Agriculture Department to be lenient, the EPA had previously stated its intent to freeze production and imports at 1994 levels by the year 2000.[41]

Mobile Sources

Prior to the 1990 CAA most reductions in air emissions were achieved by focusing on stationary sources. A key accomplishment of the 1990 law was the number of provisions included to reduce emissions from mobile sources. Eventually some reductions were accomplished in the form of tailpipe standards and a new requirement that federal highway projects conform to state implementation plans. The first of the mobile source regulations were promulgated during the final year of the Bush Administration, including new standards for reformulated gasoline and motor vehicle inspection and maintenance programs. As with the vapor canister rule earlier mentioned, the rulemaking for these standards was buffeted by election-year politics.

Consistent with the act's objective of reducing emissions from mobile sources, the EPA completed rulemaking on a new enhanced vehicle inspection and maintenance program (I/M) in 1992. The I/M rule replaced tailpipe emissions standards with a system designed to give states flexibility to design their own inspection systems to meet federal standards, but it was to become a headache for Bill Clinton. The final rule was published two days after the November election and took effect nationwide under his watch. Most drivers outside certain nonattainment areas were not accustomed to the degree of restriction on their behavior that the program imposed, and the rulemaking was faulted for discounting the costs to the individual drivers who were inconvenienced by taking their vehicles to centralized testing sites and by the cost of the repairs.[42]

The most severe backlash was in California, and after the Clinton Administration granted the state a waiver to allow testing at neighborhood service stations, the administration chose to revise the Bush-era rule in 1995.

Another regulation that became controversial at the end of Bush's term concerned reformulated gasoline. Regulators, petroleum companies, and ethanol producers began a negotiated rulemaking in February 1991, and the parties reached a deal within six months. They agreed in principle that gasoline sold in the worst nonattainment areas would emit fewer volatile organic compounds and air toxics. In addition, the rule would prohibit oil companies from dumping surplus high-volatility gas in unpolluted markets.[43] The negotiation was intended to solicit input from all sides, secure their buy-in, and inoculate the final rule against litigation. Unsurprisingly, presidential politics soon undermined the deal.

The ethanol industry complained that the rules would reduce market share for its product. While on a midwestern campaign swing before the general election, Bush declared his support for the ethanol industry and proposed a volatility waiver for reformulated gas made with ethanol blends. In order to offset the waiver for ethanol-based fuels and still meet the requirements of the law, he said he intended to increase volatility standards for other kinds of reformulated gas.[44] By the time the Clinton Administration took over the rulemaking, the deal reached by the Bush EPA had been derailed by the side agreement on ethanol. The negotiated rule was withdrawn when the EPA started over in 1993.

Indoor Air Pollution

The air pollution issue that received the most attention from policymakers was the threat from indoor sources. Congress had recently passed legislation to mitigate radon, and there was mounting evidence of health risks from environmental tobacco smoke (ETS). By a vote of 88 to 7 the Senate passed a bill by Majority Leader Senator George Mitchell in November 1991, to create an office within the EPA to coordinate indoor air programs. The Bush Administration opposed the measure, and the House never acted on a companion bill sponsored by Representative Joseph P. Kennedy before the end of the session. The issue would not go away, however, because of growing support for regulation of ETS. In June 1992, the American Heart Association caused a stir when it released a report summarizing three decades of scientific literature. The report concluded that nonsmokers who live and work in environments with smokers were 30 percent more likely to come down with heart disease, lung cancer, or other life-threatening respiratory ailments, and a Gallup Poll released at the same time found that 90 percent of Americans believed it was harmful.[45] Public health officials, the EPA, and even the White House could no longer deny the evidence of risk from secondhand smoke.

Despite a scientific consensus of a link between secondhand smoke and cancer, the first serious action toward regulation was not taken until Bush was packed and ready to leave the White House. For four years the EPA had the science and the statutory authority, but the first concrete action occurred when Administrator William Reilly released its own study on January 7, 1993. Under development ever since 1988, the EPA report concluded that secondhand smoke killed three thousand nonsmokers annually and contributed to respiratory conditions, including asthma, in as many as one million children.[46] It was prepared under the authority of the Radon Gas and Indoor Air Quality Act of 1986, which directed the EPA to study threats to indoor air quality.

Reilly was under pressure from various sources before releasing the report in his last week on the job. Before making the public declaration that passive smoke was a carcinogen, Reilly predicted his announcement would "have profound reverberations around the country," because it would trigger lawsuits that would prompt rulemaking by the EPA, OSHA, and various state agencies as well as calls for new legislation at the national, state, and local levels of government. He called the finding "one of the biggest decisions I will ever make."[47] The report was attacked immediately by the Tobacco Institute, tobacco-state legislators, and newspaper editorials questioning everything from Reilly's motives to the scientific validity of the findings.[48] By the time it was released, at least one part of the report had been watered down. It focused on deaths from lung cancer and respiratory conditions, but the section linking ETS to cardiovascular disease was dropped at the tobacco industry's urging.[49] It was a stunning omission, considering that the link between ETS and heart disease in nonsmokers had been a prominent theme in studies ranging from the surgeon general's report in 1964 to the Heart Association's 1992 report.

Occupational Safety

The Department of Labor was another arena in which significant decisions with lasting impacts were made as Bush prepared to hand the reins of the bureaucracy over to Bill Clinton. In a peculiar move, Bush reconstituted the National Advisory Committee on Occupational Safety and Health one week before leaving office, even though the committee had not held a single meeting in over four years. The purpose of calling the advisory board's single meeting of his presidency in January 1993 appears to have been to appoint new members, who would retain their seats well into Clinton's first term. Labor groups objected strongly to his choice of Kay Norton for a two-year term. The objection was due to the fact that Norton was serving as legal counsel for the ConAgra Red Meats Company of Greeley, Colorado, in litigation at the time against OSHA over worker safety violations.[50] It was a rare opportunity to entrench personnel at the last minute, and Bush took advantage of it.

Confined Space Work

Less than a week before Bush left the White House, a final rule to address the safety of workers in permit-required confined spaces was published in the *Federal Register*. OSHA had begun developing the standard in the final year of the Carter Administration, but it was not among the proposals listed before Reagan took office in 1981. Held up for most of the Reagan years, the confined space standard for general industry, published January 14, 1993, was the first of its kind. It was the only significant rulemaking for occupational safety completed during his last three months. The National Institute for Occupational Safety and Health (NIOSH) had recommended engineering controls to reduce the number of workers killed by electrocution, explosions, and suffocation while working in confined spaces.[51] This was the approach OSHA endorsed when it listed the advance notice of proposed rulemaking (ANPRM) in 1983.

Reagan's Task Force on Regulatory Relief, chaired by Vice President Bush, had conducted a review of new and existing rules and pressed for significant changes to reduce the cost of compliance in many cases. The panel urged OSHA to drop the engineering controls—requirements that toxic gas be ventilated—in favor of personal respirators. Due to concerns over effectiveness, OSHA resisted until 1988, when the reconstituted task force pressed the Labor Department to adopt the lower-cost alternative. By then Bush was campaigning for the Republican nomination to succeed Reagan, and election-year politics brought the controversy back out into the open.

In a hearing of the Senate Labor and Human Resources Committee in April, Senator Edward Kennedy asked pointed questions about Bush's involvement with the confined space standard. The director of the Office of Standards Promulgation for OSHA, Sheldon Weiner, testified that the vice president's task force had urged OSHA to prescribe the use of respirators, despite clear scientific consensus that engineering controls were more effective. "They have not been shown to be as protective, and in my view, there is no way they could be shown to be as protective," he told the committee.[52] The administration's preference for cost-effective approaches was in conflict with the agency's mandate to protect workers without regard to cost. Weiner's view was supported by other staff members from OSHA's Health and Safety Standards Division who were also summoned to testify. A former director of the Division of Safety Research at NIOSH told the committee that more than two thousand workers had lost their lives in confined space accidents during the eight years since the institute urged OSHA to create the standard.[53] The protracted controversy thus forced this to become a last-minute rule in the Bush Administration's final year.[54]

Controversy over the confined space rule subsided after Bush's election victory, and OSHA was reinvigorated briefly. Battered throughout the Reagan years, the agency reasserted its enforcement and standard-setting activities under Assistant Labor Secretary Gerard Scannell. OSHA stepped up enforcement without becoming a lightning rod, and Scannell developed a reputation as one of the most effective chiefs in the agency's history. In 1992 UAW Health and Safety director Michael Wright said that only Scannell and Eula Bingham possessed the commitment to worker safety and the administrative skills to run the agency.[55]

The revival was short-lived. Scannell had less support after Labor Secretary Elizabeth Dole stepped down halfway through Bush's term. Compared to 1990, there was a sharp decline in criminal prosecutions and fines collected in 1991. News stories of workplace fatalities appeared with greater frequency. The most prominent example in the media was a 1991 fire that killed twenty-five workers in a chicken processing plant in North Carolina. The doors had been locked from the outside. The plant had never been visited by an OSHA inspector, despite its high injury record during its eleven years of operation. The highly publicized story raised public and agency concerns, not only about the standards and enforcement in North Carolina but also in the twenty-two other states that administered their own OSHA-approved plans.[56] Within a year of Dole's departure Scannell returned to work in the private sector, being replaced at OSHA by Dorothy Strunk in 1992. Strunk was a Republican congressional staffer who was more concerned with reining in the agency than with enforcing or modifying the confined space standards.

OSHA pressed ahead with confined space regulations that focused on personal protection rather than engineering controls, as it had done previously. The confined space work rule for general industry was proposed on November 9, 1992, the week following the election victory of Bill Clinton. The final rule was published one week before Clinton's inauguration. Its implementation was suspended pending a review but was allowed to take effect. The timing of the proposal was important because there was barely enough time for the sixty-day comment period. Without a final rule in place, the incoming Clinton Administration would have faced pressure from its labor allies to start over with standards that included costly engineering controls.

Trucking

The trucking industry had long sought to relax restrictions on the number of hours that drivers could remain behind the wheel without rest. As the political parties staged their conventions in August, Transportation Secretary Andrew Card finally rolled out a proposal for the change requested by the industry and its chief lobbyist, American Trucking Association (ATA) president Tom Donohue. The proposal was to allow drivers to begin an on-duty period that could last sixty hours every seven days or seventy hours in eight days, following twenty-four off-duty hours. Under the old rules, drivers were required to get eight hours of rest for every ten hours of driving time. Since the clock would reset every twenty-four hours, it was possible to have up to sixteen hours per day of driving time, assuming it was broken up by a single eight-hour break. The hours-of-service regulations had been updated only once since they were first established in the 1930s, and there had been no major changes in thirty years.[57]

Opposition to the proposal was mobilized by the Teamsters union and a coalition of citizen groups called Citizens for Reliable and Safe Highways (CRASH). The groups organized a campaign to flood the Department of Transportation with letters before the proposal's closing date, which happened to be the day after the November election. The Interstate Truckload Carriers Conference, a subgroup of the ATA, broke with the low-key approach of its parent organization and staged its own news conference to attack the leaders of CRASH, including former NHTSA administrator Joan Claybrook. The following week tempers flared at the ATA annual convention in New Orleans, as trucking industry leaders disagreed publicly over tactics to pursue the rule change they sought. Tom Donohue, the ATA president, blasted representatives of the ITCC for calling attention to the issue by responding to CRASH and the Teamsters publicly. "The only way we could change this was quietly without mixing things up," Donohue said. "If you put the spotlight on it, the issue will not leave the Department of Transportation in one piece."[58]

Despite Donohue's best efforts, the spotlight could not be avoided. On an October morning less than a week after the groups announced their mass letter-writing campaign, a tanker truck carrying five thousand gallons of gasoline smashed into a guardrail on the Capitol Beltway and exploded. The driver was killed and several other motorists were burned, including a Virginia woman who ran from her burning vehicle engulfed in flames. Her charred body was discovered in a nearby ditch the following day.[59] The highway safety activists seized upon the deadly freeway pileup as proof of the dangers of truck driver fatigue. Two weeks after the crash Bush had conceded the election and more than forty thousand comments—overwhelmingly critical of the proposal—had been entered into the docket. Transportation Department officials complained that the voluminous response consisted mostly of form letters generated for a mass comment campaign.[60]

Transition

Following the Democrats' victory in the 1992 election and the imminent return to unitary government, some proposals stalled when it became clear that they would not be completed under Clinton's appointees. The proposal to loosen restrictions on development of wetlands was withdrawn. Nonetheless, more economically significant rules were added to the *Federal Register* during the weeks that preceded Bill Clinton's inauguration than in any transition since.

The last-minute regulatory push was met with an aggressive response modeled after the Reagan transition. The day after Clinton took the oath of office, OMB director Leon Panetta ordered a regulatory freeze and a review of all pending rules, much like the first task Bush was assigned as Reagan's vice president. The hours-of-service proposal was among those withdrawn after the regulatory review. The DOT echoed a concern raised by transportation officials in the Bush Administration that the large number of comments contained virtually no substantive answers to the questions raised in the regulatory proposal. Federal agencies were ordered to hold 125 regulations that Bush had proposed during his final weeks, although most were finalized eventually. As discussed in the following chapter, Clinton also followed Reagan's example by issuing his own directives to consolidate administrative policymaking.

Summary

The final months of Bush's term were filled with contradictions. Nowhere was this more apparent than in the implementation of the Clean Air Act of 1990. Facing an uphill reelection fight, Bush made implementation decisions with much fanfare to tout his environmental record, while simultaneously proposing regulations that would lessen the impact of the law in order to appeal to business interests. Hence Bush was later criticized for undermining the very same law on which he had staked his reputation as a legislative leader. In another paradox of his final year, Bush imposed a campaign-year moratorium on new regulations initiated by his own administration. Barry Friedman argues that these contradictions had their origins in his campaign promises on the role of government (i.e., activism to fight pollution), regulatory reform (curtailing the growth of the regulatory state), and taxes (a no-new-taxes pledge, which he famously reversed). There was considerable tension between goals of his various policies. Thus "the confusing legacy left by Bush in the regulatory arena is a consequence of his lack of a defining mission in domestic policy."[61]

The election loss after a single term forced the Bush White House to set a lame duck agenda earlier than expected. The final weeks presented an opportunity to revisit unmet priorities, although Bush's own position was weakened because he would be replaced by a Democratic president and Congress. Consequently some proposals still in their early stages were abandoned before the transition. The election loss freed EPA administrator William Reilly to follow through with important initiatives on indoor air pollution and also to resist political pressure to weaken regulations on air pollution and wetlands. The key centralizing structure, the Council on Competitiveness, was sapped of its previously powerful influence. Nonetheless, sixty-four economically significant rules took effect during his final quarter—the most of any outgoing president until George W. Bush—representing a mix of regulatory and deregulatory actions as varied and contradictory as the domestic agenda of his presidency.

As with Carter's and Reagan's final weeks, the surge of policy activity reflected a push to finalize the mixture of regulatory and deregulatory initiatives already under way. However, Bush's lame duck agenda reflected the president's own priorities to a greater extent than the midnight regulations of the Carter White House. Carter's late-term rules were developed largely under statutory and judicial mandates, begun by agencies working separately according to a model of cabinet government. Bush's last-minute burst of regulatory action was the product of a much more centralized administration that directed policymaking from the White House. The Bush Administration was not only more prolific in its final quarter than Carter's had been—it was more strategic. More of the Bush Administration's rules were finalized before the transition, so that Clinton had a difficult time reversing them. This would prove to be a lesson for Clinton.

6 | Bill Clinton's Last Campaign

A "night deposit" was the label incoming OMB director Mitch Daniels gave to the collection of rules and regulatory proposals left behind by President Bill Clinton. Six months into the presidency of George W. Bush, his administration had completed a review of Clinton's end-of-term rules and was in the process of overturning or modifying forty-five of them. One strategy in the effort to reverse Clinton's regulations was to stress their timing as part of the argument made to overturn them. In an interview with the *Washington Post,* Daniels echoed a message sounded by other administration officials, insisting that the last-minute nature of the rules suggested "they were ill-considered or ill-intentioned or both."[1] The Bush team framed their action as a measured response to capricious exercise of executive power to push through an assortment of regulations as favors to labor unions, environmentalists, and other interests. According to this narrative, Clinton took advantage of the weeks that followed the 2000 election, at an opportune time when the nation's attention was fixed upon the high-stakes battle over the Florida recount and the Supreme Court case that determined who would be his successor. Constitutionally prohibited from running for a third term, Clinton applied the tactics he had honed four years earlier when he ran for reelection and waged a new campaign for his legacy.

The policy activism at the end of Clinton's presidency was exceptional. More than 26,500 pages were added to the *Federal Register* during his last eleven weeks in office. Clinton was not only prolific; he threw himself into the process. In contrast to his predecessor, and especially his successor, both of whom floated their last-minute rule changes under the radar, Clinton trained the spotlight on his unilateral initiatives. He believed they were popular and that raising their profile would build political support. In this sense Clinton approached his midnight regulations with the zeal of a political campaign. By taking ownership of the initiatives discussed in this chapter, he could claim credit for their success long after his departure.

Following the Republican takeover of Congress in 1994, Clinton saw administration as the principal means with which to advance his domestic agenda.[2] Through such strategies as executive orders and signing statements, he scored major accomplishments while avoiding partisan battles. Even before the defeat of his health care reform proposal and the Democrats' loss of their congressional majority, an impasse over mining and grazing reform legislation prompted Clinton to abandon a legislative strategy and pursue reforms through BLM rulemaking. Several of these end runs around Congress were completed during the final weeks of his presidency, including strict new standards for levels of arsenic in drinking water, and a ban on road building in roadless areas of national forests, which the timber and mining industries opposed bitterly.[3] The end of his term also presented opportunities for unilateral action on agenda items deferred from his first term, such as mining reform.[4] There were symbolic gestures as well. Stymied by Senate refusal to confirm his judicial nominees, Clinton made a recess appointment to the U.S. Circuit Court. He even made a show of support for District of Columbia statehood by affixing a DC "Taxation without Representation" license plate to the presidential limousine in December.[5] This flurry of activity was not limited to domestic affairs, however. He negotiated trade treaties and attempted to broker a peace agreement in Israel. On New Year's Eve Clinton signed a treaty to establish an International Criminal Court that he had previously been reluctant to support.[6]

The Bush team expected a high volume of new regulations would be pushed through during the Clinton Administration's final days. As soon as Bush was sworn in as the forty-third president, the heads of all executive departments and agencies were placed on notice by a high authority. Incoming chief of staff Andrew Card Jr. issued a memorandum delaying the effective date of new regulations by sixty days and suspending rules that had been submitted but not yet published by the Office of the Federal Register. In addition, independent agencies were instructed to act "in the interest of sound regulatory practice and the avoidance of costly, burdensome or unnecessary regulation."[7] One reason the Bush team anticipated all this regulatory activity was recent history. Four years earlier Clinton had aided his own reelection victory by taking popular unilateral actions during the campaign. It was a technique he had mastered earlier in his presidency; after losing his Democratic majority in Congress, Clinton used his administrative authority to push through major policy initiatives on smoking (1995) and family leave (1999). Anticipating an additional surge of unilateral actions if Clinton failed to win reelection, Republicans sought a way to prevent interregnum abuses of executive power. This led to the Congressional Review Act of 1996, which created a process to review and repeal rules already in effect, although Congress would not exercise this power until Clinton's departure in 2001.

Reinventing the Administrative Presidency

The foundation of Clinton's version of the administrative presidency was based upon his national performance review, which took its name from "Reinventing Government" by David Osborne and Ted Gaebler. The performance review was arguably Clinton's most important administrative initiative. Reagan and Bush used the power of appointment to take control of the federal bureaucracy. Whereas their influence was based upon adding top bureaucrats to press the president's agenda, Clinton reduced the number of top administrators. The review served to strengthen presidential administration because it helped earn the trust of career staffers, who in turn were permitted to run their agencies with greater discretion. Because of the unique way Clinton took control of the federal bureaucracy to advance his own agenda, his has been called a "Reverse Administrative Presidency."[8]

One early dividend of the performance review was a greater reliance on voluntary, cooperative and market-based policies at the EPA. Norman Vig has argued that administrative reform, rather than any single policy or program, was Clinton's most enduring environmental accomplishment.[9] Partnerships were formed with stakeholder groups representing local governments, businesses, and entire industries to develop new performance-based environmental management standards. Only one of these partnerships, the Common Sense Initiative, was under way when the Democrats lost their congressional majorities in 1994. Subsequent reinvention initiatives were less effective than they could have been because they were misconstrued as defensive responses to the 104th Congress' assault on environmental protection.[10]

There were three mechanisms that steered presidential administration during the Clinton years. The first was his use of directives to agency heads to use their existing statutory authority to develop rules. Elena Kagan has described how Clinton's advisors were called upon to develop administrative directives as a way to spur administrative initiatives.[11] Second, Clinton would take ownership of their initiatives. He was willing to publicly support his advisors' proposals and show that they were his priorities as well. As Forest Service Chief Mike Dombeck explained, the road-building moratorium he proposed would not have been possible without Clinton's personal support.[12] The third tool was presidential oversight of regulatory review. As his predecessors had done, Clinton used an executive order to assert control over the process. Proposals that cleared his procedural requirements were guaranteed to move forward with the president's support.[13]

Regulatory Review

Clinton saw an opportunity in the centralized regulatory review process that he inherited from Reagan and Bush and expanded its scope to include independent agencies. Whereas his predecessors (and his successor) used the process to rein in regulatory agencies, Clinton used it to advance an activist agenda. Since it was used to such different ends, Clinton's role in creating structures favored by advocates of a unitary executive is usually overlooked.[14]

Rather than reverse the trend toward centralized regulatory review, Clinton continued it. He replaced Reagan's executive order with his own directive, E.O. 12866, which reaffirmed its key provisions, but with notable differences. Clinton's 1993 order continued the requirement that agencies submit major rules for review, and specified that OMB conduct cost-benefit analyses of proposed regulations "to the extent permitted by statute." The order also included language to enhance accountability. It limited the time allowed for reviews, which precluded the process from being used as a delay tactic, and specified that only the director of OIRA could receive outside communication regarding the rules during the review.[15] Finally, Clinton issued E.O. 13045, also requiring agencies to study the environmental, health, and safety effects of proposed regulations on children.

The obvious change from the Reagan/Bush years was reversal of White House and congressional roles over environment, health and safety policies. For two decades, Congress had usually taken the initiative in these areas. At the same time, the executive branch expanded its control over the regulatory process and developed a review process that stressed the efficiency of regulations. One consequence of this centralization is that presidents of both parties often sparred with Congress over implementation, and ideological battles became conflated with debates over costs and benefits. The politics of regulation were immediately transformed by the Republican takeover of Congress in 1994. Subsequently, the Clinton Administration used its position at the center of the policy universe to pursue an activist agenda when Congress was reluctant or unwilling to act.

This relationship was reversed for the first time when the 104th Congress pursued regulatory reform legislation based on the Republican "Contract With America" campaign pledge. For example, the House of Representatives passed a bill that revived the Reagan-era idea of strict cost-benefit analysis requirements for regulations. The Reagan Administration lacked the authority to deny proposals on that basis because many of the enabling statutes contained language prohibiting consideration of costs, but in 1995, the House passed a bill that would have imposed the requirement by law. Also in the 104th Congress, the House passed a bill to require environmental, health and safety agencies to conduct exhaustive risk assessments for new rules, and another bill was passed to discourage regulatory takings by significantly raising the cost.

If the House regulatory reform measures had been enacted, Congress could have undone decades of health and safety regulations without rewriting or repealing a single law. However, the assault on the regulatory state was blocked by a veto threat and Senate maneuvering. Clinton spent the rest of his presidency defending major regulatory policies from legislative assaults. He vetoed bills to cut funding for international family planning programs, and others to allow oil exploration in the Arctic National Wildlife Refuge and clear cutting in Alaska's Tongass National Forest. When The 104th Congress succeeded in passing legislation that would have weakened the Endangered Species Act, Clinton avoided a veto fight by using a signing statement to nullify that provision.

Clinton's Agenda and Divided Government

In addition to blocking congressional actions, Clinton asserted executive powers to advance his own priorities under the authority of existing statutes. This is exactly what he did in 1996, when he moved to withdraw hundreds of thousands of acres in Southern Utah from development. The FLPMA, enacted twenty years earlier as discussed in chapter 3, required the Secretary of Interior to inventory roadless BLM lands and make recommendations for wilderness designation by 1991. BLM reviewed 22 million acres in Utah and recommended 2.5 million for wilderness, but no action was taken for five years because Congress was deadlocked on the question of how much of the land to protect. When a new roadless inventory was ordered in June 1996, it was challenged in court by Utah's lawmakers. At the urging of Interior Secretary Bruce Babbitt, Clinton acted unilaterally in September to break through the stalemate and place a swath of coal-rich, but ecologically sensitive, land off-limits to development.[16] In the first use of the Antiquities Act since 1978, Clinton created the 1.7 million-acre Grand Staircase-Escalante National Monument with the stroke of a pen.

Even though the national monument designation caught Republicans by surprise, they had anticipated some form of late-term unilateral action if Clinton failed to win reelection in 1996. Earlier that year Congress had passed the Congressional Review Act (CRA) to give Congress the power to review and overturn rules before they went into effect. This authority was more limited in scope than the legislative veto provisions that were ruled unconstitutional by the U.S. Supreme Court's *Chadha* decision in 1983. The new law was well suited for the circumstances of the 1990s, because its authors intended it to deter last-minute rulemaking by the Clinton Administration, and only a simple majority in both houses was required for repeal. Congressional Republicans eventually used CRA after four years to repeal OSHA's ergonomic standards, which would have protected workers from repetitive motion injuries.[17]

Despite their differences, Clinton found common ground with congressional Republicans on certain issues. His reputation as a centrist and leader was enhanced by legislative achievements that include welfare reform and deregulation in the areas of financial services and telecommunications, but for the most part the agendas for those congressional sessions were controlled by the Republicans. After Clinton's own legislative agenda ran aground in 1994, no hope remained for such priorities as health care reform or the much-vilified energy (BTU) tax proposal, which stalled in the Senate after a contentious vote in the House.[18] Unlike in 1994, Clinton would not face the voters again, and his remaining months in office presented an opportunity to revisit other goals.

Figure 6.1
Review Counts, by Quarter
Economically Significant Rules, 1993–2000

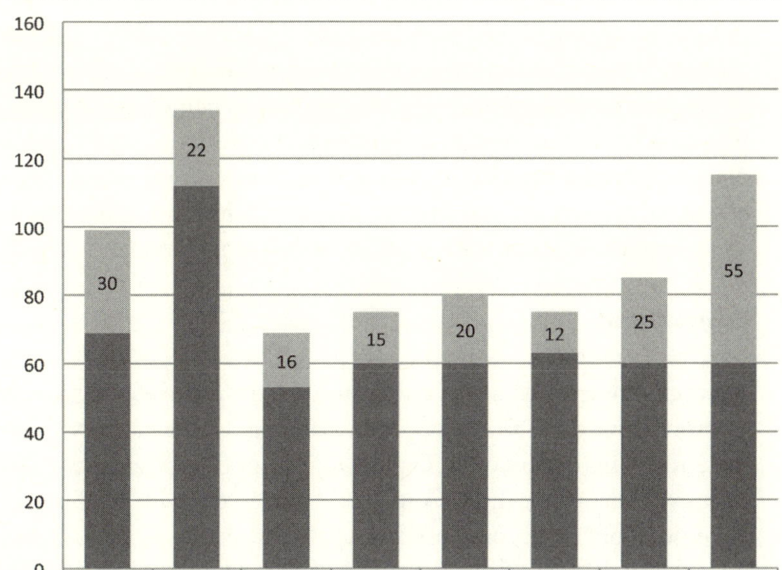

	1993	1994	1995	1996	1997	1998	1999	2000
4th Quarter	30	22	16	15	20	12	25	55
1st-3rd Quarter	69	112	53	60	60	63	60	60

Rulemaking at the End

The Clinton Administration was more willing to engage in late-term rulemaking to initiate major policy changes than any of its predecessors.[19] By the time of the transition, agencies were working overtime to finalize dozens of new regulations. White House staff worked with top administrators to develop an agenda for the final year, unofficially dubbed "Project Podesta."[20] "Starting in early 1999," John Podesta later explained, "we had people down in the White House basement with word processors and legal pads making lists of things we wanted to get done before we left."[21] The last-minute spike in rulemaking activity is illustrated in figure 6.1. Even as 2001 began, federal agencies still had twenty-five new economically significant rules under review.

Since the White House had previously demonstrated its willingness to embrace proposals from career administrators, the call for those administrative initiatives that could be enacted quickly yielded a tremendous positive response. Clinton unveiled many of those rulemaking initiatives himself, publicly announcing directives for agencies to develop rules. Altogether Clinton issued twenty directives in each of his two final years in office, the most of any equivalent period of his presidency.[22] In response to one directive, the Labor Department proposed a rule in December 2000 requiring government contractors to disclose violations of the law. The rule was supported by labor unions but panned by Republicans, and the U.S. Chamber of Commerce immediately announced it would be challenged in court, unless it was rescinded by the Bush Administration.[23] Other directives launched initiatives to impose new restrictions on hardrock mining and road building in national forests, discussed later in this chapter, and new meat inspection rules to prevent listeria contamination in processed foods. The late-term actions that Clinton initiated were popular not only with his base but with mainstream voters.[24]

Environment

A large number of Clinton's actions toward the end were calculated to advance environmental protection goals, while avoiding confrontation with an opposition Congress. This dynamic was in place for most of his presidency.[25] In the administration's final week, the EPA reached a settlement with the Natural Resources Defense Council that committed the agency to reevaluate risk and tolerance levels for certain pesticides known to be harmful to children. Even though the settlement did not result in a regulation immediately, it was unusual in that it committed the incoming administration to a course of action and restricted the EPA's discretion.[26]

Other last-minute actions were more conventional. Four weeks before the 2000 election the Department of Energy (DOE) proposed efficiency standards for four types of household appliances. In a repeat of the Carter Administration's final days of rulemaking, the final standards were listed on January 19, 2001. All were to take effect in three or more years. The energy standards were for washing machines (effective 2003), water heaters (2004), followed by air conditioners and heat pumps (2006). The appliances were among those covered by the Carter Administration's midnight rules that Reagan had overturned twenty years earlier.

Natural Resources

Clinton became determined to create a legacy through land preservation as his second term wound down. In marked contrast to the industry-friendly late-term actions of his two Republican predecessors, Clinton made sure of advertising unilateral accomplishments such as the roadless rule. Just before stepping down, he appeared at the National Arboretum near the Capitol and announced that "forest land in thirty-nine states will be preserved in all its splendor, off limits to roadbuilding and logging that would destroy its timeless beauty."[27] After he signed the California Desert Protection Act and Colorado Wilderness Act early in his first term, the reality of an opposition Congress restricted his alternatives to administrative actions. He had used the Antiquities Act only once before his last year in office, and he was cautious about invoking its authority for another action on the scale of the Grand Staircase-Escalante National Monument because of the potential backlash against his party and for the aspirations of Vice President Gore.[28] Clinton added seven more monuments in 2000 before the November election, and monument designation reached a frenetic pace. After Election Day eleven more national monuments were created, raising the total area of land Clinton preserved this way to 4 million acres.[29] Rulemaking was used to entrench major policy decisions at the end of Clinton's presidency, including restrictions on mining and timber. These represented the final attempts to revisit environmental goals that had been highlighted in his campaign and first-term legislative agenda but had been deferred.[30]

Hardrock Mining

One of Clinton's first-term priorities was to overhaul the nation's 120-year-old mining law. Royalties are not required under the Mining Act of 1872, which was designed to encourage settlement and development in the West. The arcane law effectively subsidized such destructive activities as gold, silver, and copper mining, which generate acid and cyanide runoff and involve large open-pit mines that require five times as much land to support the operations.[31] That damage had slowed since 1976, when the FLPMA required BLM to begin balancing development with ecology in its management decisions, but this merely produced a stalemate between competing interests. Reform of the 1872 law was necessary to reduce the incentives to overdevelop the land and to curb the negative externalities. The policy of encouraging mining at below-market prices was perceived as a problem by environmentalists and free market liberals alike, but they disagreed about the solution. The mining industry, which benefited most from the status quo, had the most influence over policy.[32]

Clinton and Interior secretary Bruce Babbitt thought the time was right in 1993. A rising environmental consciousness and need for deficit reduction made raising fees and limiting mining in some areas popular causes.[33] There was a gradual erosion of support for reform during the congressional debate, as mining interests and western delegations predicted the loss of hundreds of jobs. "We were just one vote away from getting the law passed," recalls Mike Dombeck, who was acting director of BLM at the time. "I never understood how the jobs argument could carry so much weight, given how few people [in western states] they employ."[34] When the reform bill died in Congress, any further possibility of legislation evaporated after the 1994 election and the loss of the Democratic majorities in Congress.

Clinton and Babbitt had another chance to do something about hardrock mining, but that opportunity came after the 2000 election. Just sixty days before Clinton left office, he changed the interpretation of the law to make it easier for the BLM to deny mining permits for ecological reasons. Under the FLPMA, the Interior secretary has the authority to "take any action to prevent unnecessary or undue degradation," but the ambiguity of the phrase made it nearly impossible to determine a standard to deny a project. The new rule, clarifying the conditions under which a permit could be denied, went into effect right before Bush's inauguration. The interpretation became "substantial irreparable harm to scientific, cultural or environmental resource values of public lands that cannot effectively be mitigated."[35] The hardrock mining rule took effect on Clinton's final day in office, but Bush's Interior secretary, Gale Norton, immediately proposed new mining regulations that removed the clarifying language. The Bush Interior Department was sympathetic to the mining industry's argument that the "substantial irreparable harm" standard was itself too vague and overly broad to serve as the basis for denying a permit.[36]

Not only was the Clinton rule popular with environmentalists; it also had broad bipartisan support in Congress. In the summer of 2001 a Republican-dominated House of Representatives voted narrowly to add a provision to an

Interior appropriations bill prohibiting the Interior Department from repealing the rule. In a twist of fate, the provision was stripped from the appropriations bill in the Senate, which switched to Democratic control after the defection of Vermont's Jim Jeffords that summer. Jeffords, who had broken with the Bush Administration and fellow Republicans over environmental issues, delivered the chamber to the usually pro-environment Democrats.[37] The new majority whip was Harry Reid of the gold and silver mining state of Nevada. Reid led the fight against the provision, and it was dropped from the final bill.[38]

The Clinton rule survived a legal challenge in 2003, when a U.S. District Court judge ruled that the interpretation was permissible because its language was consistent with the FLPMA, and that both the language and intent of the statute were clear. However, the ruling was inconsequential because the regulation was invalidated when the new one went into effect. The reversal showed how gridlocked mining policy had become, with the potential to change direction whenever there is a change in party control of the White House.

Roadless Forests

The roadless area conservation initiative that covered more than 50 million acres of national forest was the last and most ambitious of several conservation actions that Clinton claimed as his environmental legacy. It would have been too risky politically to invoke the Antiquities Act on such a grand scale. The consequences for Vice President Gore in the 2000 election were unpredictable, and congressional Republicans were threatening to amend the century-old law to restrict the president's power to create national monuments in the future.[39] The most significant legislative proposal of the second half of Clinton's second term was a $1 billion Lands Legacy bill to preserve historical sites. Since the spending-averse Republican Congress was not expected to embrace the modest bill, some other kind of action was needed to build upon Clinton's conservation record.

Protecting roadless areas became an expressed priority early in Clinton's second term, when he waded into a congressional debate over road construction.[40] In 1997, even as a Republican-dominated House championed fiscal austerity, environmental advocates, such as Representative Joseph Kennedy, were unsuccessful in their demands for cuts in the US Forest Service road budget. A bill to terminate the USFS road budget completely came within a single vote of passing. Despite the setback, Clinton took a position when a Forest Service appropriations bill was passed later in the session. He approved the legislation but added a signing statement expressing support for an ecosystem approach to forest management. For many scientists at USFS, it boosted morale to see the president acknowledge the issue and endorse principles favored by agency professionals.[41] The USFS was required to balance preservation with other goals, including the promotion of timber harvesting for the forest products industry. Road building was essential to serve that part of its mission. Once conservation scientists began to question this piecemeal approach in the 1960s, USFS began to study ecosystem preservation as an alternative.

Two earlier reviews of roadless areas, RARE (1973) and RARE II (1979), had both resulted in recommendations to suspend road construction. RARE II was considered to be more thorough and to have a stronger basis in conservation science, and appeared to have a stronger chance of successful implementation, but it was blocked by congressional action.[42] In the 1980s environmentalists began to criticize the policy on efficiency grounds, when it was demonstrated national forest timber was selling at a loss to taxpayers.[43] In 1999 Dombeck told a US Senate committee that the 343,000 miles of Forest Service roads, constructed at taxpayer expense, were contributing to the problem by subsidizing the logging of wood sold at below-market prices.[44] Furthermore, the cost of road construction escalated as new projects were forced into increasingly remote areas and onto steeper terrain, and the Forest Service lacked the resources to maintain the system it had already created.[45]

By the time Mike Dombeck became director of the Forest Service in 1997 after serving three years as acting director of the BLM because the Senate never gave him a confirmation hearing, it was clear just how dire the agency's condition had become. When Dombeck arrived he focused his attention on the growing discrepancy between the agency's mandates and its resources. For most of its century-long history, the Forest Service had funded road construction in national forests with revenue from timber sales. By the 1990s only low-yield, low-quality timber not valuable enough to pay for those operations remained. Accessing the remaining timber stock on remote terrain required the construction of longer roads, often on steeper slopes, and soon the shortfall was $8.4 billion. Dombeck tried to impress upon policymakers that the agency was losing money as it struggled to meet timber quotas set by Congress. "I began talking about this as a liability to the taxpayers," Dombeck said, "and that got their attention." He argued that taxpayers were paying a heavy price to subsidize a failing industry: "You could never run a business that way and lose so much money year in and year out." This was part of a larger strategy to reframe the discussion. He was careful to avoid language that might alienate the leaders of the new Congress, as for example in the statement, "instead of 'ecosystem' management, we began to talk about 'watershed' management . . . we sounded less like scientists, and they were more inclined to listen to us."[46]

Leadership from the top played a critical role. When Dombeck proposed a roadless area review to create a new transportation policy for the national forest system, Agriculture secretary Dan Glickman embraced the idea and indicated that the president was behind it as well.[47] The roadless forest agenda began to take shape in January 1998, when Dombeck announced the review and proposed an eighteen-month moratorium on road construction in national forests for the duration of the study. With less than three years remaining in Clinton's presidency, presidential backing gave the project fast-track status. Although the transportation policy covered only national forest land with existing roads, the swift reaction from the timber industry indicates how seriously it was interpreted as a replay of RARE II. The temporary road building moratorium went into effect in February 1999, and the policy was challenged immediately in US District Court.[48] Plaintiffs in the Wyoming case contested the policy on procedural grounds, arguing that the interim policy constituted a major rule, thus an Environmental Impact Statement was required under the National Environmental Policy Act (NEPA). The court sided with the plaintiffs, but the case was dismissed after the Forest Service agreed to complete an EIS. The proposal proved to be more popular and generated more interest than anticipated. More than two hundred thousand written comments were submitted, more than for any other rule in the history of the agency.[49]

The opponents' fears that the temporary moratorium might lead to a permanent ban were realized when Clinton announced the roadless policy in October 1999. With one year left in his presidency, and having just survived an impeachment process that resulted only in scarring his opponents in Congress, Clinton made his bold announcement in a dramatic setting. Standing in the Washington and Jefferson National Forest in autumn, with Virginia's highest mountain in the background, Clinton declared that his administration would develop a comprehensive policy to protect the remaining wild areas in the national forest system. Furthermore, this effort would be conducted on a separate track from the previously announced transportation policy.

Creating a sense of urgency, Clinton emphasized the need to move unilaterally in the face of congressional inaction. He criticized Republicans for opposing his earlier land preservation actions and for rejecting his lands legacy initiative, which had become stalled in Congress. Clinton said the bill would "allow us to meet the stewardship challenges of the new century by helping communities save small but sacred spaces closer to home. Unfortunately, this Congress seems intent on walking away from this opportunity."[50] At the same time he used the opportunity to assert his own credentials, boasting that his administration was responsible for preserving more land "than any president except Franklin or Theodore Roosevelt."

Glickman ordered the Forest Service to prepare an EIS, but the delay this caused was slight. In May 2000 the Draft Environmental Impact Statement was released, along with proposed rules for a transportation policy and conservation of roadless areas. Four alternatives were considered. The first was to maintain the status quo, which assumed the Forest Service could find a way to maintain its road building and repair obligations while meeting timber quotas. The other three alternatives banned road construction and replacement in inventoried areas, but they varied in their restrictions on timber harvesting. Those alternatives ranged from a prohibition on all timber harvesting (except for the purpose of habitat protection) to no restriction at all. Finally, in between these extremes, there was one more alternative that allowed timber harvesting in limited circumstances. This compromise is the alternative that was ultimately recommended.

The preferred alternative would ban road replacement and construction in inventoried areas and allowed timber harvesting only for purposes of stewardship, such as fuel management to reduce extreme fire risk, as well as for habitat protection. The Forest Service considered the alternatives for six months, but the volume of comments submitted during the sixty-day comment period broke all records for public participation in a rulemaking. By then 190 public meetings had been held across the country, and more than 1.1 million comments were received. Since the agency was required by law to read and consider all of them, a content analysis software firm in Salt Lake City was hired to process the letters and electronic comments.[51] More than 95 percent were in support of the proposal, in most cases urging the agency to go further.

The Forest Service made its recommendation to Glickman on November 13, just as the drama of halting the election recount in Florida thickened. The preferred alternative was to prohibit road construction and reconstruction on 49 million acres. In addition, it recommended that Alaska's Tongass National Forest be included in 2004. After the addition of the Tongass, the number of protected acres was to reach 58.5 million under the plan.[52] Clinton announced the Roadless Area Conservation Policy directive in January, after the Supreme Court's ruling in *Bush v. Gore* resolved the question of presidential succession. In a surprise move, Clinton's directive surpassed the Forest Service recommendation by including the Tongass immediately, a point emphasized when he announced the final rule at the National Arboretum: "This will include protection for the last great temperate rain forest in America, Alaska's Tongass National Forest. This initiative will provide strong, long-term protection for the Tongass, while honoring our commitment to address the economic concerns of local communities."[53]

Besides making the road building moratorium permanent, the final rule ended commercial logging and mineral leasing in all of the roadless 58.5 million acres. The final rule was adopted on January 12, 2001, and was immediately challenged in court. A request for an injunction by the Wyoming Timber Industry Association was denied because the plaintiffs failed to show that there would be damage before the rule took effect; but the legal battles had just begun. The Bush Administration would be in the position of defending the policy against new legal challenges in Wyoming and Idaho. The astonishingly efficient fifteen-month rulemaking process was followed by epic litigation that would outlast Bush's presidency.

Responding to the Roadless Rule

Less than sixty days had passed since the final roadless rule appeared in the *Federal Register*, therefore it could legally be delayed from going into effect. Once implementation was suspended by Chief of Staff Andrew Card's memorandum delaying the effective date of new regulations, the administration pursued a dual strategy to reverse the rule. First, it chose not to defend the rule against pending litigation, despite an early pledge by the newly confirmed agriculture secretary to support the policy. In response to a court challenge by the Boise Cascade Company and the State of Idaho, the Justice Department simply stated that the administration did not have a position on the merits of the rule and requested that the judge delay action until its review was completed in May. At the Justice Department's request, the implementation date was delayed a second time. When the review was released, the administration essentially took the plaintiffs' side, conceding that there had not been sufficient and meaningful opportunity for participation during the scoping phase, and the administration declared its intent to amend the rule. This was the other component of the administration's strategy: a new rulemaking process would undo the rule if the courts failed to take care of it first.

Two days before the rule was supposed to take effect in May, the judge in the Idaho case ruled that the roadless policy violated the requirements of NEPA and granted a nationwide preliminary injunction.[54] In his ruling Judge Edward Lodge echoed the objections of the plaintiffs and the administration about the process of the rulemaking. Lodge cautioned that "a rule of this magnitude should not be rushed through without adequate opportunity for public participation."[55] The ruling caught supporters of the rule and many in the Forest Service by surprise. The rulemaking groups had spent months preparing a policy to stand up to every anticipated legal challenge, and the arguments against the rule seemed to come from unexpected places. Roadless Rule Team leader Bill Supulski recalled: "I was in dozens of meetings, where I was the only non-lawyer in the room." Despite six hundred public hearings—at least two at the site of every national forest—the judge in the Idaho case embraced the view of the timber industry and the administration that the rule was made without adequate public input. Furthermore, an EIS had been conducted for the rulemaking, despite the fact that NEPA requires them for development projects, not land preservation. This struck Supulski as a redundant exercise: "What's the environmental impact of not doing something you weren't going to do anyway?" The judge had also questioned the rule's possible effect on fire management, even though the team had taken pains to address concerns in the final rule.[56] Another unexpected decision resulted from the challenge filed in Wyoming. In that case US District Judge Brimmer declared the policy illegal because, in his opinion, the Clinton Administration misused its authority to designate "wilderness," which is a power reserved only for Congress under the Wilderness Act of 1964. Many in the Forest Service found this decision bewildering, since the rule made a clear distinction between wilderness areas and a roadless forest.

The path to repeal was somewhat muddied by the administration's strategy of allowing the courts to act before resolving to undertake its own rule. The administration decided not to appeal after the rule was struck down in Idaho. Instead, officials moved quickly to develop a new rule with little advance notice and minimal public participation. The replacement rule required governors to develop their own state plans for roadless areas and allowed them to petition the federal government for a ban on road construction, if needed. It was completed in 2005 and was challenged immediately by environmental groups. Only two states, Wyoming and Idaho, submitted plans before the 2005 rule was struck down. Not all governors were pleased with the new rule, which would place them instead of the Forest Service at the center of land management disputes. A group of western states filed suit in the US District Circuit in California. In her decision Magistrate Judge Elizabeth LaPorte overturned the 2005 rule and ordered the Clinton rule reinstated. Her ruling was in direct conflict with the decision in the Wyoming case, which struck down the Clinton rule. Now there was to be scattered activity around the federal court system, and the White House was no longer directing the process. This would lead to conflicting lower court decisions and compel the administration to develop quickly a third roadless rule in the little time that remained of Bush's second term.

The Forest Service scrambled to complete a new rulemaking that would be favorable to industry and the states but would also withstand judicial review. It was issued in November 2008—sixty days before the inauguration of Barack Obama—but this failed to quell the controversy. State plans prepared while the Bush rule was still in effect were in various stages of completion. What remained was a bizarre complex of conflicting rules and court rulings that determined forest policy. Once he was confirmed, Agriculture secretary Tom Vilsack issued a directive requiring that any new road construction projects be cleared through his office, in order to "provide consistency and clarity that will help protect our national forests until a long-term roadless policy reflecting President Obama's commitment is developed."[57] The immediate effect was to halt road construction temporarily as the federal courts continued to hear challenges.

Snowmobile Ban

There were striking parallels with another late-term action that affected the Mountain West. Two weeks after the November election, the National Park Service announced a ban on snowmobiles in Yellowstone and Grand Teton national parks and on the adjacent John D. Rockefeller Memorial Parkway. The National Park Service Organic Act of 1916 required a balance between preservation and use, giving the Park Service latitude to set policy when they come into conflict. The administration determined that the preservation mandate had been neglected and that an outright prohibition on snowmobiles was justified.[58] This judgment was a political decision, but was grounded in science, since the "Winter Use Plan: Record of Decision" referenced a wealth of evidence of the impact of snowmobiles on air quality and wildlife.[59] The November 22, 2000, decision was also strategically timed, as it was adopted sixty days before the end of Clinton's term.

Reaction from opponents was swift and severe. A coalition of off-road vehicle manufacturers declared that communities surrounding Yellowstone would lose a thousand jobs and $100 million a year in tourism revenue. Wyoming Republican senator Craig Thomas threatened legislation in the Senate to reverse the ban.[60] However, judicial intervention was more effective. The Snowmobile Manufacturers Association challenged the ban in US District Court in Wyoming. Rather than defend the policy, the Bush Administration modified it by proposing a new rule explicitly declaring that snowmobile recreation was an acceptable use of the parks.[61] The Greater Yellowstone Coalition filed suit in US District Court, alleging that the new leadership of the Park Service ignored its own data regarding the adverse impact of snowmobiles. In his decision the judge determined that the new rule failed the arbitrary and capricious standard and violated the law, because it emphasized use over preservation. The administration ultimately reached a settlement, successfully arguing that the technology was the issue. Since most personal snowmobiles featured noisy and high-emission two-stroke engines, only private snowmobiles would be prohibited. Under the revised Winter Use Plan in 2007, licensed tour companies would be permitted to operate snowmobiles in the parks.[62] The compromise the Bush Administration eventually sought resembled its approach to some of the Clinton Administration's other last-minute rules. Rather than dedicate resources to an entirely new rulemaking process, it became more practical for the administration to settle.

Pollution Control

The EPA adopted more significant final rules than any other agency during the final weeks of the Clinton Administration, and the agency made a concerted effort to complete its rulemaking before the transition. Regulations still at the proposal stage were vulnerable to reversal, including water pollution standards for concentrated animal feeding operations. One week before Clinton stepped aside, the EPA proposed a permit system under the Clean Water Act to limit runoff from feedlots, only to have this withdrawn after Bush's regulatory review.[63]

Following the Bush Administration's review, most late-term final rules were allowed to take effect without contest. These included new emission standards for diesel buses and trucks, which were mandated by the 1990 Clean Air Act amendments. Industry and conservative think tanks disliked the rule and were urging the new appointees at the EPA to reconsider it. Political pressure notwithstanding, OIRA director John Graham determined there was no justification for revisiting the rule. Following the review, he noted that the cost-benefit analysis had limitations due to gaps in scientific knowledge and the difficulty of expressing some ecological and health benefits in monetary terms. However, Graham noted that those benefits that could be expressed in monetary units had been used in the EPA's analysis, and "they were roughly 20 times larger than the estimated costs."[64] The new administration stood by the rule, to the surprise of supporters and opponents who expected intervention on behalf of the affected industries.

The Bush Administration also chose not to withdraw proposed emission standards for nonroad diesel engines. The proposed rule set new standards for the sulfur content of diesel fuel in order to cut emissions from heavy equipment, such as tractors and bulldozers, by 90 percent. This brought nonroad source emissions in line with the new standards for bus and truck engines. Politically, the nonroad diesel standards were easy for the Bush Administration to support. These previously unregulated sources spewed more particulates into the air than the nation's entire fleet of cars, buses, and trucks.[65] The major industry groups representing affected industries, the Diesel Technology Forum and the Engine Manufacturers' Association, chose to work with the EPA rather than oppose the rules. The two largest manufacturers of nonroad diesel engines, Cummins and Caterpillar, were based in Indiana and Illinois—two states that would not be in play during the 2004 election.[66]

Arsenic

Even among Clinton's numerous last-minute rules that began as presidential directives, most were promulgated under statutory or judicial mandate. One was a long overdue standard that the EPA had proposed in May 2000 for arsenic in drinking water. The final rule was published in the closing days of his presidency despite the objections of many local governments, and it immediately became a problem for the incoming Bush Administration. The Safe Drinking Water Act had already authorized the EPA to set standards for contaminants like arsenic, and a standard of 50 parts per billion (ppb) left over from World War II was called inadequate by environmentalists. Amendments to the act in 1996 required the EPA to concentrate on those contaminants that posed the greatest risk to public health. In response, a new standard of 5 ppb for arsenic was proposed in June 2000.

Water utilities protested the new standard as too strict and costly to implement. Instead, they argued for standard of 10 ppb, a level that would bring the United States in line with other industrial nations. The World Health Organization had adopted 10 ppb as the maximum level for drinking water years earlier, as the European Union and Japan had done previously. A stricter standard, the utilities argued, would be too burdensome for small communities; moreover, another drawback was monetary, as the additional health protection of a 5 ppb standard was not worth the cost. The Clinton Administration yielded to these arguments and approved the 10 ppb standard in a final rule issued during its last week in office. Since the new arsenic rule had yet to go into effect, it faced an uncertain future after it was suspended by the Card memo. The new EPA administrator, Christine Whitman, complained that the previous administration had rushed it through at the last minute. Citing the need for more scientific research and a review of costs and benefits, she initiated a new rulemaking, which was to consider an array of alternative standards, ranging from 3 ppb to 20 ppb.[67]

Opponents of the proposed standard sought to reframe the health risks of arsenic levels. Even though opponents had succeeded in persuading the Clinton Administration to lower the proposed standard from 5 to 10 ppb, they were elated by the Bush Administration's decision to suspend the rule. Key opposition came from those groups charged with implementing the new standard, including the American Water Works Association, a trade group with 57,000 members; the American Water Works Research Foundation, a think tank funded by water utilities; and the National Rural Water Association, which represented more than 20,000 small communities. To a lesser extent, there was some opposition from industries whose wastewater contributed to arsenic contamination, such as the mining and wood preserving industries. Each of these groups made appeals to relax the standard by challenging perceptions of the risk as involuntary, intentional, and universal.

Environmentalists put the administration on the defensive over its decision, and a Republican-dominated House of Representatives responded by passing legislation directing the EPA to implement a stricter arsenic standard. Even though a scientific review vindicating the tougher standard was completed later that year, the opposition's success at delaying the rule by calling for more scientific research, or "paralysis by analysis," was seen as a cynical but effective tactic.[68] Congress was feeling pressure from the public to enact the stricter standard through legislation, and even congressional Republicans began calling for the rule's reinstatement. One Republican critic was Vermont's Jim Jeffords, who denounced the administration's environmental stances before switching parties to become an independent. That summer, the Republican-dominated House of Representatives passed a bill endorsing the standard, and the administration backed down. On October 31, 2001, the EPA published a final arsenic rule that was unchanged from Clinton standard in January.

Earlier in 2001, Bush reversed a campaign pledge to regulate carbon dioxide emissions and withdrawing from the Kyoto Protocol. Likewise, suspending the arsenic standard probably seemed like a safe move at the time. The administration might have noted the lack of salience of environmental issues and gambled that the backlash to its decisions would be slight. According to a Pew Center survey from spring 2001, only 20 percent of the public knew about the decision to withdraw the arsenic standard, even though 57 percent said they disagreed with the decision when informed about it.[69] The numbers are similar to public opinion on the Kyoto treaty. Only 20 percent reported that they knew about the administration's decision to withdraw, but in that case only 47 percent of respondents disagreed with the move when it was explained to them. The arsenic decision was little known to the public, but unlike Kyoto, withdrawing the arsenic standard proved to be very unpopular in the aftermath of the move.

Ironically, the Bush Administration's arsenic reversal may have helped bring about a stricter regulation. Under a loophole in the Clinton Administration's regulation, 10 ppb was to be measured as 0.01 milligrams per liter (mg/L). Municipalities that detected arsenic levels up to 0.015 mg/L could easily comply by rounding their measurements down. That was closed in 2002, after the EPA published a clarification to the revised final rule setting the standard at 0.010 mg/L.[70] For Bush the controversy over the arsenic rule was an early political setback with no lasting impact. By the time it was resolved in October 2001, the threat from arsenic in drinking water was no longer on anyone's mind. Since the Clinton Administration would not be the one to enforce the rule, it is tempting to suspect that this "hot potato" was passed to the Bush White House. Had the Supreme Court ruled differently in *Bush v. Gore*, and had the final arsenic rule been issued on schedule, Gore would have inherited the controversy along with responsibility for implementation.

Pipeline Regulation

Like the arsenic rule, the pipeline safety standards adopted in Clinton's final weeks were required by legislative mandate and were long overdue. A 1992 law required the Department of Transportation (DOT) to identify environmentally sensitive areas and develop a plan to increase the frequency of inspections for pipelines that traversed those areas. Those regulations might have continued to languish if a combination of environmental disasters, deadly accidents, and election-year politics had not thrust the issue onto the agenda near the end of Clinton's presidency.

The *Exxon Valdez* disaster was fresh in the memories of lawmakers when the Pipeline Safety Act was reauthorized in 1992. For the first time the statute required that the DOT consider the environmental impact of pipeline operation. The law mandated new inspection and reporting standards for environmentally sensitive areas by 1994. Responsibility for all this was assigned to the tiny Office of Pipeline Safety (OPS), a unit within DOT with 107 employees. The statute mandated the use of new electronic monitoring equipment and robotic technology, often referred to as "smart pigs," to inspect pipelines from the inside for cracks and corrosion, and it also created new certification requirements for pipeline operators. OPS proposed certification standards after two years, but industry complained that testing requirements to establish operator qualifications would be too prescriptive and burdensome. The administration backed off the proposal after Democrats suffered heavy losses in the midterm election of 1994. At the end of 1998 OPS proposed a new certification program based on periodic performance evaluation, and the testing requirement was dropped.

With the exception of the certification proposal, efforts to implement the 1992 law stalled. Industry representatives negotiated with OPS over the environmental provisions while simultaneously lobbying the 104th Congress to consider rolling them back. Representatives of Koch Industries, Colonial, and several other pipeline companies met with OPS in 1995 to explain their objections, presenting regulators with an American Petroleum Institute–commissioned report showing that compliance with proposed requirements for environmentally sensitive areas would cost the industry up to $4 billion.[71] Three oil-state senators, John Breaux of Louisiana, Trent Lott of Mississippi, and Kay Bailey Hutchison of Texas—the largest recipient of petroleum industry campaign contributions—pushed through a bill in 1996 that instructed OPS to focus on worst-case scenarios and submit proposed regulations to advisory committees for review.[72] The bill also ensured that new regulations would face harsh scrutiny in the two committees—one for oil pipelines and one for natural gas—by increasing the number of industry representatives on both panels.

The regulatory rollback continued despite shocking stories of industry negligence. One disaster due to negligence was a ruptured pipeline that spilled more than one million gallons of fuel into South Carolina's Reedy River in 1996. The pipeline's owner, Colonial Industries, was one of the companies arguing for a relaxed definition of environmentally sensitive areas. In August of that same year, another fatal accident resulting from industry negligence occurred when two teenagers were killed by the explosion of an underground pipeline transporting butane near Lively, Texas, engulfing their pickup truck in flames. An investigation revealed that the Texas pipeline's owners, Koch Industries, had known of a severe corrosion problem since 1982.[73] When the parents of the two victims sued Koch for $100 million, they were awarded $296 million by the jury. In the same year the EPA fined Koch Industries a record $30 million for hundreds of oil spills during the 1990s, after the EPA determined that Koch had intentionally deferred inspections and repairs on its pipelines.[74]

Only four weeks after the 1996 Texas disaster, Koch and other pipeline companies managed to block new safety regulations by lobbying both Congress and OPS. Lott, Hutchison, and Breaux's bill, which was supported by industry, sailed through Congress four weeks after the explosion. The Senate passed it by unanimous consent with no floor debate or even a vote, and the House passed the very same bill the following day after less than one hour of debate. The ironically titled Accountable Pipeline Safety and Partnership Act of 1996 (S.1505) relaxed safety provisions that Congress had imposed four years earlier, but the new provisions were never implemented. In negotiations with regulators, industry had been seeking a definition of "environmentally sensitive" that was narrower than the definition applied by the EPA and other agencies. The 1996 law gave industry what it wanted. A new category of "unusually sensitive areas" (USAs) was created to replace the language in the 1992 act.

The new regulations for enhanced pipeline monitoring and reporting requirements were to apply only to these newly designated USAs, a definition applied only to densely populated areas and a limited range of ecosystems, such as navigable waterways. The proposed rule excluded 80 percent of the area that would have been covered under the standard definition of "environmentally sensitive."[75] Despite the pipeline owners' victory on the definition, OPS made little headway in implementing the scaled-back safety program. By 1999 neither the map of USAs nor the inspection rules had been adopted, and they might have been delayed beyond the end of Clinton's second term had pipeline regulation not suddenly returned to the agenda.

The focusing event in 1999 that thrust the issue onto the agenda was a deadly explosion caused by a leaking gasoline pipeline in Bellingham, Washington. Two ten-year-old boys were playing beside a creek when the BP-operated pipeline spilled more than 200,000 gallons of gasoline into the water and the spill ignited. The boys were severely burned by the fireball, and they died in a hospital the following day. Prior to the explosion, a fly fisherman was drowned when he was overcome by fumes.[76] The Bellingham tragedy refocused attention on the environmental and safety risks from aging pipelines. Both Congress and the White House attempted to show leadership on the issue, even though both branches were complicit in dismantling pipeline safety policies that had been in place during Clinton's first term. A representative of the American Petroleum Institute was on Capitol Hill several weeks before the explosion to argue against new safety legislation, stating in his testimony, "we do not recommend any major change in the pipeline safety program in the 106th Congress. We just need to keep the progress coming in what is basically a well run program."[77]

After the Bellingham explosion, the administration announced that the overdue pipeline safety rules would be promulgated during its remaining two years. A negotiated rulemaking by the Department of Transportation produced an operator certification program, the first pipeline safety rule to implement the 1996 law. New pipeline safety bills were introduced by Senators Patty Murray of Washington and John McCain of Arizona, then a candidate for the 2000 Republican nomination for president. The Clinton Administration also proposed its own bill.[78]

As chair of the Senate Commerce, Science, and Transportation Committee, McCain called hearings on the Pipeline Safety Act following the Bellingham tragedy. McCain used the hearings to promote his own bill, considered the friendliest to industry because it required industry to disclose information about pipeline locations but did not feature the rigorous testing schedule of the other two. In the hearings, lawmakers questioned the delays in the regulations Congress had mandated years earlier. A General Accounting Office report requested by Congress stated that pipeline accidents had caused 220 deaths between 1989 and 1998.[79] Furthermore, in 1987 the National Transportation

Safety Board had made thirty-nine recommendations to improve pipeline safety, none of which had been implemented.

In McCain's hearing, senators grilled the OPS administrator over the delay in regulations for USAs. In response, she pointed to the restrictions that Congress had placed on the agency when the law was last amended:

> Under the statute, the first requirement is that we have to be able to define what an unusual area is. That is an environmental term not existing in any other statute, and that definition in fact was changed by Congress in 1996 in terms of what the parameters would be. It is an important but exceedingly complicated effort in terms of not only defining what would fall in that area, but also identifying where it would be on the pipeline.[80]

As the election of 2000 approached, the competition between Congress and the executive branch to show leadership intensified. OPS pressed ahead and completed final regulations defining unusually sensitive areas and new standards for inspections. The industry opposed the administration's rules, arguing that compliance would be too costly without uniform national standards. Pipeline companies hoped favorable legislation would preempt the regulations, but they considered the Murray bill unacceptable because of its provision allowing states to set more protective standards than were allowed at the federal level.

The industry finally dropped its opposition to new regulation after another tragedy reminded the public of the dangers of decaying pipelines. In August 2000 a natural gas pipeline exploded near Carlsbad, New Mexico, killing twelve people camping under a bridge that supported the pipeline at the Pecos River. The fireball engulfed the campsite and destroyed nearby cars.[81] Pipeline legislation seemed inevitable, and the oil-state senators, such as Hutchison and Breaux, agreed to support it after securing deals to limit amendments. Senators passed the administration bill by unanimous consent, but it received a cool reception from their counterparts in the House. No House version of the bill had been marked up or debated, and many representatives balked at the idea of holding a vote to rubber stamp the Senate bill. Furthermore, some influential House Democrats felt the Senate bill did not go far enough, and they were skeptical of the industry's sudden embrace of the legislation. When the House adjourned before the November election without voting, Transportation secretary Rodney Slater announced the new inspection rules for USAs.

With Congress in gridlock, executive action was the only certain way to respond to the Washington and New Mexico disasters and address the lax enforcement of the industry. Since no legislation was passed before the 2000 election, the administration's inspection rule was the only safety measure enacted before George W. Bush and the new Congress took over. All along, OPS proceeded to update the safety standards under the authority of the 1996 statute, despite a concurrent effort in Congress that could have invalidated the rules if a new law were passed. Those rules were adopted in January, after the legislative session ended without passing a pipeline safety bill.

Paradoxically, one consequence of the administrative action was to undermine efforts in the next Congress to update pipeline safety. Two weeks after Bush's inauguration, Senate Democrats revisited the issue and attached an amendment requiring testing every five years to a new pipeline safety bill, which passed 98–0, but ran aground in the House because of the same divisions that had derailed the previous bill.[82] Even though the new regulations were stricter, state regulators retained the responsibility for enforcement. This offered more certainty than new legislation, which threatened to change the inspection regime significantly. The Clinton Administration's unilateral move to enhance pipeline safety was prompted by industry's resistance to legislation. In 2001 industry representatives told Congress that legislation was unnecessary because the new rules were sufficient to protect safety.[83]

The Bush Administration reaffirmed the need to reform pipeline safety but appeared even more determined to pursue the solution administratively. Bush called for improved safety standards, but left specific policy recommendations to Vice President Cheney's Energy Task Force, which was created during his second week in office. The task force released its report in May 2001, recommending expanding the nation's energy pipeline network and streamlining the approval process by eliminating requirements for some environmental and safety studies.[84]

Occupational Safety and Health

The lone example of Congress invoking its new powers under the CRA was when it overturned regulations to prevent on-the-job musculoskeletal disorders. OSHA's standards to prevent injuries from repetitive motions took effect just four days before Clinton left office. At the urging of President Bush, congressional Republicans replaced what they alleged were last-minute ergonomics rules, despite the fact that OSHA had begun to develop the program ten years earlier in his father's administration. A draft ANPRM was circulated in 1991 before Gerard Scannell stepped down as the first OSHA administrator in the administration of George H. W. Bush, but following the congressional election of 1994, work was held up by a series of legislative riders that prohibited the agency from completing its work on the standard.

Completing the ergonomics standard during the remaining years of Clinton's term became OSHA's priority, once the last legislative rider postponing the rule expired in 1998.[85] Even though progress was interrupted for nearly four years, a wealth of data had accumulated regarding the causes and costs of repetitive-motion disorders. The proposed rule, published in 1999, noted that carpal tunnel syndrome and other cumulative trauma disorders accounted for almost half of workplace injuries, and such injuries were common for such occupations as poultry processors, grocery checkers, and users of video terminals. According to the preamble, employers reported to the Bureau of Labor Statistics that such injuries accounted for one dollar of every three dollars spent on workers' compensation in 1997.[86] OSHA decided to publish the final rule the week after the November election, which was safely within the sixty-day deadline to protect it from reversal by the incoming president. The date was also chosen because Congress was not in session, and OSHA officials predicted the matter would attract less attention.[87]

Industry groups protested that it was a one-size-fits-all standard that offered too little flexibility. John Morrall, who conducted the economic analysis for OIRA in 2000, had misgivings because he suspected there were better ways to give industry incentives to reduce the number of ergonomic injuries. "It was very controversial all along," he recalls. "We were not very thrilled with some of the analysis OSHA did. Sometimes they just guessed at the benefits."[88] Anticipating industry objections, OSHA published a 600-page preamble to the rule to explain fully the rationale for the ergonomics program and to ensure that employers would be aware of their options for compliance. The rule was eight pages in length. OSHA officials complained of a misinformation campaign by the rule's opponents, who were alleging that the government was imposing a "600-page regulation."[89] In addition congressional Republicans assailed OSHA's "midnight regulation," a characterization that caused the rule's author to bristle: "It was delayed by riders until '98 . . . they're the ones that held it up."

By January Bush had been declared the election winner, and OSHA received a barrage of requests to extend the comment period rather than allow the final rule to take effect. It was also clear that any delay in the final rule would allow the incoming Bush Administration to withdraw the rule unilaterally and erase a decade of work. In his final press briefing, Deputy Labor Secretary for Occupational Safety and Health Charles Jeffress conceded that the Bush Administration was likely to postpone implementation of the standards and would probably propose its own regulatory program. He speculated that it would take years for the courts to decide the fate of the rule and expressed the hope that businesses would develop their own ergonomics programs despite the lack of legislation: "I urge people to look at what they can do to make a difference now. Yes, specific requirements could change, but put a program in place that fits your workplace. Clearly, the message on ergonomics is that musculoskeletal disorders are a problem and many businesses have had success."[90]

The response was quicker and more severe than Jeffress predicted. Bush considered but did not seek a consent decree on ergonomics.[91] Rather than involve the administration in a new rulemaking, a dual strategy of encouraging action in Congress and the courts was planned.[92] Much as they handled the roadless rule challenge, the Bush team would not defend this policy against the inevitable lawsuits. Concurrently, they could expect business allies in Congress to explore reversal under the CRA.

The Bush Administration's strategy was to intervene sparingly, acting unilaterally only if Congress or the courts failed to overturn the Clinton-era rules. Since businesses had until October to comply, there was ample time for the courts to intervene if Congress did not act within sixty days. Congress finally acted under the direction of the White House after six weeks had gone by without a court striking down the rule. With the window to use the CRA about to close, President Bush issued a statement calling for a repeal of the ergonomics program.[93] The Senate took up the reversal the very same day.

In the floor debate Senator Edward Kennedy criticized the bill as "special-interest legislation" for friends of the Bush White House. The resolution's author, Senate Republican Whip Don Nickles, countered that "the only thing that was 'special interest' was the Clinton Administration trying to jam this thing through in the last four days."[94] Since the 1996 law included a provision that precluded a filibuster, the Senate passed the repeal in a 56–44 vote, sending it on to the House the same day. Within weeks, Labor secretary Elaine Chao began a series of information-gathering meetings to develop a new ergonomics program based on voluntary guidelines, with no enforceable standards.[95] Bush signed the bill repealing the OSHA ergonomics program on March 20, 2001.

Transition

Just as the Clinton Administration was more willing to use late-term rulemaking to initiate major policy changes, the incoming Bush Administration was more aggressive about overturning them.[96] When Bush Administration officials complained to the press about Clinton's "night deposit," it was one symptom of a larger breakdown of decorum during the transition. Other members of the administration leaked stories, later refuted, that departing Clinton staffers had vandalized the White House, and political operatives raised hackles about some of Clinton's controversial last-minute pardons. Stories of "midnight rules" were part of a broader campaign to discredit the policies the new administration hoped to reverse. In Congress, Republican committee chairs scheduled hearings and provided a platform for disaffected groups. Marshall Whitenton, representing the National Association of Manufacturers, told the House Committee on Government Reform: "A number of rules that were hurried through the promulgation process in the final days of this last administration suffered from a serious deficiency in these essential qualities of responsible rulemaking. As a result, some recently finalized rules could require huge expenditures even for modest, let alone any genuine, protection of human health, the environment, and worker safety."[97]

The Bush team assumed office with a tool-kit of responses at the ready, beginning with the Card memorandum. Agencies were ordered to withdraw rules sent to the Office of the Federal Register and to delay of the effective dates of new rules not yet in effect. Unlike the regulatory moratoriums of 1981 or 1993, which were announced by the incoming OMB directors, this order came directly from the chief of staff. The scope of the review plan was also unprecedented. By ordering both suspensions and withdrawals, on the Bush Administration's first day in office, the Card memo exceeded the boundaries of both the Reagan and Clinton reviews.[98]

While many unfinished rules were simply withdrawn, the new administration was forced to be selective about the final rules it would attempt to modify. Opportunities for administrative reversal were limited because of the time and resources agencies required to commit to new rulemaking. Whenever possible, the administration preferred to rely on litigation and legislation. In some cases in which interest groups threatened litigation, as in the case of the roadless forest initiative, the administration chose not to defend the policy in the courts. In other cases, such as the snowmobile ban, the litigation presented the administration with an opportunity to remake the rule in a settlement. Finally, the administration could rely on Congress for some of the heavy lifting. The outcome of the 2000 election was one-party rule, and even though the ergonomics standard was already in effect, congressional leaders were able to use the CRA to push through its repeal with a simple majority vote and no floor debate. The decision to be selective in its response to Clinton's late-term actions made sense, considering that there are costs associated with unilateral action. The arsenic rule and the surrounding controversy became a distraction during the first hundred days, forcing the Bush Administration to divert energy and resources from other priorities.

The ergonomics standard notwithstanding, most of Clinton's rules were left intact. Only a handful of significant rules were reversed. The EPA issued twenty-six final rules during Clinton's last weeks—thirteen economically significant and thirteen nonsignificant—but three of the four targeted for amendment or repeal were significant. The contrast can be seen more clearly in the fate of OSHA's late-term rules. Of the six OSHA rules, three were significant and three were nonsignificant, and both the OSHA rules that were successfully repealed or amended were significant.[99]

When the Bush Administration chose to reverse late-term rules, it had mixed success with settlements. Even if an incoming administration prefers to repeal, new rules produced in negotiated settlements are advantageous because they may be perceived as more legitimate.

For example, one of the final actions by the Clinton Agriculture Department was to cancel the Pork Information Program, which taxed hog producers for the industry-funded national advertising campaign "The Other White Meat." The program was unpopular with independent producers, and in a referendum in 2000 they voted overwhelmingly to ask for its repeal. After the transition, corporate hog farmers complained of voting irregularities in the referendum and sued. The Bush Agriculture Department reached its own settlement with the big pig producers and the program was reinstated.[100] In the same sort of rulemaking settlement as the snowmobile ban, the pork information case shows that settlements are tenuous and can backfire.

Summary

The end of Bill Clinton's presidency featured a concerted last-minute effort to entrench policies to protect the environment, health, and safety. Whereas fewer economically significant rules were promulgated during the Clinton Administration's final months in comparison to the Bush Administration eight years earlier, Clinton's agenda included a number of discretionary rules that served a coherent partisan agenda. The timing ensured that the new rules would be final and in effect early enough to deny his successor opportunities to rescind them unilaterally, leaving legislation and judicial review as the best strategies. In this sense, Clinton was a far more strategic lame duck president than the three who preceded him.

Clinton approached his midnight regulations with the zeal of a political campaign. Since his unilateral initiatives resonated with the political mainstream as well as his party's base supporters, training the spotlight on them served a dual purpose. Clinton helped shore up consensus for individual initiatives while simultaneously building his policy legacy. The approach was a sharp contrast with that of his predecessor and especially his successor, as the following chapter shows, both of whom floated their last-minute rule changes under the radar.

The Bush-Cheney Administration's response to Clinton's late-term actions was equally sophisticated. After the initial suspension and review of new rules, incoming officials were selective about their fights. Because of the cost of committing resources to an entirely new rulemaking process, only a few rules were withdrawn entirely. In other cases, regulatory settlements provided more expedient solutions. The administration anticipated that some rules would be reversed by the courts, because of the inevitable litigation from interest groups whenever the procedural bases for rules were called into question. And the White House had a partner in the Republican-dominated Congress to preempt rules through legislation. One additional instrument in their arsenal was the CRA, which the Bush Administration and Congress used to reverse OSHA's ergonomics standards.

When Congress stepped in to repeal the ergonomics standards, the Republican leadership was in agreement with the White House and conditions were ideal for invoking the recently enacted CRA. The reversal of the ergonomics standards represents the only time Congress has used this law for its intended purpose. As such, it is the rare exception that proves how intractable policy entrenchment through rulemaking has become. The strategy of relying upon other institutions has limitations as well. In the case of the roadless rule, allowing battles to play out in the courts before engaging the policy directly resulted in conflicting court decisions that prolonged the administration's own efforts to replace the rule. For all the complaints about the Clinton team's last-minute policy measures, the experience did not dissuade Bush from taking very similar actions eight years later.

7 | Bush, Cheney, and Midnight Deregulation

Two weeks after George W. Bush left the presidency, environmental activist and attorney Robert F. Kennedy Jr. was on Capitol Hill offering the new Congress his interpretation of the Bush legacy. Kennedy told the House Judiciary Subcommittee on Commercial and Administrative Law that the outgoing administration had undermined environmental laws when it issued a number of rules to benefit its friends in the oil and coal industries. The Bush Administration, Kennedy claimed, "took shortcuts in order to get these out the door, as gifts to the industry."[1]

The new Congress was still sorting through the numerous policy changes the administration managed to complete during its final weeks. Lawmakers sought to understand how the federal government was bound by these late-term rules, but their mistrust of the Bush Administration was so severe that the hearings focused on the question of how they could be reversed. The previous eight years had been filled with public fights over the environment, even when Republicans controlled both houses of Congress. However, the administration usually prevailed when it avoided public fights over controversial rulemaking by acting without Congress. The same approach was used to initiate a number of last-ditch deregulatory actions at the end of the term.

Bush's eleventh-hour agenda focused on actions that would have lasting impact on policy, while avoiding actions that could be undone easily. He issued only three executive orders in January 2009—the fewest of any contemporary president—concentrating instead on a large volume of late-term regulations. Similar large numbers of late-term rules had been left behind by his predecessor and by his father, but many were able to be withdrawn or modified easily because they had not yet taken effect. When Bush and Cheney took office, 254 of the Clinton Administration's proposed and final rules were effortlessly withdrawn or modified in order to reflect the new administration's preferences.[2] In 2008 the administration avoided this problem by issuing most of its final rules sixty days before the transition: early enough that there was little the Obama Administration could do about them.

There had not been a clear domestic policy agenda since the beginning of Bush's second term, when he proposed legislation to reform social security and immigration policy. Following a razor-thin reelection victory, Bush declared that he had political capital, and intended to use it, but the mandate was soft and was limited by a divided public. His proposals failed to attract widespread support, even among his own party in Congress. By late 2005 the worsening conditions in the Iraq War and botched response to Hurricane Katrina had dashed any hope of major legislative accomplishments.

There was greater success with initiatives that did not require significant use of political capital. As their recent predecessors had done, Bush and Cheney took control of the bureaucracy right away. Cheney was primarily responsible for fashioning a "unitary executive." From the advisory groups he created for the transition, Cheney selected the heads and deputy administrators of agencies with authority over energy, the environment, and natural resources.[3] Using the power of appointments and a series of directives, the White House was able to implement a number of policies without Congress. Because of this preference to act alone, Bush's approach has been likened to the administrative presidency of Reagan.[4]

Several of the administration's policy initiatives originated with the Energy Task Force that Vice President Cheney convened at the outset of the administration in 2001, as mentioned in the preceding chapter. The National Energy Plan Development Group held a series of closed meetings with corporate executives and lobbyists, although no guest lists or meeting records were made available at the time. When Representatives Henry Waxman and John Dingell, the senior Democrats on the House Energy and Natural Resources Committee, demanded the names of the participants, Cheney's legal counsel David Addington responded that the vice president was not obligated to reveal any information about the individuals with whom he met with or why meetings were held. They later demanded the details of the development of the energy strategy, but that request was similarly rebuffed. After more than a year, a list obtained through the Freedom of Information Act confirmed what many had suspected. The groups who had access to the panel were predominantly oil, gas, and coal interests. Cheney and Energy secretary Spencer Abraham met with more than 400 representatives from 150 businesses in the three months of secretive deliberations.[5]

The main recommendations of the proposed national energy strategy were to increase oil and gas drilling and relax restrictions on coal production.[6]

Subsequent legislative proposals would reflect some of its recommendations, including opening the Arctic National Wildlife Refuge oil exploration; $33 million in tax credits and subsidies for the oil, gas, and nuclear industries; and relaxing New Source Review requirements under the Clean Air Act. Other recommendations were pursued administratively, including an Interior Department rule relaxing regulations on mountaintop removal mining, and a proposal to allow limited mineral development in the national monuments designated in the final weeks of Clinton's term.[7]

Another round of deregulatory initiatives was launched in 2004. At the invitation of the White House, the business community proposed a list of 189 existing regulations to be reconsidered. In March 2005, the OMB announced that it had selected seventy six for review.[8] The concerns that were communicated to the White House became the basis for proposals to relax existing regulations during Bush's second term. Among these were changes to the Family and Medical Leave Act (FMLA) that allowed employers to subtract sick days from vacation time and changes to hours-of-service limits for truck drivers, rule changes that were finalized during the last weeks of 2008. Thus the administration's eleventh-hour agenda was in place four years in advance.

Regulatory Review

Previous administrations had used regulatory review effectively to influence agency rules and put their stamp on policy. Management of this process was more assertive under the Bush White House. In a significant departure, OIRA took an active role by suggesting issues for the regulatory agenda. Among the "prompt letters" sent to agencies during his first term were a suggestion that OSHA consider the benefits of defibrillators in the workplace, and another encouraging the Agriculture Department to consider voluntary and market-based policies to promote environmental stewardship as alternatives to command-and-control policies.[9]

The continued centralization of regulatory review not only enhanced presidential control over regulation; it contributed to the decline in the independence of regulatory agencies. Another factor was a recently enacted law that aided the Bush Administration's business allies. In 2000 Congress passed the Data Quality Act, which allowed regulated interests to challenge information used to formulate rules. In essence, the DQA created an additional step in the rulemaking process, allowing parties to question whether rules were indeed formulated on the basis of "sound science."[10] The act accomplished legislatively what prior administrations had often done informally: moving the "back door" for business interest appeals out into the open.

The administration continued to follow the procedure established under Clinton's E.O. 12866 for six years. Following the Democrats' takeover of Congress during his second term, Bush issued E.O. 13422 to consolidate presidential control of the executive branch. The 2007 directive required agencies to define the problem and identify a specific market failure that the proposed regulation would be intended to solve. It also required agencies to designate a political appointee as the organization's regulatory compliance officer, whose approval is required before any proposal can be listed on the semiannual regulatory agenda. Now that the White House was forced to share oversight with an opposition Congress, the already centralized structure inherited from the Clinton Administration was no longer enough.

The White House continued to tighten its control over the regulatory state in 2008 when it took the unprecedented step of extending executive privilege to EPA communications.[11] The move was sparked by the EPA's denial of California's request to impose stricter greenhouse gas emissions standards under the Clean Air Act. After the waiver was rejected, the White House refused a congressional request for communications between OIRA and the EPA. As House Oversight and Government Reform Committee chair Henry Waxman protested, "the President has asserted executive privilege to prevent the committee from learning why he and his staff overruled the EPA. There are thousands of internal White House documents that would show whether the president and his staff acted lawfully, but the president has said they must be kept from the public."[12] The waiver was eventually granted, but the standoff over executive privilege was unresolved. The episode came to symbolize the degree to which regulatory decisions were subordinated to the administration.

Rulemaking at the End

The last year of the Bush-Cheney Administration featured a frenzy of executive policymaking. Far more economically significant final rules were submitted to the Office of the Federal Register in 2008 and the first three weeks of 2009 than in the last year of any previous administration. As figure 7.1 shows, the 142 significant rules greatly exceeded the total for each of the administration's previous years. Moreover, the forty-seven final rules completed in the fourth quarter of 2008 exceeded the fourth quarter totals from each of the previous seven years. Similarly, the ninety-five final rules completed during the first three quarters of 2008 dwarfed the output of the equivalent period from the previous seven years.

Aside from surpassing his predecessor's record in terms of quantity, the surge of regulatory activity at the end of Bush's presidency differed in some

Figure 7.1
Review Counts, by Quarter
Economically Significant Rules, 2001–2008

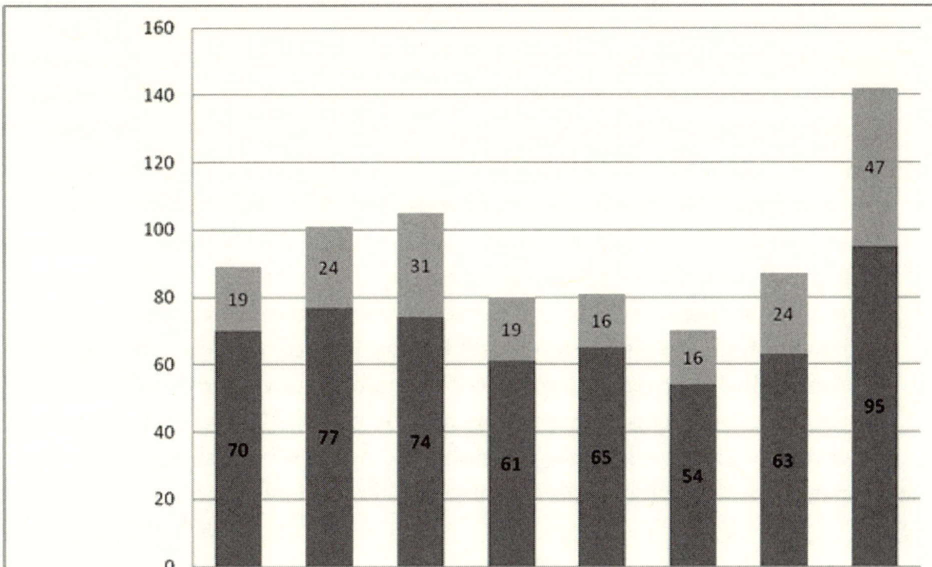

	2001	2002	2003	2004	2005	2006	2007	2008
4th Quarter	19	24	31	19	16	16	24	47
1st-3rd Quarter	70	77	74	61	65	54	63	95

important ways. First, the White House consciously tried to limit the regulatory logjam as the end approached. In May 2008 Chief of Staff Joshua Bolten wrote to executive departments and regulatory agencies requesting them to forward proposals for rule changes that could be accomplished by the end of the year.[13] In addition Bolten instructed the agencies that all rulemaking must be final by November 1, essentially a prohibition of "midnight" rules. Nonetheless, federal agencies submitted twenty-six economically significant final rules for review in November, December, and January. This number is fewer than the Clinton Administration had during the equivalent time period. In the two months leading up to the election, however, the Bush Administration submitted fifteen and sixteen final rules, respectively, roughly double the number under his predecessor in September and October of 2000. As figure 7.2 shows, the submission rate peaked before the election in October, whereas in the final year of the Clinton Administration, November was the month when the most economically significant final rules (nineteen) were submitted to OIRA.

The Bush Administration was just as prolific in November, if nonsignificant rules are included. Altogether, fifty-three final rules were submitted during the first three weeks of November, nearly double the number the Clinton Administration submitted during the equivalent period of time.[14] By front-loading these actions, they advanced an eleventh-hour agenda but carefully avoided the "midnight" label.

Finally, the quiet approach to the eleventh-hour agenda is the most striking difference between Bush and his predecessor. Bush said little publicly about the priorities that were planned for administrative action in 2008. Whereas many of Clinton's last-minute initiatives were announced with news releases and even some press appearances by the president himself, this White House downplayed its eleventh-hour agenda. By late summer the political parties were getting ready to hold their national conventions, and little attention was paid to the outgoing president. His name was scarcely mentioned by the Republican candidate running to replace him. With the spotlight off the administration of George W. Bush, the remaining weeks presented a final opportunity to revisit unfulfilled agenda items. In September and October OMB had 103 final rules under review. One week before Election Day, eighty-four final rules were still under review, including fourteen controversial economically significant rules.

Figure 7.2
Economically Significant Rules,
Final Five Months of the Clinton and Bush Administrations

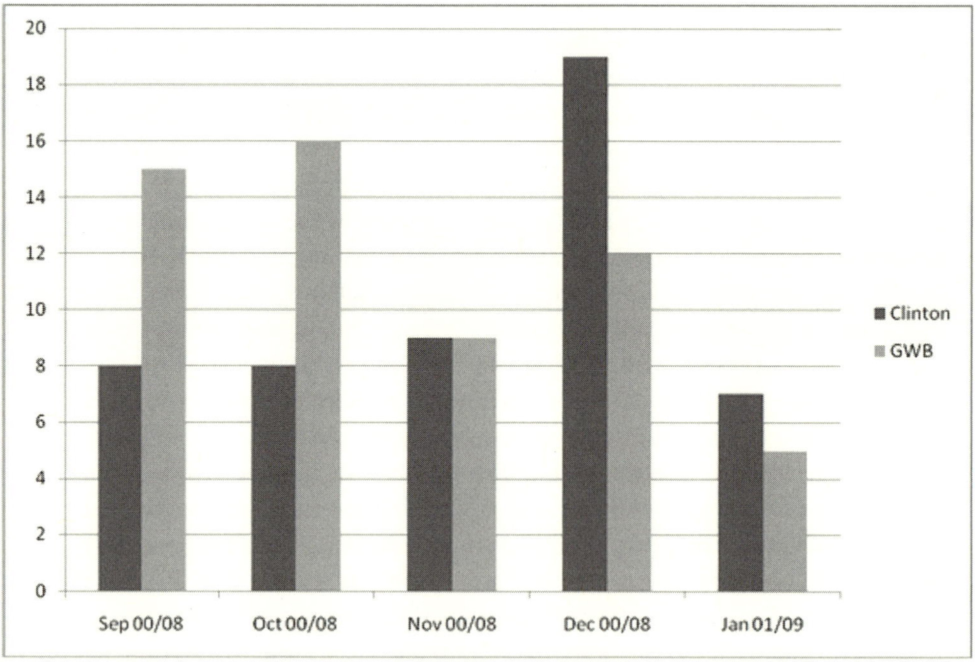

Natural Resources

The unilateral policy initiatives of the eleventh hour included a backlog of deferred environmental policy measures that had been on the Bush agenda since Vice President Cheney convened his Energy Task Force. Despite the Bolten memo, a number of these initiatives appeared in August, as the political world and media were focused on the major parties and the countdown to their national conventions. Late summer and fall were marked by an administrative push to loosen all manner of environmental regulations. Examples are the procedural requirements of the Endangered Species Act and the Magnuson-Stevens Fishery Conservation and Management Act, the air quality regulation in 156 national parks and wilderness areas under the Clean Air Act, and SMCRA regulations to limit erosion damage from strip mining in Appalachian valleys.

In one initiative, abandoned after the election, the Department of Commerce proposed a rule to relax the environmental review requirements used to set catch limits for commercial fishing. The proposal was to give regional councils, often dominated by commercial fishing interests, the power to review fisheries management plans conducted by the National Marine Fisheries Service, and to allow those councils to determine whether the environmental assessments were conducted fairly.[15] The fishing industry had lobbied unsuccessfully for the change two years earlier, as Congress negotiated the Magnuson-Stevens Act. However, powerful Alaska senator Ted Stevens inserted vague compromise language providing for greater participation by the advisory councils.[16] This ambiguous language presented an opportunity for a clarification in the form of a rule change. The proposal was still under review the week of the election and consequently was suspended before the transition. The administration did advance other last-minute proposals, including one that would have relaxed a key provision of the Endangered Species Act.

Endangered Species

The unfinished business at the end of the Bush years included an older priority that had little chance of succeeding as part of his legislative agenda. Conservative and pro-development Republicans had spoken of repealing or weakening the Endangered Species Act since the 1994 "Contract with America" campaign promise when they won their congressional majorities over a decade earlier after forty years in the minority. The 104th Congress effectively barred new listings of species with a legislative rider and even considered a takings bill, which would have curtailed the use of the ESA severely.[17] A legislative assault on the ESA was out of the question by the end of the Bush years, so the new focus was on administrative channels. For example, there were allegations of political appointees interfering with scientific reviews when these conflicted with the interests of influential industries. In 2004 the Union of Concerned Scientists reported that more than 20 percent of US Fish and Wildlife Service scientists acknowledged they had been directed to alter or exclude technical information.[18]

A rule proposed in August 2008 by the US Fish and Wildlife Service gave federal agencies the discretion to decide whether their projects posed a threat to endangered species, without having to submit to an independent scientific review. Without doing the consultation prescribed under the act, the Army Corps of Engineers could decide to undertake a construction project, or the Forest Service would be allowed to sell timber, if either agency determined that such a review was unnecessary. Just before the final rule was published on December 11, 2008, Interior Secretary Dirk Kempthorne declared that the ESA would no longer be used as a "back door" to block construction projects. A *New York Times* editorial characterized the action as another attempt "to rewrite the law, albeit through regulatory means."[19] Bush's rule fell short of rewriting the law, but Obama's subsequent response fell short of completely overturning the rule. Five weeks after his inauguration, the new president used the occasion of the Interior Department's 160th anniversary to announce that independent scientific reviews would still be mandatory.[20] In a speech before a crowd of cheering Department of Interior employees, Obama repeated his pledge from the campaign that his administration would restore science to its rightful place, citing the ESA as a prime example. However, Obama did not select this as one of his battles. Instead of committing resources to a new rulemaking, as he did with the surface mining rule, he issued a directive that advised the Interior Department to continue the reviews. This changed agency practice but left the Bush rule intact.

Surface Mining

A December 2008 rule easing a key restriction on mountaintop removal mining was the product of an effort begun eight years earlier. Loosening restrictions on coal mining was a priority for the Bush Administration from the beginning, despite the fact that Bush had not discussed the issue in the 2000 campaign, and that neither he nor his Democratic opponent Albert Gore bothered to campaign seriously in coal country. During the Clinton years the states were under pressure to curb degradation of Appalachian rivers and streams from mountaintop removal, a particularly destructive form of strip mining. Environmentalists were beginning to succeed with their legal challenges, arguing that the practice violated a Reagan-era regulation against mining runoff.[21] A Bush White House promised to be a more sympathetic venue for the coal industry.

There had been tremendous growth in mountaintop removal during the two decades following the passage of SMCRA in 1977. West Virginia had granted permits for only 300 acres of mountaintop removal in 1973, but this figure exceeded 12,000 acres by 1997, and 300,000 acres of hardwood forest had been destroyed in the process.[22] The growth in mountaintop removal mining was partly a consequence of one of the compromises that allowed the law to pass. When senators from coal states fought restrictions on mountaintop removal mining that were in the House version of the bill, they were dropped in the conference committee because of such objections.[23]

SMCRA included a mandate to "minimize the disturbances to the prevailing hydrologic balance at the mine site and in associated offsite areas and to the quality and quantity of water in surface and groundwater systems both during and after surface mining operations and during reclamation."[24] To implement this mandate, the Office of Surface Mining, Reclamation and Enforcement developed the stream buffer zone rule, finalized in 1983 (revised and expanded in 2008 and revisited through litigation in 2009). The 1983 rule prohibited all mining activities within a hundred-foot buffer zone of rivers, headwaters, and streams. OSMRE could grant waivers, but only if a mining operation would not adversely affect water quality.

In mountaintop removal mining, as the name of the procedure suggests, coal operators blow a mountain to pieces with explosives to access the valuable low-sulfur coal that lies deep in the ground beneath the mountain range. The practice is considered safer than traditional mining techniques because there are fewer deaths from accidents and mine collapses, but it requires only a few days and a small number of workers with explosives to pulverize a mountain completely. Once the surface vegetation is clear-cut and the charges are detonated, the dirt and rock fill neighboring streams and gullies. Rock dams are constructed to retain the infill as well as the runoff and other mining wastes. By one estimate, 724 miles of Appalachian streams were buried under strip mining infill between 1985 and 2001.[25] The valley fills tend to stay indefinitely, except when floods and dam collapses send mudslides and mining debris rushing into Appalachian streams.[26]

For many years, these fills were permitted under the rule because OSMRE interpreted its own rule to apply only to the extraction of coal, not the waste produced from the blast. After a number of accidents, Appalachian residents of downstream communities began to challenge these waivers in the 1990s.

The movement scored a victory in 1999, when US District Court Judge Charles Haden ruled that the buffer zone rule also applied to valley fills.[27] The Clinton Administration's Justice Department sided with the plaintiff. The administration decided to embrace the court's ruling as its own policy, rather than undertake a rulemaking process to clarify the policy. "There was a fear of opening it up," one OSMRE official explained. "It put the states on notice that the plaintiff's interpretation is what they support."[28] The ruling was later overturned on appeal, but coal operators wanted a clarification of the policy. The White House promised to be a more receptive venue after the arrival of Bush and Cheney, and they soon made a gesture toward the industry. In 2004 the Interior Department proposed a new rule to clarify the policy. Although more favorable to industry, the language was still open to further interpretation. The proposal would have allowed mining within one hundred feet of a stream as long as operators could show that they took steps "to the extent possible" to avoid harm to fish and wildlife and protect water quality. It was soon struck down, and a new proposal was issued the following year.

The 2005 proposal contained stricter language prohibiting mining within one hundred feet of streams, but it explicitly exempted valley fills from the buffer zone. This includes slurry impoundments and other waste dumps. A draft EIS was released in April 2007, and despite a large number of negative comments, the final rule took effect in December 2008. There was a push to complete the rule by the end of the year, according to the rule's author, Dennis Rice. The Bolten memo instructing agencies to complete rulemaking before November had no effect on the agency's timetable, Rice insists. "It left me scratching my head. I've never seen anything like that before."[29]

By listing the final rule more than sixty days before the transition, the Bush Administration made it very costly for the Obama Administration to reverse the policy. Incoming Interior Secretary Ken Salazar announced his intent to overturn the rule, at first filing a lawsuit in US District Court to block its implementation.[30] When the suit was rejected, the new administration's only recourse was to begin a new rulemaking. Having committed publicly to reversing the rule, Salazar directed OSMRE to begin work on a new rule, which was proposed at the end of 2009. Even though the buffer zone rule was ultimately withdrawn, this came at a cost to the new administration because it was forced to undertake a new rulemaking at the same time it needed to focus on its critical first hundred days' agenda. Thus, the buffer zone rule is an example of how eleventh-hour rules, even when rescinded, can impose limitations upon the next administration.

Oil Shale

Yet another controversial late-term mining rule was proposed to open nearly 2 million acres of public lands in Colorado, Wyoming, and Utah for oil shale leasing. There had been previous efforts to open public land for oil shale development at the end of both the Reagan and George H. W. Bush Administrations, and the persistence of oil shale supporters was surprising considering the slow development of a cost-effective technology to extract hydrocarbons from the land and questions about the amount of water that the mining operations would require.[31] The BLM proposed a framework for oil shale development in July, and after four months on the fast track, the final rule was issued on November 17. The rule was heralded by the American Petroleum Institute and denounced by Colorado senator Ken Salazar, who criticized the administration for "allowing political deadlines to trump sound policy."[32] The timing ensured that it would be in effect more than sixty days before Inauguration Day. After the oil shale rule took effect, there was one more development. Five days before Bush relinquished the White House, BLM leased 640 acres for exploration. The deal included an option for conversion into a thirty-year commercial lease with a low royalty rate of 5 percent.

In addition to the oil shale rule, the administration held a controversial interregnum sale of oil and gas leases. On Election Day plans were announced to sell leases for hundreds of thousands of acres in Utah. The National Park Service was not consulted about the planned sale, even though it included parcels adjacent to national parks.[33] The auction of 131 leases took place December 19. One of Salazar's first acts as interior secretary was to cancel seventy-seven of the leases for sites adjacent to national parks and monuments in Utah.

Pollution Control

Improving the physical condition of the national parks was one of candidate Bush's two environmental promises (the other, a pledge to regulate carbon dioxide emissions, was quickly abandoned when he turned against the Kyoto treaty). As president, Bush increased the operating budget of the park system, but other policy initiatives threatened to undermine the parks in other ways.[34] Even as the 2008 election neared, environmentalists were alarmed when the EPA proposed rule changes that would have allowed new coal-fired power plants upwind from ten national parks.[35] The Class-1 air quality proposal would have degraded air quality in the parks by changing the way air pollution was monitored.

Class I Air Quality

The Clean Air Act amendments of 1977 created a system designating certain areas of the country as Class I zones that would enjoy a higher level of protection from air pollution. These zones included national parks, wilderness areas, and "other places of scenic and historical value," which were to have ambient air quality beyond the standards established in the 1970 law. Air quality standards for these areas were to be based on Prevention of Significant Deterioration, meaning that no permits may be granted for new pollution sources or upgrades to existing sources under New Source Review if the emissions increased the pollution in a Class I zone.

Many of the open spaces designated as Class I zones are vulnerable to damage due to their proximity to coal-fired power plants. Such facilities emit high levels of sulfur dioxide, which kills trees and causes acid rain; and of nitrogen oxides, which increase smog; and of mercury, which accumulates in streams and kills fish and wildlife. However, the most apparent effect for the public is reduced visibility in some of the nation's most-visited national parks, including the Great Smoky Mountains National Recreation Area, Yosemite National Park, and the Badlands, Great Basin, and Wind Cave national parks.

The proposal was to change the way ambient pollution in Class I zones had been measured for more than three decades. First, it substituted an annual average for the maximum emission level calculated over three hours in a single twenty-four-hour period. Second, the new metric excluded existing sources that had been granted variances from the total output. An additional change allowed state regulators to select what they considered any "representative time period" for the two most recent years. Then they would be allowed to calculate emissions on the basis of the selected monitoring period and were granted the discretion to use whatever data they considered more reliable. The March 2008 proposal was the latest in a series of regulatory initiatives during the Bush years intended to reduce restrictions on the use of coal. Bush's 2003 "Clear Skies" initiative (later withdrawn) would have weakened the New Source Review program, allowing power generators to replace equipment without meeting the higher emission standards required by law. The Clean Air Interstate Rule of 2005 was designed to reduce emissions from power plants east of the Mississippi but also exempted some of the dirtiest plants from adding pollution controls. Remanded by DC Circuit Court in 2008, the rule was later reproposed by the Obama Administration.[36] In 2006 the EPA weakened a proposed rule to reduce particulate matter in national parks.

There were 156 Class I zones when the rule was proposed. Its immediate impact would have been to allow permits for twenty-four new coal-fired power plants upwind from ten national parks. Perhaps the site most at risk, Virginia's Shenandoah National Park was adjacent to six of the proposed plant sites. Critics immediately countered that the change would obscure pollution spikes as well as blur the monitoring process, making it harder to identify the major sources of emissions.

The proposal drew fire not only from environmentalists but also from officials within government. Mark Bunyak, a policy analyst for the National Park Service, drew an analogy that became quoted widely after it was circulated by Representative Henry Waxman. The comment compared the use of averaging emissions over the course of a year in evaluating permit applications to "allowing a person to average all the variations in his driving speed over (an) entire year to see whether he is complying with the 55-mile-per-hour speed limit.[37] The theme was echoed in a statement from the Washington, DC–based National Parks Conservation Association:

> It's like if you're pulled over by a cop for going 75 miles per hour in a 55-mile an hour zone, and you say, "If you look at how I've driven all year, I've averaged 55 miles per hour. . . . It allows you to vastly underestimate the impact of these emissions."[38]

In the weeks following the November 2008 election, the *Washington Post* reported that EPA was working to finalize the rule quickly. Time was of the essence, as the final rule had to be published sixty days before Obama's inauguration or face likely reversal. However, stories of opposition to the rule by scientists and administrators within the EPA began to surface. The proposal was criticized by nine of the agency's ten regional directors, four of whom objected in written comments, and five others formally dissented.[39]

When the unofficial November 19 deadline passed, neither the Class I air quality rule nor the Bush Administration's controversial New Source Review proposal had appeared in final form. The administration abruptly reversed course, despite "weeks of frantic work trying to complete the rules."[40] On December 10, 2008, the EPA issued a news release announcing that it was withdrawing the proposal. No explanation was given, although an EPA spokesperson stated that the administration did not wish to impose a "midnight regulation" upon the incoming Obama Administration and added, referencing the Bolten memo, that the White House had said "no new rules should be imposed in the administration's final days."[41] Several other rules that the agency had either recently finalized (or was continuing to develop) during the administration's final days were not mentioned.

Occupational Safety and Health

The Bush era was not a particularly busy time for policymaking regarding occupational safety and health. During the first seven and a half years, OSHA issued just one significant health rule: a court-ordered standard for exposure to hexavalent chromium. For this reason, no one expected any major regulatory action so late in Bush's second term. When Congress learned that a major occupational health rule was planned prior to the 2008 election, a controversy erupted because the Department of Labor had not disclosed that any such rule was under development.

Workplace Toxics

A Department of Labor proposal to soften regulations for toxic substances in the workplace was particularly controversial. The proposed change in risk assessment procedures would have made it easier for employers to challenge studies OSHA and the Mine Safety and Health Administration (MSHA) used to set exposure limits for toxic chemicals. The Department of Labor had not published notice of the rulemaking in the semiannual Unified Agenda the previous December or May. It was not until the summer of 2008 that OIRA acknowledged it was reviewing a draft proposal, and the ensuing rumors of a "secret rule" drew the ire of administration critics in Congress.[42]

News of the rulemaking broke just days before the proposed rule appeared in the *Federal Register.* The potential effects were far-reaching because OSHA and MSHA were given the responsibility for regulating the use of toxic substances in occupational settings. The rulemaking was not publicly acknowledged until the proposal was under review and OIRA listed a reference to its status online on July 7.[43] Once the *Washington Post* obtained documents and reported on the proposal later that month, labor and public health groups orchestrated a media campaign to feed the backlash.

The initiative was finally acknowledged two weeks later, when the department acknowledged to the *Washington Post* that it was fast-tracking a rule. According to the report, the Labor Department explained the lapse by saying the rule change had not been disclosed previously "because they were uncertain until recently whether they wanted to follow through and pursue a regulation."[44] OIRA director Susan Dudley later attributed the controversy to the irregular way the administration rolled out the proposal. The Labor Department "just didn't think it would be that controversial," she later explained. "If you look at the substance of the proposal, it's pretty benign."[45] A former OSHA official expressed doubt that it was an oversight because the proposal came from the top: "It came from the assistant secretary for policy, not from OSHA. It was shopped around but OSHA warned them not to do it. They said it wasn't necessary. This was your classic midnight regulation . . . they were trying to sneak it through at the end."[46]

Details of the proposal were not made public until the notice of proposed rulemaking appeared in the *Federal Register* on August 29. The proposed change effectively made it more difficult to control toxic chemicals in the workplace by altering the risk assessment practices used to determine the level of exposure that could be considered safe. Instead of continuing the established assumption that workers stay in the same job for forty-five years, it recommended the use of industry-specific data. This would allow employers to substitute estimates based on shorter terms of employment, resulting in significantly higher exposure limits for workers.[47] On the basis of these estimates, employers would be allowed to challenge the risk assessments used by OSHA and MSHA.

The new round of risk assessment challenges added one more step to the standard-setting process as well as more opportunity for delay. Among other procedural requirements, it mandated a separate formal ANPRM for every occupational health rule. In another provision that opponents found infuriating, OSHA and MSHA were required to place background documents for their proposed regulations into the docket within two weeks of the ANPRM, although the Department of Labor had not done its own risk assessment proposal. Combined, the provisions threatened to add significant delays to any future administration's efforts to develop health standards, even though the typical OSHA rulemaking already lasted eight years. Moreover, the requirements would have ensured that the rulemaking process would last longer than the term of any single president; even a two-term president.

By the time the notice appeared in the *Federal Register*, unions, environmental groups, and several members of Congress had already called for its withdrawal. Senator Edward Kennedy and Representative George Miller, who both chaired committees with oversight in the areas of environment and labor, protested that the department was "moving this proposal over the objections of career staff in the relevant health and safety agencies." The chairmen issued a joint written request for the text of the proposed rule as well as documents related to meetings and communications regarding the development of the proposal. Finally, they expressed their feelings in no uncertain terms:

> There are long-established directives to ensure that the Administration acts in a transparent manner so that the public has the time and ability to properly consider all proposals. It appears that the Department may be violating those rules. We are likewise concerned that the Department would seek a rule change in near total secrecy to this point.[48]

The request was sent to the secretary of labor on July 10, just two days after the reference on reginfo.gov was noticed by a blogger.[49] After several days without a response, Miller sent a second letter that included a pointed criticism of the "secret regulation," calling it "an attempt by the Bush Administration and the Business community to fundamentally weaken the scientific process for enacting new regulations that protect American workers." Since the notice of proposed rulemaking appeared at the end of August, the thirty-day public comment period would expire before October. Labor and progressive groups immediately requested a thirty-day extension of the comment period and demanded that the Department of Labor schedule hearings to give the public more opportunity for input. It was unlikely that the request for hearings would be granted, but a thirty-day extension of the comment period would have delayed the effective date of the final rule until the winner of the November election took office.

Powerless to affect the content of the rule or slow its development, opponents made an issue of the timing and transparency of the process. Besides calling for more time and opportunities for input, critics accused the administration of ignoring the May memo from Chief of Staff Bolten. Writing on behalf of the OMB, OIRA director Susan Dudley explained that "the memorandum was not meant to be a moratorium on proposed regulations."[50] The proposal became a campaign issue when the request to extend the comment period was denied. In a September hearing on "The Secret Rule" staged by the House Subcommittee on Workforce Protection, witnesses took aim at the timing as often as the content. As Peg Seminario of the AFL-CIO told the panel,

> The Bush Administration started its tenure in 2001 by repealing OSHA's ergonomics standard, and for the past 7½ years it has refused to take action to issue new safety and health standards unless under court order or in response to Congressional mandates. Now in its waning days, the Administration is attempting to put into place new regulatory requirements that would make it much more difficult for the next administration to take action to protect workers.[51]

In the midst of the general election campaign, Senator Barack Obama and four other senators introduced a bill to prohibit the Labor Department from issuing the final rule.

The Democratic presidential nominee also appealed in writing for Labor Secretary Elaine Chao to intervene to extend the comment period and release the results of a study the Labor Department had commissioned to formulate the rule.[52]

Days after the comment period closed, the political landscape was transformed on November 2 with Obama's election victory and enlarged Democratic majorities in Congress. Even as the Democrats' threat to overturn the rule became more credible, the rulemaking continued on the fast track through the end of November.[53] With less than sixty days remaining until the transition and still no final rule, the proposal finally stalled. In December Dudley told her staff that she would not allow the review of the final rule to go forward. By then the calendar, as well as opposition from both Congress and the president-elect, guaranteed that the proposal would be dead on arrival.

When the new secretary of Labor, Hilda Solis, formally withdrew the proposal in 2009, the *Federal Register* notice acknowledged that the comments included several requests for an extension. However, the circumstances of the proposal for the process were not among the reasons given for the reversal. It simply stated that the rule's requirements were unnecessary. A separate ANPRM for each proposed standard would "unduly delay the rulemaking . . . this in turn could harm workers by unnecessarily delaying the introduction of the health protections of the standard."[54] In addition, the announcement cited several instances when the Department of Labor had rejected earlier claims that industry-specific risk assessments be conducted by OSHA and MSHA, and it noted that the forty-five-year working life assumption had been upheld in federal court as conforming to the intent of Congress.[55]

Family and Medical Leave

Another last-minute rule by the Department of Labor aimed to weaken a policy dating back to the previous Democratic administration. President Clinton had signed the Family and Medical Leave Act into law in 1993 following years of congressional lobbying by unions and women's rights groups. The National Association of Manufacturers, representing fourteen thousand businesses, had opposed the law fiercely for years, but legislative repeal was out of the question because of a likely veto by President Clinton. The law's enduring popularity limited the options even for the extremely pro-business Bush-Cheney Administration. The business group had lobbied for rule changes that would reduce its impact on employers, naming this as a priority when the administration solicited requests for rule changes four years earlier.[56]

In 2008, fifteen years after FMLA became law, the business groups succeeded in obtaining their goal. The Labor Department proposed new regulations that allowed employers to seek information from health care providers to determine whether an employee's medical leave is necessary and to subtract family leave days from an employee's sick days or vacation time. The under-the-radar approach required the business groups to wait patiently for the right moment.

The moment arrived during the campaign of 2008. The final rule was listed two weeks after the November election and took effect during Bush's final week in office. The nature and timing of the action allowed the Labor Department to avoid a public debate altogether. Leaving the statutory language untouched, the rule altered its impact simply by changing its interpretation.

Transition

Bush's successor took the reins during an unprecedented crisis. Between a financial panic and two wars, Obama's plate was filled. However, his team was able to consider matters beyond the economic policy and national security issues. The new administration had to assess the domestic policy implications of Bush's eleventh-hour initiatives. No one was better prepared for the last-minute surge than Obama's transition chief, John Podesta. As chief of staff under President Clinton, Podesta had coordinated an administrative push to make lasting changes in several areas of domestic policy during the administration's last two years. As his predecessors had done, Obama began his presidency with a review of his predecessor's last-minute rules. Incoming chief of staff Rahm Emmanuel announced the suspension of new rules, but many were unaffected because most had been finalized before Election Day and had taken effect more than sixty days before the transition.[57]

In certain cases the outcome of the review was a foregone conclusion. Incoming Labor secretary Hilda Solis easily withdrew OSHA's risk assessment proposal because it was halted in its tracks by OMB before Bush left office, even though it had been on the fast track. After stating his opposition to OSMRE's stream buffer rule, Interior secretary–designate Ken Salazar found that it could not be reversed so easily. He was forced to initiate a new rulemaking, diverting resources from other priorities.

Obama made a number of decisions right away that signaled a break from Bush-Cheney policies. He vowed to restore science as a primary factor in decisions on public land and natural resources, winning praise for creating a position of scientific integrity officer at the Department of Interior, and appointing administrators with strong scientific credentials, including leading marine ecologist Dr. Jane Lubchenco to lead the National Oceanic and Atmospheric Administration. Despite these high-profile gestures, many of Obama's policies represented continuity with the Bush years. For example, even with large Democratic majorities, he was frustrated in his effort to persuade Congress to create an emissions trading program for carbon dioxide. Since most of his predecessor's eleventh-hour rules were in effect already, initiating new rulemaking procedures to reverse them was no easier than building consensus for new legislation.

Summary

In the transition from Bush to Obama, the evolving practice of eleventh-hour rulemaking came into fruition as an effective strategy of policy entrenchment. Through careful advance planning, the Bush-Cheney Administration succeeded in delivering much of its late-term agenda without political consequences and unencumbered by the practical limitations of separation of powers. The White House policy establishment was more centralized compared to those of previous administrations, giving the Bush Administration the means to pursue an ambitious lame duck agenda through administrative channels.

The timing of the initiatives was instrumental. The surge of late rulemaking activity occurred not at "midnight," but during the run-up to the election, just early enough to inoculate those initiatives from reversal by the Obama Administration. In this sense the Bush Administration used last-minute rulemaking preemptively. The Bush Administration favored rulemaking for a large number of policy changes during its final months, just as its predecessors had done. What distinguished the Bush team's approach was their sensitivity to the calendar. The larger number of rules finalized in the lead-up to the election, as opposed to in the last sixty days as was more typical for his predecessors, ensured that the incoming administration would have a more difficult time reversing their actions.

The quiet approach the Bush Administration used to advance its deregulatory measures in 2008 stands in sharp contrast with Bill Clinton's advocacy for his own policies. Easing surface mining regulations and pollution standards for Class I areas had been identified as priorities ever since Vice President Cheney convened his Energy Task Force in 2001. The Department of Labor's proposal to change risk assessment procedures caught many off guard, but OSHA had been reluctant to create new rules to protect workers during the entire Bush presidency. Well before the rumors of a "secret rule" began, the Labor Department had already commissioned a study and circulated a draft proposal at OSHA. Each of these initiatives was planned far in advance, and timing was an important part of the administration's strategy.

8 | Conclusion

Digging in and Running out the Clock

A year before President Obama's reelection, progressives were nervous. The stakes in any presidential election are high, but it was clear that the winner in 2012 would gain control of the federal bureaucracy and determine the direction of domestic policies discussed in the preceding chapters. The Washington, DC-based Center for Progressive Reform sounded this alarm in the title of its report *Twelve Crucial Health, Safety, and Environmental Regulations: Will the Obama Administration Finish in Time?* The reported faulted industry lobbying, congressional interference, and OIRA reviews for delaying regulations ranging in scope from mine safety and workplace accident prevention to addressing pollution from stormwater runoff and coal ash.[1] A Republican victory, the report warned, meant that rules stuck in the pipeline were in danger of being rescinded by the new president or reversed through the Congressional Review Act.

Mindful of the clock, President Obama rolled out a series of unilateral policy initiatives known as the "We Can't Wait" campaign.[2] From an executive order to prevent prescription drug shortages to the recess appointment of Richard Cordray to lead the new Consumer Financial Protection Bureau, each of his actions was calculated to bypass Congress and leave a lasting mark on public policy. Legislative accomplishments such as the Affordable Care Act notwithstanding, the first two years of Obama's presidency were filled with frustration. A unified Republican opposition and skittish Democrats thwarted many of his other legislative priorities. The congressional midterm elections of 2010 proved the final nail in the coffin for his legislative agenda, as no fewer than sixty-six seats in the House of Representatives flipped from Democrat to Republican control. The party's gains from the 2006 and 2008 elections were washed away by an anti-incumbent wave, which also managed to take out powerful veteran committee chairs such as John Spratt, Ike Skelton, and James Oberstar in the process. Even though the president's party held onto a majority in the Senate, the House vote was a rebuke at least as severe as his two predecessors experienced in the midterm elections of 1994 and 2006.

There was little hope for Obama's agenda in the 112th Congress. Since most of the defeated Democrats were moderates—unlike the freshman Republican class—the House of Representatives was expected to be the most conservative and ideologically polarized of the modern era.[3] The midterm election put the brakes on other initiatives, such as comprehensive immigration reform and climate change legislation, which were deferred when Obama essentially "bet his domestic presidency on health care."[4] Just as his predecessors had done, he would have to be content governing without Congress.

Democrats were still counting the casualties a week after the election, as an executive-centered policy agenda began to take shape. The Center for American Progress, a think tank led by former Clinton chief of staff John Podesta, released a report and a series of recommendations that the president use administrative tools to enact a progressive agenda rather than waste his energy courting an obstructionist Congress.[5] Rulemaking, executive orders, and agency management led the list of policy instruments that Podesta singled out: "The U.S. Constitution and the laws of our nation grant the president significant authority to make and implement policy."[6] The Center for American Progress report identified several urgent issue areas as well as administrative actions that could be implemented by the end of 2012. Some of the thirty-four recommendations involved using executive authority under recent statutes to overcome compromises made in Congress. For example, Obama could ensure that the new consumer financial protection agency had a strong and independent regulatory authority. He was urged to promote preventative health care by actively guiding rules to implement the Affordable Care Act. Other more modest goals might be accomplished in such policy areas as education, simply by advocating rules that would make college financial aid more transparent. In addition, the president was urged to stop jailing undocumented immigrants and to direct Immigration and Customs Enforcement to prioritize immigrants with criminal records. Another of Podesta's recommendations, to "conserve federal lands for future generations" by executive action, seemed as if it were lifted from Clinton's playbook.[7]

The menu of unilateral actions proposed in the aftermath of the disastrous midterm election was the foundation for the "We Can't Wait" campaign. Obama arrived at the slogan in a White House strategy meeting in the fall of 2011, after several weeks of arduous budget negotiations with the Republican House leadership. Accordingly, the neglected domestic policy areas of occupational safety, environmental protection, and conservation were prominent among the initiatives. Appearing with Clinton at a construction site in Washington,

DC, Obama announced a green building initiative. He reiterated his call for energy efficiency tax credits, adding, "But we can't wait for Congress to act. And if they won't act, I will."[8] Since Congress was less than accommodating to his energy and climate goals, Obama directed federal agencies make more than $2 billion dollars in efficiency upgrades to buildings. Harnessing the vast economic power of the federal government, he bolstered the domestic market for renewable energy by committing the navy to buy 450,000 gallons of biofuels—the largest biofuel purchase in US history.[9] Invoking the Antiquities Act, Obama created a new national monument of Fort Monroe, Virginia, a refuge for escaped slaves during the Civil War.

The issue of domestic violence presented Obama with another opportunity to circumvent a "do-nothing" Congress. When the Violence against Women Act (VAWA) expired in 2012 and Congress was unable to reach an agreement to reauthorize the 1994 law, Obama used the authority he had to address violence affecting the federal workforce. Domestic violence that spills over into the workplace had been identified as a leading threat to worker safety in a NIOSH report from the Bush-Cheney era. Workplace homicides had fallen to a sixteen-year low in 2010, but workplace homicides against women had increased. According to NIOSH, one-fourth of the female victims were killed by people they knew, and the majority of those homicides were cases of domestic violence carried out in the workplace. Although the general duty clause of the Occupational Safety and Health Act gives OSHA some authority to create regulations reducing risk from workplace violence, in the absence of a specific mandate the agency did little more than provide information and voluntary guidelines to employers.

With the impasse over VAWA, Obama issued a directive that would at least protect the federal workforce. "As the nation's largest employer, the federal government should act as a model in responding to the effects of domestic violence on its workforce," Obama stated in the directive.[10] By the end of December 2012, all federal agencies were required to develop policies to prevent domestic violence against employees or by employees and to establish procedures to intervene and assist employees affected by domestic violence. Obama prefaced his announcement by touting the benefits of the recently expired VAWA, and as a statement from Vice President Biden explained, "While we wait for Congress to reauthorize this critically needed legislation, the federal government is doing its part."[11]

Obama continued to tout his unilateral initiatives going into his reelection campaign against Republican Mitt Romney. This showed his determination to define himself in relation to a "do-nothing" Congress, while at the same time building a list of accomplishments that would be difficult to reverse should he lose to Romney. The administration had been pondering additional land preservation initiatives, and congressional Republicans cried foul when a BLM memo detailing Interior secretary Ken Salazar's proposal to consolidate fourteen parcels of western lands to create conservation areas was leaked to the Utah congressional delegation.[12] As noted in chapter 7, the eleventh-hour rules of the Bush-Cheney Administration on oil shale and surface mining were a major distraction for Salazar when he took over as Interior secretary. There would be a certain irony if presidential proclamations were used to set aside land as conservation areas, tying the hands of Obama's successor. Such a move would not be unexpected, considering the circumstances parallel with those of Clinton and Bush at the end of their terms and the incentives for modern presidents to use executive policymaking generally.

The Strategic Lame Duck

Late-term rules are worth studying because they have consequences lasting beyond the partisan squabbles that occur around presidential elections and transitions. From John Adams's midnight appointments of judges to Jimmy Carter's lame duck executive orders and environmental legislation at the dawn of the 1980s, outgoing presidents have used the tools available to them to ensure the longevity of their own preferences and to tie the hands of their successors. In 1980, end-of-term rulemaking became a feature of presidential transitions. Beginning with the ambitious lame duck policy agenda of the Carter Administration, presidents have increasingly relied on unilateral actions late in their terms to advance domestic policy goals that they were unable to accomplish with legislation. As we have seen in the subsequent transitions, the trend that Carter began has evolved into a vital tool for every administration since.

Since the Carter Administration engaged in fervent last-minute rulemaking in 1980–81 and "midnight regulations" became a familiar term, the *Federal Register* has repeatedly been filled with last-ditch efforts to further the policy agendas of outgoing presidents. Late-term rulemaking is more than just tying up loose ends, particularly for rules that have taken a long time in the preparation and planning stages—more than just taking care of the unfinished business of a lame duck administration. Since it gives more power to federal agencies and to executive decision making, it is an effective method of circumventing the approval of Congress.

There are clear advantages to rulemaking as an instrument of policy entrenchment. Rules carry the force of law, and they are resistant to reversal if they are well planned and properly formulated. The frequency of eleventh-hour rulemaking suggests that the optimal time to list a final rule is after the November election, but before November 21, thus ensuring that the rule will take effect sixty days prior to Inauguration Day. Others not classified as economically significant can be listed in December. When an outgoing administration attempts to leave a policy legacy in the form of rules, some are invariably overturned by its successor. However, as we have seen, rescinding a rule can impose cost upon the successor administration. The constraints new presidents face limit the number of new battles they can afford to undertake, and the opportunity cost to the new president's agenda can be very high. Even those last-minute rules that appear destined for rescission are potent forms of symbolic policy that can set the stage for policy change in the future. For example, most of the auto safety, occupational safety, and health rules withdrawn by the incoming Reagan Administration in 1981 were eventually reinstated or revisited within a few years.

Major Findings

The political cycle of the presidency creates incentives to use executive action to pursue policy change, and a reliable opportunity occurs in the final months of a president's term. The preceding chapters illustrate how presidents routinely exploit this opportunity. Rulemaking for policy entrenchment is a strategy of two-term presidents, single-term presidents, Democrats and Republicans alike.

The longitudinal analysis in chapter 2 of late-term economically significant rules identified two significant trends. First, discretionary rules account for an increasing share of late-term policymaking. As outgoing presidents have increasingly relied upon rulemaking for their own initiatives, the proportion of discretionary rules finalized at the eleventh hour has been higher. Fewer of the last-minute rules of the two most recent administrations (Clinton and Bush) were mandated by statutory or judicial requirements, compared to previous administrations. Second, discretionary late-term rules, as opposed to mandatory rules, are more likely to be withdrawn without going into effect. This pattern is most apparent in the rules promulgated at the end of the Clinton and Bush-Cheney Administrations.

The major conclusion we may draw from each case study is that eleventh-hour rulemaking is used most often and most effectively to serve particular goals. As a tool of policy entrenchment, it is more effective for regulatory action than deregulatory purposes. Even though the technique has been applied by presidents in the service of regulatory agendas as well as antiregulatory agendas, the activist regulations of the Clinton Administration largely weathered efforts to reverse them. This is consistent with Loring and Roth's observation that procedural and legal obstacles work against presidents who try to reverse regulatory actions without justification.[13] Conversely, deregulatory actions that relax or undermine the intent of the statute are more difficult to justify and therefore easier to reverse.

The cases also illustrate that eleventh-hour rulemaking is a preferred strategy for presidents to affect policy areas where legislative politics are deadlocked. This is a common feature of social regulation, a form of regulatory policy that has grown since the 1970s and is characterized by more conflict between policymakers and more adversarial relationships between agencies and regulated firms than is the case for traditional economic regulation.[14] Mining policy is a prime example. As with Clinton's hardrock mining rule, presidents are tempted to use executive authority to break stalemates to advance their policy preferences, and the final months in office present the best opportunity to act without fear of consequences. Clinton attempted to modify mining policy not by changing the law but by influencing the way it is implemented. Since Congress did not clarify what the law meant by prohibition of "unnecessary" and "undue" damage to the environment, his reform consisted of offering an interpretation of their meaning and giving the Interior secretary discretion to deny permits on that basis. Besides mining, other policies have been revisited regularly at the time of presidential transitions, beginning with the Carter transfer of power to Reagan. These include air and water pollution, regulation of toxic substances, and workplace safety and rights.[15] Subsequent administrations have used the same tool to enact new protective policies, and others have used the strategy to relax or reverse the very same policies.

Through the records of five presidential transitions, we can trace the development of eleventh-hour rulemaking, beginning with the scattershot suite of last-minute rules and regulatory proposals that followed Carter's defeat in 1980. With some variations, this phenomenon was imitated by each successive president, culminating with George W. Bush's calculated, coordinated, and ideologically coherent effort to cement a pro-business legacy at the end of his second term. The evolution of that strategy comes into focus when we review the presidential transitions from each of the preceding chapters.

Carter faced policy stalemates over controversial energy and environmental issues, and he used his executive authority at the end of his term to force the changes he wanted. He issued several executive orders and directives to preserve federal land, extend conservation measures, and impose restrictions on hazardous waste exports. Ironically, these unilateral actions had little to do with the surge of last-minute rulemaking that was also part of his legacy. Agencies promulgated dozens of rules during Carter's final weeks in office, despite his efforts to increase regulatory oversight and impose discipline upon regulatory agencies. Most of the action was concentrated among the relatively new agencies assigned to implement social regulations, especially OSHA, NHTSA, OSMRE, and the EPA. Leaders of these agencies were known for their commitment to meeting the requirements imposed by Congress, which sometimes placed them at odds with the White House. Since the Carter Administration began under a model of cabinet government, each regulatory agency pursued its own lame duck agenda that originated in the decentralized environment at the start of Carter's term. Although Carter's critics characterized his rulemaking as hasty, the case study in chapter 3 demonstrates that on the contrary, the Carter Administration interregnum rulemaking was deliberate and strategic. Agencies staffed by civil service employees were working independently of the White House to implement statutes.

Reagan's final quarter was the least active in terms of regulatory output, due in part to the intraparty transition. Although there was no increase in quantity, Reagan contributed to the midnight rulemaking phenomenon by making the public more aware of it. By institutionalizing regulatory review within the executive office of the president, Reagan created a system that tracked regulatory proposals and monitored their costs and benefits. This had the effect of increasing the scrutiny of last-minute regulations, including his own.

Under Reagan the power of the administrative presidency was used to the fullest in the service of a deregulatory policy agenda. Priorities that could be enacted unilaterally were deferred until the end of Reagan's presidency, when he would be free to make politically risky decisions without fear of retribution from the voters. The White House continued to pursue a coordinated agenda throughout his presidency, culminating in last-minute decisions to grant licenses for nuclear power plants, new rules for mandatory drug testing, and proposals to reduce meat inspections and open federal land for strip mining. Even though he was transferring power to a successor of his own party, some of Reagan's late-term rules may have been deliberately timed to take the heat for unpopular decisions off the incoming Republican administration. Thus Bush was spared some contentious decisions. The midnight strategy nonetheless evolved under Reagan's watch. The end of his term also featured strict new pollution rules that Congress had mandated when major environmental laws were renewed during the 1980s. The irony was that the high volume of regulations promulgated by the EPA at the end of 1988 was the result of Reagan's own aggressive pursuit of regulatory relief at the beginning of his presidency.

In marked contrast with Reagan, the administration of George H. W. Bush listed a record-setting number of economically significant final rules during the last ninety days. His approach resembled Reagan's in other ways, however. Bush frequently used rulemaking for deregulatory actions, and the centralized regulatory review system he inherited from Reagan was designed to ensure that agency rules reflected the president's priorities. In this sense Bush expanded upon the eleventh-hour strategy of his predecessor and used it more aggressively. The unilateral actions at the end of his presidency followed a trajectory of diminishing cooperation with an opposition Congress. Following his election defeat, administration officials pushed last-minute proposals intended to roll back restrictions on activities from wetland development to strip mining, and even the amount of rest required for truck drivers between shifts, all of which were unsuccessful. Comparatively few of Bush's last-minute rules were discretionary. Even though most were mandated by Congress, Bush was instrumental because of his advocacy for the civil rights, agriculture, and environmental legislation that accounted for the majority of the new rules.

The Clinton Administration took a different approach to late-term rulemaking. The Clinton White House expanded the use of executive agencies to advance its domestic agenda in 1995. Clinton's use of interregnum rulemaking was part of this overall strategy and represents a significant increase over the way previous presidents had made use of eleventh-hour rules. Not only was there an increase in the quantity of rules, but unlike in his predecessor's actions, a larger share of Clinton's last-minute rules were discretionary. Clinton, again facing a gridlock with Congress on policy, was responsible for the largest number of written rules in the *Federal Register* recorded in his last ninety days, with more than 26,500 pages of new rules. Even though the Carter Administration pre-dated Clinton in advancing an activist agenda on the way out the door, Clinton's activity was distinct because of the degree of coordination and presidential involvement. Several of Clinton's initiatives were directed by the White House, resulting in a more cohesive set of priorities than the outgoing Carter Administration had.

The eleventh-hour strategy of George W. Bush was the most sophisticated, as he incorporated lessons from each of his predecessors. For example, the Bush-Cheney agenda featured the coordination of the Reagan Administration's late-term rules, since agency initiatives were cleared by the OMB and reflected the president's priorities. The agenda was also ambitious, since it included the largest volume of economically significant rules since his father's last quarter. Like the Clinton initiatives, most of the Bush-Cheney rules were not promulgated under statutory or judicial mandates. Therefore the surge of rulemaking included priorities that originated with the administration. Agencies were not simply implementing statutory requirements under deadlines imposed by Congress or the courts. Bush did what both of his predecessors had done: increase the quantity of rules as well as the proportion of discretionary rules as his second term came to an end.

The Bush White House further refined the use of interregnum rulemaking by taking precautions to ensure that they could not easily be undone. Many of Clinton's rules that had not yet taken effect were reversed or modified, so the Bush White House was wary of the potential for the incoming Obama Administration to do the same. Developing techniques to make these last-minute rules "stick" was an important part of the evolution of interregnum rulemaking as an administrative tool. Although administration officials complained bitterly about Clinton's eleventh-hour rulemaking, they were just as prolific eight years later but sought to avoid the negative label by directing agencies to finish rules by November 1. Nevertheless, federal agencies issued fifty-three rules in November and continued throughout December and January.

The cases also demonstrate that incoming administrations have developed increasingly sophisticated strategies for responding to their predecessors' late-term rules. When considered together, the case studies demonstrate an overall evolution of interregnum rulemaking. Every president since Carter has honed the effectiveness of this powerful policymaking tool. It grew to be so institutionalized that before the end of the Clinton years in the White House, Congress moved in 1996 to limit the power of interregnum rulemaking with the Congressional Review Act; it has still grown to be used and relied upon by every administration since. The reversal of OSHA's ergonomics standards in 2001 represents the only time Congress has used this law for its intended purpose. As such, it is the rare exception that proves how intractable such rulemaking has become.

Discussion

Now that midnight rulemaking has become routine for outgoing presidential administrations, scholars need to rethink the implications of this strategy in terms of democratic accountability and the implications if the will of the people is regularly thwarted in the period following elections, when administrative agencies face less oversight and presidents are less accountable as they relinquish power.

Accountability and democracy are at the heart of partisan criticism of midnight rulemaking. The fact that mining reform legislation had stalled in Congress years earlier raised a cloud of suspicion over Clinton's administrative push to restrict hardrock mining at the end of his term. In regard to the hardrock mining rule, House Republican Whip Roy Blount said, "The kind of things you haven't been able to do during your term, you shouldn't do as you're closing the door."[16] Not surprisingly, mining interests and their congressional allies did not share the administration's view that administrative policymaking offered the means to transcend partisan gridlock and enact policies for the common good.[17]

Presidents now enter office with the intention of immediately overturning many of their predecessors' actions. Thus durability is an important question in investigating the effectiveness of eleventh-hour rules (as studied by Loring and Roth). Rules are fairly resistant to repeal because of the constraints operating on new presidents. For example, even though Reagan withdrew many of the incomplete rules left over from the Carter Administration, most of the withdrawn initiatives returned in some form. Only one NTSHA standard was killed permanently.[18] New versions of the withdrawn OSHA rules were promulgated during the Reagan and Bush years. After initially withdrawing the chemical labeling rule, the Reagan Administration reluctantly issued a new hazard communication standard the following year.

The Republican administrations that followed Carter both launched controversial initiatives during their final months that were blocked before they could take effect. The Reagan Administration proposed to relax restrictions on strip mining and relax meat inspection regulations, but both initiatives were withdrawn amid opposition from congressional Democrats and Reagan's Republican successor. Before handing power off to Bill Clinton, the Bush Administration also proposed to relax restrictions on strip mining but was preempted by Congress. None of these initiatives made it past the proposal stage, however. The late-term final rules that both administrations added to the *Federal Register* on their way out were not altered by their successors. Under Reagan, the EPA promulgated a handful of hazardous waste and water pollution standards, and OSHA completed a long-awaited lockout/tagout standard before his vice president succeeded him. The Bush Administration sent a larger volume of final rules to the *Federal Register* on the way out, including new air pollution standards and an OSHA rule for confined space work that went unchallenged by his successor.

The Bush-Cheney Administration was determined to reverse Clinton rules it opposed but had little success with final rules already in effect. As with the other cases reviewed, the durability of Clinton's late-term rules is evidence of a general deference to presidential actions by Congress and the courts.[19] Clinton's rule limiting road building in national forests is a prime example of how sticky late-term rules can be. The Bush Agriculture Department suspended the rule following a lawsuit, but the Bush-Cheney Administration, its allies in Congress, and various interest groups never succeeded in reversing the rule entirely because they were thwarted by conflicting court rulings.

The Clinton Administration's arsenic rule is another case in point. The Safe Drinking Water Act authorized the EPA to set standards for arsenic, but the statute did not specify an acceptable level of risk, how to balance the cost of regulation, or how to balance these factors in its decision. There were years of inaction because these weighty decisions were left to the EPA. When the controversial final rule was finally adopted, the Clinton Administration treated it as a political hot potato, which was lobbed to the incoming Bush Administration. The Clinton Administration avoided promulgating the controversial rule until after the 2000 election. After Bush was inaugurated as the forty-third president and the EPA withdrew the rule to consider a weaker standard, there was a swift backlash from environmentalists. Despite its original inclination to weaken the arsenic restrictions, the administration could not ignore the resulting political firestorm. This included a rebuke by congressional Republicans and was further fueled by a National Academy of Sciences study—done at the administration's request—that found even greater health benefits than previously expected. The rule was reinstated before the end of the year.

The eleventh-hour rules of George W. Bush were the most resistant to change. As I have described, the administration's strategy was to complete its surge of final rulemaking earlier in the calendar than had the Clinton Administration. Taking effect before the transition, the administration's more controversial rules, including the buffer zone policy for mountaintop removal mining and the scientific review exemption under the Endangered Species Act, were largely immune to the suspensions that Bush used to delay and impede Clinton's rules. Just as Howell and Mayer found that earlier presidents paid a price for reversing their predecessors' rules, the Bush White House seemed determined that the policy agenda it enacted administratively could be reversed only at a high cost to his successor.[20]

A Question of Accountability

The growing use of eleventh-hour rulemaking for discretionary policy initiatives, and the persistence of such rules in spite of best efforts to reverse them, raise legitimate questions about the accountability of executive power. Various proposals have been made to restore the accountability for regulatory policy that congressional oversight of agencies is meant to provide.

These consist largely of general solutions formulated in response to unique circumstances. The most recent transitions occurred under conditions of intense partisanship, as presidents governing alongside an opposition Congress relied upon parallel policymaking structures within the White House to advance their priorities. In every transition since 1992, the surge of administrative policymaking fostered mistrust. As divided government gave way to unitary government, partisan frustrations exploded over administration attempts to circumvent the legislative process, leading to congressional hearings, heated rhetoric about midnight regulations, and calls for reform.

The Congressional Review Act figured prominently in the debates around the two most recent transitions. Even though the legislative veto was determined to be an unconstitutional violation of separation of powers in 1983, this 1996 law is a permissible instrument to repeal rules under specific conditions. In theory the threat of congressional review under the act is a deterrent to executive branch excess. As explained in chapter 6, there are so many restrictions on its use that Congress has invoked the CRA to overturn only one rule, in 2001. Congress is more apt to use the normal legislative process to preempt midnight rules. Chapter 5 describes the response to a last-minute rule the Bush-Quayle Administration proposed that would have opened protected public lands, including some national parks, for strip mining. The Interior Department's rule exploited the ambiguity of a phrase in the 1977 Surface Mining law, "valid and existing right," to resolve a long-standing dispute. The rule clarified the term to award mining permits to holders of mineral rights that were purchased even after the lands were preserved. Congress preempted the rule by passing an amendment that clarified the term to be consistent with the previous interpretation, finally settling the controversy through law.

Congress could also take action to delay further the effective date of last-minute rules, giving the incoming administration greater latitude to rescind them. For example, a change in the law to permit the administration to repeal final rules adopted during the interregnum period without going through the notice-and-comment process would give agencies an incentive to complete them before the election. However, granting too much power to incoming administrations to reverse their predecessors' regulations would have perverse consequences. It would create incentives for interest groups to lobby the new administration to weaken or overturn all sorts of rules, resulting in an inaugural frenzy of crack-of-dawn rulemaking.[21] Andrew Morriss and colleagues suggest that a better alternative is to limit how much agencies should be allowed to do before a transition, perhaps with legislation allowing agencies to work only on emergency regulations during the interregnum period. They would be forced to budget their time and to complete more regulatory activity when they and the administration could still be forced to pay a price for overreach.[22]

Another approach to reform would involve subjecting interregnum rules to greater scrutiny in the courts. Virtually all major rules are challenged in court, and litigation is inevitable in cases of controversial last-minute rules. Some scholars have urged that the remedy for midnight regulations be focused at this stage. For example, Jack Beermann argues that timing should be a consideration in judicial review of rules.[23] The courts treat final rules adopted at the last minute by an outgoing administration no differently than any other rules.

Both of these proposals, while giving the judiciary and the incoming administration greater latitude to reverse eleventh-hour rules, also have the effect of tipping the balance of power toward the legislative branch. Congress has the means to create significant delays by using the appropriations process, enacting legislative amendments to restrict agency actions, trimming budgets, and conducting oversight hearings. Chapters 5 and 6 describe examples of Bush and Clinton Administration midnight rules that might have been completed earlier but were delayed significantly because of these tactics. Any reforms that limit the durability of last-minute rules would give an adversarial opposition Congress an incentive to grind the rulemaking process to a halt, rather than encouraging lawmakers to use their power more constructively. For example, instead of reacting to executive branch initiatives, Congress could assert itself by reforming legislation to reduce agency discretion. If lawmakers are willing to resolving political conflicts during the formulation of legislation, then the rulemaking process is less likely to produce the type of controversial outcomes that erupt into hostilities around presidential transitions. Moreover, Congress could amend the enabling statutes to reduce the ambiguities that presidents and top administrators use to justify policy activism by the executive branch. As an institution, Congress has been reluctant to use its available powers to reduce the incentives for midnight rulemaking.

Eleventh-Hour Rules and the Democratic Process

An issue tied closely to accountability is the democratic legitimacy of eleventh-hour rulemaking. The practice of adopting final rules following an election—rules that do not reflect the preferences of the winner—challenges an important assumption of the democratic process: that policymaking is responsive to the will of the people. Critics have pointed out that the timing circumvents congressional oversight because it occurs at the end of the legislative session as well as the president's term. Thus strategically timed executive policymaking can be used to bypass the deliberation and debate provided by the only representative body that keeps agency rulemaking in check under normal conditions. Congressional delegation of legislative authority is a legitimate concern about agency rulemaking generally.[24] The growing frequency of executive policymaking at the eleventh hour implies that more important decisions are made without the scrutiny of the normal political process.

In addition to the familiar concerns about bypassing the democratic deliberation and oversight of Congress, Morriss and colleagues suggest that late-term rulemaking is prone to partisan mischief. An incoming administration has the option of withdrawing a rule that is not consistent with its priorities if it chooses to dedicate resources to a new rulemaking procedure. The political capital this requires can be a tremendous opportunity cost because it diverts resources that the new administration would rather use for its own policy agenda. Similarly, the growing practice of eleventh-hour rulemaking is said to encourage bureaucratic overreach in an effort to embarrass the incoming administration. By finalizing a rule that the incoming administration is known to oppose, the outgoing administration invites controversy upon its successors, who will inevitably come into conflict with political interests that support the rule.[25]

The actions of incoming presidents to respond to their predecessors' eleventh-hour initiatives have equally serious implications for democracy. The Supreme Court's *State Farm* decision established that the Administrative Procedure Act provision for public input applies to rule changes and withdrawals as well as to the formulation of new rules, but this has not deterred presidents from seeking ways to circumvent this procedural requirement. George W. Bush waged an elaborate repeal campaign, beginning with his chief of staff's order to suspend Bill Clinton's last-minute rules. The Card memo went as far as to suspend final rules without a notice-and-comment process. The opportunity for participation required by the APA is bypassed when rules are withdrawn unilaterally. Future research should examine the elaborate strategies that incoming presidents have developed to repeal predecessors' lame duck activities.

Summary: The Clock Is Always Ticking

The expansion of the policy role of the presidency has coincided with two parallel if incongruous trends: a growth in institutional domestic policy capacity and a tendency of recent presidents to limit the scope of the domestic agenda. Pursuing an ambitious domestic agenda can be risky because it spreads the administration's resources thin and increases the likelihood of failures. Modern presidents face significant expectations to deliver on their promises, and they have more resources to devote to domestic policy leadership than ever before. The results of this study support the observations in recent literature that late-term rulemaking is on the rise. Since rulemaking is not purely unilateral, it is more effective as an instrument of policy entrenchment than are prerogative powers that presidents employ independently. At the end of a presidential term it can be used more successfully than trying to persuade Congress at a time when a president's influence is usually waning. Thus presidents have incentives to be prolific at the end and to begin planning early.

The case studies invite four conclusions about late-term rulemaking. First, it can be an effective technique to promote regulatory as well as deregulatory goals. Presidents of every political stripe are tempted to employ administrative rulemaking for entrenchment of their policies because rules are more resistant to reversal by successive administrations than are other unilateral tools. Late-term rules also tend to be used for specific policy areas. Where newer issues of social regulation are concerned, more policy decisions are made through bureaucratic discretion because gridlock makes legislative reform unlikely. In all cases, the strategy was used in occupational safety and health as well as environmental policy. Third, there is a rise in discretionary policymaking at the eleventh hour. Prior to Clinton's exit, most late-term rulemaking was used to promulgate rules mandated by Congress. This changed when the outgoing Clinton Administration promulgated a large number of discretionary rules for initiatives that originated within executive departments and the White House, a trend that George W. Bush continued. Finally, late-term rules are becoming more resistant to reversal. As recent administrations have forced policy decisions on their way out, and have projected their preferences into the future, they have also developed elaborate strategies to minimize the chances of rescission.

The use of this instrument threatens to undermine democratic accountability because the executive branch can act with less congressional oversight or fear of recrimination from the voters at the end of a president's term. Due to policy stalemate in Congress, the executive branch has become the part of government most likely to affect domestic policy in the absence of legislative action, especially in times of divided government. The rise of eleventh-hour policymaking has also coincided with changes in the political environment. The twenty-four-hour news cycle, the rise of cable networks, and the Internet have all expanded the public access to information, so perhaps in the future, executive branch officials will be cautious about using this strategy for policy goals without broad-based support. Conversely, the conditions that seem to encourage eleventh-hour policymaking for controversial ends, including favors for interest groups and partisan mischief, can also liberate presidents to act in the national interest. In this sense, the president can act more as a "free bird" than a lame duck.[26] Many of the initiatives discussed here advanced popular safety, health, and environmental objectives. If Congress is seen as obstructing those goals, or catering to narrow economic interests in their opposition, then the president will be in a strong position to pursue ambitious and resilient eleventh-hour policy initiatives.

Appendix

Economically Significant Fourth-Quarter Rules

George W. Bush		
Rule	*Department/Agency*	*Received*
Secure Flight Program	Homeland Sec	10/20/2008
Physician Fee	HHS	10/29/2008
Changes to Payment	HHS	10/29/2008
Employment Eligibility	FAR	10/31/2008
Abandoned Mine Program	Interior	10/31/2008
Family & Medical Leave	Labor	11/4/2008
Security Filing	Homeland Sec	11/6/2008
Internet Gambling	Treasury	11/7/2008
Mortgages	HUD	11/7/2008
Oil Shale	Interior	11/7/2008
Child Support	HHS	11/10/2008
Ozone Monitoring	HHS	11/13/2008
Driver Hours	Transportation	11/13/2008
Patient Safety – Ext.	HHS	11/14/2008
Fuel Economy	Transportation	11/14/2008
Premiums & Cost Sharing	HHS	11/17/2008
Spill Prevention	EPA	11/18/2008
Salmonella	HHS	11/19/2008
Medicaid Flexibility	HHS	11/21/2008
Safety Assurance	Transportation	11/26/2008
DC Special Flight Rule	Transportation	12/3/2008
TRICARE-OPPS	Defense	12/4/2008
Public & Assisted Housing	HUD	12/9/2008
Cyclical Program	Agriculture	12/12/2008
Refrigeration	Energy	12/18/2008
Equipment Supplier	HHS	12/19/2008
Coal Mines	Labor	12/19/2008
Medicare Benefits	HHS	12/30/2008

George W. Bush, *continued*		
Rule	*Department/Agency*	*Received*
Environmental Quality	Agriculture	1/9/2009
Wetlands Reserve	Agriculture	1/9/2009
Medicare Benefits	HHS	1/9/2009
HIPPA Code Sets	HHS	1/9/2009
Electronic Transactions	HHS	1/9/2009
Investment Advice	Labor	1/9/2009
Country of Origin	Agriculture	1/9/2009
Sugar Program	Agriculture	1/22/2009
Loan Assistance	Agriculture	1/22/2009
Nondiscrimination – Disability	Justice	1/22/2009
Nondiscrim. – State & Local	Justice	1/22/2009
Conservation Reserve	Agriculture	1/23/2009
On-Board Recorders	Transportation	1/23/2009
Service Exemption	Labor	1/26/2009
Outer Continental Shelf	Interior	1/26/2009

Bill Clinton		
Rule	*Department/Agency*	*Received*
Disaster Assistance	Agriculture	10/24/2000
Market Assistance	Agriculture	10/24/2000
Physician Fees	HHS	10/25/2000
Outpatient Payment	HHS	11/2/2000
Bioenergy Program	Agriculture	11/7/2000
Contractors & Affirm. Action	Labor	11/8/2000
Ergonomics	Labor	11/9/2000
Munitions Ranges	Defense	11/13/2000
Mining Claims	Interior	11/14/2000
Food Stamp Eligibility	Agriculture	11/15/2000
Retirement Security	Labor	11/16/2000
Description Rules	Labor	11/16/2000
Livestock Price	Agriculture	11/20/2000
Labeling Shell Eggs	HHS	11/29/2000

Bill Clinton, *continued*		
Rule	*Department/Agency*	*Received*
Electronic & Tech Access	ATBCB	12/11/2000
Diabetes Coverage	HHS	12/14/2000
Chem. Recovery Combust.	EPA	12/15/2000
Organic Program	Agriculture	12/15/2000
Privacy Standards	HHS	12/19/2000
Sulfur Control	EPA	12/21/2000
Nondiscrimination in Coverage	HHS	12/22/2000
Prohibit Health Discrimination	Labor	12/22/2000
Lead-Based Paint	EPA	12/22/2000
State Child Health	HHS	1/4/2001
Medicaid Pay Limit	HHS	1/4/2001
Fed. Financial Participation	HHS	1/4/2001
Farm Storage Loan	Agriculture	1/5/2001
Roadless Areas	Agriculture	1/5/2001
Boating Grant Program	Interior	1/5/2001
Occupational Injury	Labor	1/5/2001
Food Stamp	Agriculture	1/8/2001
Steel Erection	Labor	1/8/2001
Lead	EPA	1/8/2001
Water Heater Efficiency	Energy	1/9/2001
Juice	HHS	1/10/2001
Drinking Water – Arsenic	EPA	1/10/2001
Medicaid – Managed Care	HHS	1/12/2001
Sea Lion, Groundfish	Commerce	1/16/2001
Central Air/Heat Pumps	Energy	1/17/2001
TRICARE	Defense	1/25/2001
Property Acquisition	FEMA	1/31/2001
Consolidated Emission	EPA	2/14/2001
Primary Drinking Water	EPA	2/16/2001

George H. W. Bush		
Rule	*Department/Agency*	*Received*
Drug Claims Medicaid	HHS	10/23/1992
Acid Rain	EPA	10/23/1992
Real Estate	HUD	10/28/1992
Food Labeling	HHS	10/28/1992
Food Labeling – Zinc	HHS	11/1/1992
Food Labels – Dairy, Syrup	HHS	11/1/1992
Labels Tuna, Soft Drinks	HHS	11/1/1992
Label Omega-3	HHS	11/5/1992
Butter	HHS	11/5/1992
Food Labeling – Special Diet	HHS	11/5/1992
Labeling – Sodium	HHS	11/5/1992
Labeling – Fat & Cancer	HHS	11/5/1992
Wheat	Agriculture	11/10/1992
Labeling – Calcium	HHS	11/10/1992
Labeling – Heart Disease	HHS	11/10/1992
Labels – Vitamins & Cancer	HHS	11/10/1992
Medicare Fee Schedule	HHS	11/13/1992
Sewage Sludge	EPA	11/25/1992
Water Quality	EPA	12/1/1992
Food Labels – Folic Acid	HHS	12/8/1992
Food Labels – Fiber	HHS	12/21/1992
Labeling – Fiber, Cancer	HHS	12/21/1992
Food Labeling – Healthy	HHS	12/22/1992
Labeling – Daily Intake	HHS	12/22/1992
Food Labeling	HHS	12/22/1992
Label Health Claims	HHS	12/22/1992
Nutrition Labeling	HHS	12/22/1992
Nutrient Content	HHS	12/22/1992
Food Labeling	HHS	12/22/1992
Grain	Agriculture	12/23/1992
Nutrition Labeling	Agriculture	12/24/1992
Confined Spaces	Labor	12/31/1992
Feed Grain	Agriculture	1/7/1993
Nonpoint Pollution	EPA	1/8/1993

George H. W. Bush, *continued*		
Rule	*Department/Agency*	*Received*
Corrective Action	EPA	1/11/1993
Evaporative Emission	EPA	1/15/1993
Marine Transportation	Transportation	1/19/1993
Vessel Response	Transportation	1/19/1993

Ronald Reagan		
Rule	*Department/Agency*	*Received*
Thrifty Food	Agriculture	10/21/1988
Anti-Drug Aviation	Transportation	11/4/1988
Controlled Substance	Transportation	11/4/1988
Guaranteed Loans	Agriculture	12/30/1988
Exposure Limits	Labor	1/10/1989
Emergency Loans	Agriculture	1/11/1989
Fair Housing	HUD	1/13/1989
Auto Fuel Economy	Transportation	1/18/1989
Mortgage Payment	HUD	1/26/1989
Wheat Feed Cotton	Agriculture	1/27/1989
Flight Recorder	Transportation	1/27/1989
Hazardous Waste	Labor	1/30/1989

Notes

Short citations in these notes include year of publication for ease of matching to the reference listing that follows.

Introduction

1. Clinton, 2001, "Remarks on Action to Preserve America's Forests," 18.
2. Clinton's executive actions are discussed at length in chapter 6 of the present volume. For a comprehensive list of national monument designations in his final year in office, see John T. Wooley and Gerhard Peters, *The American Presidency Project* (online), Santa Barbara, California, http://www.presidency.ucsb.edu/proclamations.php?year=2000&Submit=DISPLAY.
3. Clinton, 2001, "Remarks on Action to Preserve America's Forests," 19.
4. This was the lead sentence of a news report on the Clinton speech. See Rogers and Hutcheson, 2001, "Clinton in Thick of Fight." The story quotes lobbyist Chuck Cushman of the American Land Rights Association as comparing the forest preservation initiative to "Sherman's march to the sea."
5. Representative James Hansen of Utah, quoted in Rogers and Hutcheson, 2001, "Clinton in Thick of Fight."
6. Clinton, 2001, "Remarks on Action to Preserve America's Forests," 18.
7. Moe, 1985, "The Politicized Presidency."
8. See Nie, 2008, *Governance of Western Lands.*
9. Dombeck et al., 2003, *From Conquest to Conservation.*
10. Light, 1999, *President's Agenda.*

Chapter 1

1. The coal industry, which supported Bush and Cheney in the previous year's election, was one of the groups represented on the influential task force. See Warshaw, 2009, *Co-Presidency of Bush and Cheney*.
2. Coleman, 2001, "Gov. Bob Wise."
3. Ward, 2001, "DEP Backs Off."
4. Dennis G. Rice, policy and regulatory analyst, US Department of Interior, Office of Surface Mining, Reclamation and Enforcement, interview with author, December 23, 2010.
5. Nie, 2008, *Governance of Western Lands*.
6. See Klotz, 1997, "On the Way Out"; Cochran, 2001, "Cinderella Constraint"; Howell and

Mayer, 2005, "Last One Hundred Days"; Brito and de Rugy, 2008, "Midnight Regulations"; O'Connell, 2008, "Political Cycles of Rulemaking."

7. Mendelson defines agency burrowing as the attempts by departing presidents to entrench policies by making patronage appointments and moving political appointees into civil service positions. See Mendelson, 2003, "Agency Burrowing."
8. Cooper, 2002, *By Order of the President.*
9. For the now dated but seminal work on the power of persuasion, see Neustadt, *Presidential Power*.
10. For recent studies that examine a range of prerogative powers, see Howell, 2003, *Power without Persuasion*; Cooper, 2002, *By Order of the President*; and Shull, 2006, *Policy by Other Means*. Others that focus narrowly on executive orders are Mayer, 2001, *With the Stroke of a Pen,* and Warber, 2006, *Executive Orders and the Modern Presidency*.
11. Light, 1999, *President's Agenda*.
12. Nathan, 1983, *The Administrative Presidency.*
13. Warshaw, 1994, "The Carter Experience."
14. Hugh Heclo has noted a tendency for newly elected presidents to affirm their belief in cabinet government, which he attributes to the desire to reassure the public that the new president is not power-hungry, rather than to a concrete plan to manage his administration: "It is significant that no president has ever left office extolling the virtues of cabinet government" (see Heclo, 1983, "One Executive Branch or Many?" 26).
15. Friedman, 1995, *Regulation in the Reagan-Bush Era.*
16. Pfiffner, 2005, *The Modern Presidency*.
17. The successful enactment of George W. Bush's first-term agenda was facilitated by key personnel who wasted no time taking the reins of the White House policy apparatus. There were dedicated advisors for each of his domestic policy priorities. Lawrence Lindsey, who chaired the National Economic Council, managed the president's tax cut legislation. The education reform was managed by Margaret Spellings, and until his resignation at the end of 2001, the Office of Faith-based Initiatives was led by John DiIulio (Warshaw, 2009, *Co-Presidency of Bush and Cheney*).
18. Pfiffner, 1996, *The Strategic Presidency*.
19. Ibid.
20. Light, 1999, *President's Agenda*.
21. President Obama was likely sensitive to this when he decided to pursue health care reform legislation during his first year in office despite pleas from his senior advisors to delay such a bold policy proposal (Alter, 2010, *The Promise*).
22. O'Connell, 2008, "Political Cycles of Rulemaking."
23. Light, 1999, *President's Agenda*.
24. Of these sources, public opinion is the best indicator to predict which emerging problems will receive the president's attention, particularly in election years. See Yates and Whitford, 2005, "Institutional Foundations."

25. The decision in *Motor Vehicle Manufacturers Association v. State Farm*, 463 U.S. 29, 42 (1983), stated: "An agency changing its course by rescinding a rule is obligated to supply a reasoned analysis for the change beyond that which may be required when an agency does not act in the first instance."
26. Mendelson, 2003, "Agency Burrowing."
27. Susan E. Dudley, director, Office of Information and Regulatory Affairs, interview with author, September 3, 2010.
28. Mendelson, 2003, "Agency Burrowing."
29. Morrow, 2001, "Midnight Regulations: Natural Order of Disorderly Governance."
30. Power et al., 2008, "White House Pushes through a Flurry."
31. Fahrentold, 2008, "Bush Administration Pushes."
32. Klotz, 1997, "On the Way Out."
33. Howell and Mayer, 2005, "Last One Hundred Days."
34. See, for example, Dudley, 2001, "Reversing Midnight Regulations." This is also known as the "clean plate" theory of transitions. See Pfiffner, 1983, "The Carter-Reagan Transition."
35. Johnson, 1986, "Portrayal of Lame-Duck Presidents."
36. Howell and Mayer, 2005, "Last One Hundred Days."
37. Loring and Roth, 2005, "After Midnight."
38. Cochran, 2001, "Cinderella Constraint."
39. Quarterly figures were generated from OIRA's Database of Historical Reports, http://www.reginfo.gov.
40. The final quarter of the presidency is defined as the ninety days that precede the transition. For the purposes of comparison, the first quarter of the year begins with Inauguration Day or its anniversary (January 21–April 20). The other quarters of the year are designated by the same interval: April 21–July 20 (second), July 21–October 20 (third), and October 21–January 20 (fourth).
41. Bolten, 2008, "Issuance of Agency Regulations," http://www.ombwatch.org/files/regs/PDFs/BoltenMem0050908.pdf.
42. 463 U.S. 29 (1983). An agency must examine the relevant data and provide a satisfactory explanation of its decision.
43. Loring and Roth, 2005, "After Midnight."
44. See Rose, 1991, *The Post-Modern President*.
45. Goldstein, 2001, "Last-Minute Spin."
46. 467 U.S. 837 (1984). The Chevron decision established a doctrine of deference to agency discretion. Following a two-step test, the court first determines the clarity of the statute. If the language is clear and the agency exceeds its authority, it would be grounds to overrule the agency's decision. Most successful challenges to agency rules are decided at the first step. If the statute is ambiguous, then the court must determine whether the agency's interpretation is permissible under the statute. For this, courts usually defer to the agency; see Lubbers, *A Guide to Federal Agency Rulemaking*.

47. Rossi, 2001, "Bargaining in the Shadow."
48. *Immigration and Naturalization Service v. Chadha,* 462 U.S. 919 (1983). Prior to the ruling, statutes often included provisions for Congress to overrule implementation decisions with a one-house vote.
49. CRA is the more common name of the Small Business Regulatory Enforcement Fairness Act of 1996, P.L. 104–121, 110. Stat. 857–874.
50. Even staunch critics of Clinton's late-term rulemaking predicted that the CRA would be used sparingly. It was possible only because of the conditions that existed during the first sixty days of the Bush-Cheney Administration. Dudley, "Reversing Midnight Regulations."

Chapter 2

1. Hamilton et al., *Federalist Papers*.
2. Moe, 1985, "The Politicized Presidency."
3. Fishel, 1985, *Presidents and Promises*.
4. Howell, 2003, *Power without Persuasion*.
5. Shull, 2006, *Policy by Other Means*.
6. Mayer, 2001, *With the Stroke of a Pen*.
7. Cooper, 2002, *By Order of the President*.
8. Kerwin, 2003, *Rulemaking*.
9. The exception to this trend was the presidency of George H. W. Bush. After succeeding his fellow Republican Ronald Reagan in office, Bush chose to retain most top managers in the federal bureaucracy (see Lewis, 2008, *Politics of Presidential Appointments*, 53).
10. Kagan, 2001, "Presidential Administration."
11. Lewis, 2008, *Politics of Presidential Appointments*, 73.
12. Moe, 1985, "The Politicized Presidency."
13. Nathan, 1983, *The Administrative Presidency*. Cooper, 2002, *By Order of the President,* describes how contemporary presidents have expanded their use of these policy instruments.
14. Daynes and Sussman, 2010, *White House Politics and the Environment*.
15. Edwards and Wayne, 1999, *Presidential Leadership*.
16. Gerhard Peters, "Executive Orders," *The American Presidency Project* (online), *www.presidency.ucsb.edu/data/orders.php*. Clinton began issuing these orders on his first day in office, when he rescinded the Reagan-Bush-era "gag rule" on abortion counseling at military hospitals. This policy is reversed by executive order every time the White House changes party control.
17. Shull, 2006, *Policy by Other Means*.
18. West, 2004, "Formal Procedures, Informal Processes," 79.
19. Despite its origins and location within the Executive Office of the President, OIRA has been a stable organization with low turnover. Except for two leadership positions, it is staffed with civil service employees valued for their expertise as opposed to loyalty or partisanship (West, 2004, "Formal Procedures, Informal Processes").

20. Lewis, 2008, *Politics of Presidential Appointments*.
21. McGinness, 2001, "Regulatory Review as Constitutional Restoration."
22. Triano and Walzman, 1991, *All the Vice President's Men*.
23. Eisner et al., 2006, *Contemporary Regulatory Policy*.
24. Cahn, 1995, *Environmental Deceptions*.
25. Congress has various means to do this, for example a legislative rider, change in statute, or the Congressional Review Act, a form of legislative veto used to reverse President Clinton's ergonomics rule in 2001 (see chapter 6).
26. Lewis, 2003, *Presidents and the Politics of Agency Design*.
27. Kerwin, 2003, *Rulemaking*.
28. Stone, 2002, *Policy Paradox*.
29. Regulation is defined as "public policies explicitly designed to govern economic activity and its consequences at the level of the industry, firm, or individual unit of activity" (see Eisner et al., 2006, *Contemporary Regulatory Policy*).
30. Meier, 1985, *Regulation*.
31. Friedman, 1995, *Regulation in the Reagan-Bush Era*.
32. Eads and Fix, 1984, *Relief or Reform*.
33. It is significant that independent regulatory commissions were excluded from Reagan's initial regulatory freeze and regulatory review directive in 1981.
34. Meier, 1985, *Regulation*.
35. Capture theory, advanced by Samuel Huntington (1952) and others, was limited to the sphere of economic regulation and describes regulatory commissions that oversee a single industry.
36. Heclo, 1978, "Issue Networks and the Executive Establishment."
37. Berry and Portney, 1995, "Centralizing Regulatory Control."
38. These are among the policy areas most likely to be delegated by Congress. David Epstein and Sharyn O'Halloran show that in addition to appropriations committees, congressional committees on environment, energy, and labor are the most likely to hold oversight hearings (Epstein and O'Halloran, 1999, *Delegating Powers*).
39. Social regulation is usually forced upon regulated industry at the request of public interest groups, in contrast to regulation established at the encouragement of the regulated industry. Social regulation is not exclusively concerned with control of entry to the market or prices, although these policies do affect economic activity (see Fuchs, 1988, *Presidents, Management and Regulation*).
40. Szasz, 1984, "Industrial Resistance."
41. A worker's right to accompany OSHA inspectors without losing wages, "walkaround pay," was challenged in *Chamber of Commerce v. OSHA* (1978); the chemical industry challenged the cost of OSHA's benzene standard, which was upheld in *AFL-CIO v. American Petroleum Institute* (1980); and the right to access medical records was challenged in *Louisiana Chemical Association v. Eula Bingham* (1981). See Szasz, 1984, "Industrial Resistance."

42. See Morrow, 2001, "Midnight Regulations: Natural Order of Disorderly Governance"; Howell and Mayer, 2005, "Last One Hundred Days."
43. See O'Connell, 2008, "Political Cycles of Rulemaking," for a discussion of the differences between midnight and crack-of-dawn rules.
44. For example, see Furlong, 1995, "The 1992 Regulatory Moratorium"; Golden, 1998, "Interest Groups in the Rule-Making Process."
45. Berry, 1984, *The Interest Group Society.*
46. Kerwin, 2003, *Rulemaking*.
47. Furlong, 1995, "The 1992 Regulatory Moratorium."
48. West, 2004, "Formal Procedures, Informal Processes"; Webb Yackee, 2005, "Sweet-Talking the Fourth Branch"; Shapiro, 2007, "Why Do Agencies Change Their Proposed Rules?"
49. See Golden, 1998, "Interest Groups in the Rule-Making Process," as well as Kamieniecki, 2006, *Corporate America and Environmental Policy*.
50. O'Connell, 2008, "Political Cycles of Rulemaking."
51. Ibid.
52. Under the Congressional Review Act, economically significant rules take effect sixty days after they become final; the span is thirty days for all others.

Chapter 3

1. Light, 1999, *President's Agenda*.
2. The "Lau Regulations" were proposed on August 4, 1980, to establish compliance standards for bilingual education following the 1974 US Supreme Court ruling in *Lau v. Nichols*. Not only was the Reagan team opposed to the Lau Regulations; a backlash was brewing in Congress. A legislative rider in 1980 blocked the Department of Education from issuing final bilingual education rules until 1981, following the transition. One week after the election, Women's Issues adviser Debbie Hyatt wrote, "We need to decide whether any form of ED staff work on these regulations should continue during the next two months." Memo from Hyatt to Stuart Eizenstat, November 12, 1980, Domestic Policy Staff, Hyatt 21, Jimmy Carter Library, Atlanta, Georgia (hereafter cited as JCL, with folder and file names and box number if applicable).
3. See Fix and Eads, 1985, "Regulatory Reform." Reagan and the Task Force for Regulatory Relief (active 1981–83) were responsible for Executive Order 12291, "Federal Regulation," and Executive Order 12498, "Regulatory Planning Process," which were to be game changers under the new administration, because from then on, new regulations would have to be disclosed when in their preliminary planning stages and then get past OIRA (see Friedman, 1995, *Regulation in the Reagan-Bush Era,* 3–4).
4. Vice President George H. W. Bush, "Statement Regarding Actions Taken by the President's Task Force on Regulatory Relief," CFOA 88, Martin Anderson, Subject File, Task Force on Regulatory Relief, March 25, 1981, Ronald Reagan Presidential Library, Simi Valley, California.

5. Calavita, 1983, "Demise of the Occupational Safety and Health Administration."
6. Derthick and Quirk, 1985, *Politics of Deregulation*; also Kingdon, 1995, *Agendas, Alternatives and Public Policies.*
7. See Eads and Fix, 1984, *Relief or Reform*, for what the Ford Administration introduced.
8. Rattner, 1979, "Carter Announces Legislative Plan."
9. Warshaw, 1994, "The Carter Experience."
10. Warshaw, 2009, *Co-Presidency of Bush and Cheney.*
11. Carson, 1962, *Silent Spring.*
12. When President Kennedy was asked at the Presidential News Conference of August 29, 1962, if he considered asking the Department of Agriculture or the Public Health Service to look at the growing concerns of scientists about pesticides, he said, "Yes, and I know they already are. I think, particularly, of course, since Miss Carson's book." Carson's work was criticized by the chemical industry and by some agronomists, but it nonetheless catapulted the environmental movement into action and successfully advocated for state and federal regulation of DDT and other substances, once her study was vindicated.
13. Caudill, 1962, *Night Comes to the Cumberlands.*
14. Caudill, 1963, *Night Comes to the Cumberlands.*
15. Public Health Service, 1965, *Protecting the Health of 80 Million Americans.*
16. Noble, 1989, *Liberalism at Work*
17. Ibid.
18. Ibid., 4.
19. Ibid.
20. Ibid.
21. Gus Speth, 1980, Memorandum, "Environmental Issues" (JCL: CEA-15).
22. Nivola, 1986, *Politics of Energy Conservation.*
23. Ibid.
24. Interview with the President, June 13, 1980. *Public Papers of the Presidents of the United States: Jimmy Carter,* vol. 1: 1113.
25. Federal Land Policy and Management Act (1976).
26. Cawley, 1993, *Federal Land, Western Anger.*
27. Klyza and Sousa, 2008, *American Environmental Policy.*
28. Williss, 1985, *"Do Things Right the First Time."*
29. Udall, 1988, *Too Funny to Be President.*
30. Shabecoff, 1980, "Andrus Prohibits Coal Strip Mining."
31. McElfish and Beier 1990, *Environmental Regulation of Coal Mining.*
32. Stern, 1976, *The Buffalo Creek Disaster.*
33. Montrie, 2003, *To Save the Land and People.*
34. Ibid.
35. Rosenbaum, 1989, *Environmental Politics and Policy.*
36. Montrie, 2003, *To Save the Land and People.*

37. Hayes, 1992, *Incrementalism and Public Policy.*

38. Menzel, 1983, "Redirecting the Implementation of a Law."

39. Omang and Behr, 1981, "Rules Freeze."

40. Hayes, 1992, *Incrementalism and Public Policy.*

41. US Environmental Protection Agency, 2001, Douglas M. Costle interview.

42. In a well-publicized memo to Reagan's transition team, Stockman wrote: "A cradle to grave hazardous waste control system under RCRA will take effect in 1981 at an annual cost of up to $2 billion. While prudent national waste disposal standards are clearly needed, the RCRA system is a *monument to mindless excess:* it treats degreasing fluids and PCBs in the same manner; and the proposed standards for generators, transporters and disposers, along with relevant explanations and definitions, encompass more than 500 pages of the Federal Register" (Stockman and Kemp, 1980, "Avoiding an Economic Dunkirk," emphasis in original).

43. Carnes, 1982, "Confronting Complexity and Uncertainty."

44. Landy et al., 1990, *The Environmental Protection Agency*.

45. Knight, 1980, "Toxic Wastes Hurriedly Dumped."

46. Cutler, 1981, Memorandum to President Carter, "Proposed Executive Order Re Export of Hazardous Substances," January 14 (JCL: Staff Offices-Cutler, box 74).

47. The order required the State Department to work with the Commerce Department to identify substances to be placed on the Commodity Control List. Anticipating industry objections, it provided for the Commerce Department to "consult with affected industries" and "consider the likely effects of proposed controls on the export performance of the U.S. before imposing controls." It also contained language to "assure that trade secrets or other confidential commercial or financial information are not disclosed to foreign governments," unless authorized by law (See Cutler, 1981, Memorandum).

48. White House Office of the Press Secretary, "President Reagan's Initiatives to Reduce Regulatory Burdens," February 18, 1981. Copy in author's possession.

49. A. Allan Hill, Letter to Natural Resources Defense Council, November 23, 1982, WHORM: Subject File, NR-CEQ, Ronald Reagan Presidential Library.

50. Implementation was a point of controversy because the policy threatened to create tension between the federal government and the states. The law required states to enforce the building efficiency standards, but according to Robert B. Reich, who conducted the regulatory review, half the states had no building codes in 1979. Therefore the federal government would have required the states to enforce federal standards, or it had to enforce federal standards directly. See Aderman, 1979, "Energy Standards for New Buildings."

51. President Jimmy Carter, Proclamation 4813 (January 13, 1981), *The American Presidency Project* (online), http://www.presidency.ucsb.edu/ws/?pid=44498.

52. President Ronald Reagan, Proclamation 4820 (February 17, 1981), *The American Presidency Project* (online), http://www.presidency.ucsb.edu/ws/?pid=43421.

53. Stockman claimed: "Three thousand pages of appliance efficiency standards scheduled for implementation in thirteen categories of home appliances in 1981 . . . threaten to create

multi-billion dollar havoc in the appliance industry" (Stockman and Kemp, 1980, "Avoiding an Economic Dunkirk").

54. Council on Wage and Price Stability, 1980, "Background Memorandum on the Department of Energy's Proposed Energy Efficiency Standards for Consumer Products," July 25 (JCL: Domestic Policy Staff-Government Reform, Bernick 1).
55. Meier, 1985, *Regulation*.
56. Joan Claybrook, NTHSA administrator, interview with author, October 18, 2010.
57. Nivola, 1986, *Politics of Energy Conservation*.
58. Holsendolph, 1981, "Miss Claybrook Initiates 2 Rules."
59. Claybrook interview, 2010.
60. Eula Bingham, OSHA administrator, interview with author, December 14, 2010.
61. Bingham interview, 2010.
62. Bingham interview, 2010.
63. In 1986, following the deadly chemical release in Bhopal, OSHA began to require complete workplace inspections on every tenth visit. In 1988 the records-only inspection rule was abandoned after a worker in Illinois died of cyanide poisoning. The manufacturing plant had not received a full inspection because of its prior above-average safety record. See Blosser, 1992, *Primer on Occupational Safety*.
64. Ibid.
65. Noble, 1989, *Liberalism at Work.*
66. Lofgren, 1989, *Dangerous Premises.*
67. Council on Wage and Price Stability, 1976, "Council Criticizes OSHA Approach to Reducing Occupational Noise Exposure," September 22 (JCL: CEA-Shultze 59).
68. Memorandum, Nina Cornell to Charles Schultze, "OSHA's Noise Standard," February 1977 (JCL: CEA-Schultze 59).
69. Katherine Bernick, 1980, Memorandum to Stuart Eizenstat, "OSHA's Noise Standard," December 12 (JCL: FG 21–5).
70. Ibid.
71. Barringer, 1981, "Job Noise Rules Stretched."
72. Bingham interview, 2010.
73. Bernick, 1980, Memorandum to Stuart Eizenstat.
74. Bingham interview, 2010
75. Weinstein, 1981, "Disputed Work-Hazards Film to Air."
76. Ibid.
77. Bingham interview, 2010.
78. McDowell, 1982, "Government Car Guide."
79. Claybrook interview, 2010.
80. McDowell, 1982, "Government Car Guide."
81. Cannon, 1981, "U.S. Rules Frozen 60 Days."
82. Stockman, 1981, Memorandum for the President.

83. The lone exception was a standard for automobile rear-window visibility, proposed before the Carter Administration left office. The auto industry opposed the rule bitterly, and it was never reconsidered (Claybrook interview, 2010).
84. Davis, 1993, *Energy Politics*.
85. Stockman, 1981, Memorandum for the President.
86. Vice President George H. W. Bush, "Statement Regarding Actions Taken by the President's Task Force on Regulatory Relief," letter to business groups, March 25, 1981, OA 9588, Robert Carleson Files, Ronald Reagan Presidential Library.
87. *Motor Vehicle Manufacturers Association v. State Farm*, 1983.

Chapter 4

1. Furlong, 1995, "The 1992 Regulatory Moratorium."
2. Domestic Policy Council, "Memorandum on Federal Preemption of State Food and Drug Regulations," July 27, 1988.
3. Quoted in McAllister, 1988, "White House Rejects Request."
4. Anderson, 1990, *Revolution*.
5. See Nathan, 1983, *The Administrative Presidency*; also Durant, 1992, *Administrative Presidency Revisited*.
6. Fishel, 1985, *Presidents and Promises*.
7. Pfiffner, 1983, "The Carter-Reagan Transition."
8. Prominent among reports provided by the interest groups and think tanks was the Heritage Foundation's 1980 *Mandate for Leadership*, which contained 1,270 specific recommended actions for the administration.
9. Pfiffner, 1983, "The Carter-Reagan Transition."
10. Nathan, 1983, *The Administrative Presidency*.
11. Heclo, 1983, "One Executive Branch or Many?" 45.
12. Lewis, 2008, *Politics of Presidential Appointments*.
13. McGarity and Shapiro, 1993, *Workers at Risk*.
14. Ibid.
15. Cawley, 1993, *Federal Land, Western Anger*.
16. Quoted in "Justices Uphold Strip Mining Curbs Opposed by Watt," *New York Times*, June 16, 1981, B9.
17. McCurdy, 1986, "Environmental Protection."
18. The MMS undertook surveying and leasing operations formerly housed within the BLM, the US Geological Survey, and the Bureau of Indian Affairs. Therefore the new agency's emphasis was on revenue generation, rather than on environmental protection (Dickinson, 2011, "The Presidency and the Executive Branch").
19. Moe, 1985, "The Politicized Presidency."
20. White House Office of the Press Secretary, "President Reagan's Initiatives to Reduce Regulatory Burdens," February 18, 1981. Copy in author's possession.

21. They included sexual harassment guidelines issued by the Equal Opportunity Employment Commission, Title IX athletics directives for women's athletic programs and hiring discrimination guidelines, Rehabilitation Act guidelines to ensure building access for people with disabilities, the EPA's lead phasedown program, and CPSC standards prohibiting flammable material in children's sleepwear.
22. Raines, 1981, "U.S. Begins Deregulation Review."
23. Anderson, 1990, *Revolution*.
24. Ibid., 261.
25. Untermeyer, 1997, "Looking Forward."
26. See Hockstader, 1988, "Judge Lifts Development Ban."
27. Shabecoff, 1989, "Interior Dept. Acts."
28. Ibid.
29. Ibid.
30. Shabecoff, 1988. "U.S. May Open Some Parklands to Coal Mining."
31. Durant, 1992, *Administrative Presidency Revisited*.
32. Heritage Foundation, 1980, "Mandate for Leadership."
33. James Watt, Memo to Reagan, "Withdrawal of Wilderness," OA 11833, Meese 39, Folder "James G. Watt-Interior," Ronald Reagan Library.
34. Ibid.
35. Soden and Steel, 1999, "Evaluating the Environmental Presidency."
36. Bosso, 1997, "Seizing Back the Day."
37. Russakoff, 1982, "Watt Agrees to Postpone."
38. Montrie, 2003, *To Save the Land and People*.
39. Dennis G. Rice, policy and regulatory analyst, US Department of Interior, Office of Surface Mining, Reclamation and Enforcement, interview with author, December 23, 2010.
40. McCurdy, 1986, "Environmental Protection."
41. Shabecoff, 1988, "U.S. May Open Some Parklands to Coal Mining."
42. Keith Schneider, 1992a, "Campaign Concerns."
43. Powell, 1999, *Science at EPA*.
44. Bryner, 1995, *Blue Skies, Green Politics*.
45. Ibid.
46. Markey, 1988, "Letters."
47. Vig, 2006, "Presidential Leadership and the Environment."
48. Rassmusen, 1997, "Managing Hazardous Waste."
49. MacKerron, 1989, "Has OMB Been Out of Bounds on EPA?"
50. See Fishel, 1985, *Presidents and Promises*, for a discussion of Reagan's bureaucracy bashing.
51. Richard H. Thaler and Cass R. Sunstein cite OSHA's hazard communication standard as an exemplary use of information to "nudge" individuals and firms as an alternative to the coercion of command-and-control regulation. See Thaler and Sunstein, 2008, *Nudge*.
52. OSHA considered publishing a proposed lockout standard before Reagan took office, as it had done with other regulations that were still under development. The administrator

of OSHA during the Carter Administration, Eula Bingham, felt the necessary work of building political consensus for a rule had not been completed. These activities included dialogues with workers, consultation with Congress, and working with the news media to inform the public better (Eula Bingham, interview with author, December 14, 2010).

53. Swoboda, 1988, "OSHA Rule Delays."
54. Swoboda, 1989, "U.S. Issues Safety Standards for Machinery."
55. Thaler and Sunstein, 2008, *Nudge*.
56. Schroeder and Nelson, 1986, "Drug Testing."
57. Ibid.
58. Sensitive positions were defined as those previously designated as critical/sensitive positions, or having access to classified information, presidential appointees, law enforcement personnel, and "other positions that the agency head determines involve law enforcement, national security, the protection of life and property, public health or safety, or other functions requiring a high degree of trust and confidence." See Thompson et al., 1991, "Drug Testing in the Federal Workplace."
59. Wicker, 1988, "Rescuing the Drug Bill."
60. Nash, 1988, "Rail Safety Proponents Dismayed."
61. Thompson et al., 1991, "Drug Testing in the Federal Workplace."
62. Because of industry complaints that such warnings depressed sales of ground beef, the new rule allowed "calcium" to be listed as an ingredient instead (Tolchin, 1983, "The Rush to Deregulate").
63. Havemann, 1986, "How Prime Forces of Government Killed a Cutback."
64. Eads and Fix, 1984, *Relief or Reform*.

Chapter 5

1. Rauch, 1991, "The Regulatory President."
2. Bryner, 1995, *Blue Skies, Green Politics*.
3. George H. W. Bush, "Remarks at Dedication Ceremony for Social Science Complex at Princeton University in Princeton, N.J.," May 10, 1991, *The American Presidency Project* (online), http://www.presidency.ucsb.edu/ws/?pid=19573.
4. Tiefer, 1994, *Semi-Sovereign Presidency*.
5. Ibid.
6. Quoted in MacKerron, 1989, "Has OMB Been Out of Bounds on EPA?"
7. McGarity and Shapiro, 1993, *Workers at Risk*.
8. Victor, 1991, "Quayle's Quiet Coup."
9. Berry and Portney, 1995, "Centralizing Regulatory Control."
10. Duffy, 1996, "Divided Government and Institutional Combat."
11. Friedman, 1995, *Regulation in the Reagan-Bush Era*.
12. Henry Waxman, "Opening Statement, Business Meeting Regarding the Contempt Resolu-

tion," Committee on Oversight and Government Reform, U.S. House of Representatives (June 20, 2008), *http://oversight-archive.waxman.house.gov/documents/20080620121418.pdf*.

13. Woodward and Broder, 1992, "Quayle's Quest."
14. Germond and Witcover, 1991, "Bush Resisting Domestic Policy Debate."
15. Carcasson, 2004, "Global Gridlock."
16. Friedman, 1995, *Regulation in the Reagan-Bush Era.*
17. Letter, Ken Lay to President George H. Bush, March 30, 1992, ID# 320118, HE007-01, WHORM: Subject File, Bush Presidential Records, George Bush Presidential Library.
18. Furlong, 1995, "The 1992 Regulatory Moratorium."
19. Weisskopf and Lippman, 1992, "From Fumes to Water."
20. At the time, vapor traps were required only in those cities with the worst air quality.
21. Keith Schneider, 1993, "U.S. Court Orders Gas-Vapor Traps."
22. Weisskopf and Lippman, 1992, "From Fumes to Water."
23. Furlong, 1995, "The 1992 Regulatory Moratorium."
24. Keith Schneider, 1992b, "President's Strip-Mining Plan."
25. Ibid.
26. Letter, President George H. W. Bush to Richard Cheney, December 3, 1991, ID# 294506, NR 004, WHORM: Subject File, Bush Presidential Records, George Bush Presidential Library.
27. Ede Holiday, 1991, Memo to John Sununu.
28. Robert E. Grady, Memo to George H. W. Bush, "Governor Hickel and Alaska Issues," January 8, 1993, WHORM: Subject File, NR 004, Bush Presidential Records, George Bush Presidential Library.
29. Rosen, 1992, "Bush Exempts Alaska."
30. Kenworthy, 1992, "Bush Air, Wetlands Proposals."
31. Keith Schneider, 1992a, "Campaign Concerns Prompt."
32. US Representative Henry Waxman, quoted in Triano and Walzman, 1991, *All the Vice President's Men.*
33. Cohen, 1992, *Washington at Work.*
34. Bryner, 1995, *Blue Skies, Green Politics,* 191; on policy fatigue see Bailey, 1998, *Congress and Air Pollution.*
35. Quoted in Duffy, 1996, "Divided Government and Institutional Combat."
36. Friedman, 1995, *Regulation in the Reagan-Bush Era.*
37. Weisskopf, 1992, "Administration Considers Weaker Protections."
38. Ibid.
39. Noah, 1993a, "EPA Declares 'Passive' Smoke a Human Carcinogen."
40. The complete phase-out exceeded even the standard recommended by the Montreal Protocol.
41. Noah, 1993b, "EPA Sets Rules."
42. Ramsden, 1997, "Vehicle Inspection/Maintenance."

43. Bryner, 1995, *Blue Skies, Green Politics*.
44. Ibid.
45. "Ban Is Urged on Cigarette Smoke in Public Places," 1992.
46. US Environmental Protection Agency, 1993, *Respiratory Health Effect*.
47. Noah, 1993b, "EPA Declares 'Passive' Smoke a Human Carcinogen."
48. For example, the *Washington Times* ran editorials accusing the agency of acting from political correctness and of questioning the science by (perhaps willingly) confusing measures of significance with confidence intervals.
49. Epstein, "Ronald McDonald vs. Joe Camel."
50. Kamen and Swoboda, 1993, "Bush Angers Organized Labor."
51. National Institute for Occupational Safety and Health, 1979, *Criteria for a Recommended Standard*.
52. Sheldon Weiner, "Oversight of the Occupational Safety and Health Administration" (testimony), Labor and Human Resources Committee, U.S. Senate Hearing, 100th Congress, *Congressional Record* 100-719 (April 18, 19, and 20, 1988). Weiner, 1988, "Oversight of the Occupational Safety and Health Administration."
53. John Moran, "Oversight of the Occupational Safety and Health Administration" (testimony), Labor and Human Resources Committee, U.S. Senate Hearing, 100th Congress, *Congressional Record* 100-719 (April 18, 19, and 20, 1988).
54. The testimony included other evidence of the administration's indifference. As Moran explained, when NIOSH wanted to produce a public service announcement on the risks of confined space work, the Department of Health and Human Services refused to clear the spot for production, even though it had widespread support and popular "Karate Kid" actor Ralph Macchio had offered his time "free of charge."
55. Victor, 1992, "Is the Honeymoon Over?"
56. Ibid.
57. A Reagan Administration proposal to relax hours-of-service rules in 1981 was withdrawn because it failed its cost-benefit test.
58. Hamilton, 1992, "Hours of Service Proposal."
59. Jennings, "Bridge Repaired After I-270 Crash."
60. DOT officials complained that the torrent of interest group–generated postcards urged them to reject the rule but lacked content that might have helped them improve it.
61. Friedman, 1995, *Regulation in the Reagan-Bush Era,* 173.

Chapter 6

1. Goldstein, 2001, "Last-Minute Spin."
2. Kagan, 2001, "Presidential Administration."
3. Turner, 2009, *Roadless Rules*.
4. Morriss et al., 2003, "Between a Rock and a Hard Place."

5. Landers, 2001, "Sprint to the Finish."
6. Cannon et al., 2001, "The Long Goodbye."
7. F.R. 66 (January 24, 2001): 7702.
8. Vig, 2006, "Presidential Leadership and the Environment."
9. Ibid.
10. Fiorino, 2006, *The New Environmental Regulation.*
11. Kagan, 2001, "Presidential Administration."
12. Mike Dombeck, USFS director, interview with author, January 6, 2011.
13. Kagan, 2001, "Presidential Administration."
14. Kelley, 2010, "Unitary Executive."
15. Kagan, 2001, "Presidential Administration."
16. Leshy, 2001, "Babbitt Legacy."
17. Between the enactment of the CRA in March 1996 and the March 2001 reversal of the ergonomics rule, resolutions of disapproval for twelve other regulations were introduced in Congress. None was successful, and most died in committee. See Rosenberg, 2008, *Congressional Review of Agency Rulemaking*
18. See, for example, Cloud, 1993, "Clinton's Energy Tax Plan."
19. Loring and Roth, 2005, "After Midnight."
20. Kagan, 2001, "Presidential Administration," 2296.
21. Quoted in Broder, 2007, "A Legacy Bush Can Control."
22. The forty directives in 1999–2000 exceeded the number Clinton issued during any equivalent period of his presidency (Cannon et al., 2001, "The Long Goodbye").
23. Greg Schneider, 2000, "Government Issues Guide on Contractors."
24. Bert Rockman noted that the unilateral actions put forth at the end of Clinton's term were all popular policies: "How, exactly, will President Bush explain why he is suspending a last-minute Agriculture Department regulation requiring meat-packing plants to conduct regular testing for listeria, a bacteria responsible for killing 21 Americans?" (quoted in Cannon et al., 2001, "The Long Goodbye").
25. Leshy, 2001, "Babbitt Legacy."
26. Rossi, 2001, "Bargaining in the Shadow."
27. Clinton, 2001, "Remarks on Action to Preserve America's Forests," 18.
28. Klyza and Sousa, 2008, *American Environmental Policy*.
29. Monument creation intensified at the very end of his final year. During January 2001, in his last three weeks as president, Clinton created or expanded nine national monuments (see Ranchod, 2001, "Clinton National Monuments").
30. Hahn et al., 2003, "Environmental Regulation during the 1990s."
31. Jehl, 2001b, "Gold Miners Eager."
32. Rothenberg, 2002, *Environmental Choices.*
33. Leshy, 2001, "Babbitt Legacy."
34. Dombeck interview, 2011.

35. F.R. 43 Part 2090, "Mining Claims under the General Mining Laws" (November 21, 2000): 69999.
36. See Jehl, 2001b, "Gold Miners Eager."
37. On Earth Day, 2004, Jeffords made a statement on the Senate floor that summarized his frustrations: "This Bush administration has a growing credibility gap, maybe even a credibility chasm, on environmental policy. The President has lost the trust of the American people when it comes to the environment." *Congressional Record* 50, Part 6 (April 20–May 4, 2004): 7179–80.
38. Morgan, 2001, "New Mining Regulations."
39. Turner, 2009, *Roadless Rules.*
40. Ibid.
41. Dombeck interview, 2011.
42. Dombeck et al., 2003, *From Conquest to Conservation.*
43. Hays, 2009, *The American People, the National Forests.*
44. Dombeck, 1999, Memorandum to Personnel.
45. Hays, 2009, *The American People, the National Forests.*
46. Dombeck interview, 2011.
47. Ibid.
48. The Wyoming Timber Industry Association immediately challenged the moratorium in US District Court, beginning more than a decade of litigation over the rule (Turner, 2009, *Roadless Rules*).
49. Dombeck interview, 2011.
50. William J. Clinton, Remarks at George Washington National Forest, Virginia, October 13, 1999, *The American Presidency Project* (online), http://www.presidency.ucsb.edu/ws/?pid=56702.
51. Bill Supulski, planning specialist, USDA Forest Service, interview with author, December 20, 2010.
52. Klyza and Sousa, 2008, *American Environmental Policy.*
53. Clinton, 2001, "Remarks on Action to Preserve America's Forests," 18.
54. *Kootenai Tribe of Idaho v. Veneman*, 142 F. Supp. 2d 1231 (D. Idaho 2001).
55. Quoted in Turner, 2009, *Roadless Rules.*
56. Supulski interview, 2010.
57. US Department of Agriculture News Release, "Agriculture Secretary Vilsack Announces Interim Directive Governing Roadless Areas in National Forests," Document 0185.09, May 28, 2009.
58. National Park Service, 2000, "Winter Use Plan."
59. Nie, 2008, *Governance of Western Lands.*
60. Stein, 2000, "Snowmobile Ban Set."
61. F.R. 68 (December 11, 2003): 69,268.
62. Nie, 2008, *Governance of Western Lands.*

63. In another example of serial midnight rulemaking, the Bush Administration proposed its own more industry-friendly rule at the end of 2008 (see chapter 7).
64. Graham, 2007, "The Evolving Regulatory Role."
65. Lee and Revkin, 2003, "E.P.A. Plans Crackdown."
66. Janofsky, 2004, "Tougher Emission Rules."
67. Jehl, 2001a, "EPA to Abandon New Limits."
68. Andrews, 2006, "Risk-Based Decision-Making," 225.
69. Pew Research Center, 2001, "Tepid Opposition."
70. Sutton, 2003, "The George W. Bush Administration and the Environment."
71. Nesmith and Haurwitz, 2001, "Pipe Owners' Clout."
72. The *Austin American-Statesman* reported that Hutchison received $290,777 and Breaux received $148,873 from petroleum interests between 1996 and 2000 (see Nesmith and Haurwitz, 2001, "Pipe Owners' Clout").
73. National Transportation Safety Board, 1998, Pipeline Accident Summary Report, Lively, Texas.
74. Nesmith and Haurwitz, 2001, "Pipe Owners' Clout."
75. The 1996 law exempted several places of ecological and historical value, including sites of previous pipeline leaks. Among them were Pennsylvania's John Heinz National Wildlife Refuge, the site of a 170,000-gallon crude oil spill in 2000; Florida's Big Cypress wetland, where a pipeline had leaked 150,000 gallons of crude oil since the 1970s; and the *USS Arizona* Memorial at Pearl Harbor, which was briefly closed to tourists in 1996 when a corroded oil pipeline dumped 36,000 gallons of fuel into the water (Nesmith and Haurwitz, 2001, "Pipe Owners' Clout").
76. National Transportation Safety Board, 2002, Pipeline Accident Summary Report, Bellingham, Washington.
77. Richard C. Wilson, "The Reauthorization of the Natural Gas Pipeline Safety Act and the Hazardous Liquid Pipeline Safety Act" (testimony), Commerce Committee, Subcommittee on Energy and Power, U.S. House of Representatives, *Congressional Record* 55-139 (February 3, 1999).
78. Senator Patty Murray introduced a bill to restore the requirement from the 1992 law that pipelines be tested every five years. Murray's bill also gave states the right to impose safety requirements that exceeded federal standards, making it the strictest of three competing Senate bills. The Clinton Administration offered an alternate pipeline safety bill, which was announced by Vice President Gore and introduced into the Senate by Ernest Hollings of South Carolina. The administration bill restored the testing requirement, with the stipulation that testing be conducted with the Best Achievable Technology, which the industry also opposed.
79. US General Accounting Office, 2000, Report to the Ranking Minority Member.
80. Frances Coyner, Testimony before US Senate Committee on Energy, May 19, 2000.
81. National Transportation Safety Board, 2003, Pipeline Accident Summary Report, Carlsbad, New Mexico.

82. Cohn, 2001, "New Jersey Senators Mollified."
83. Ibid.
84. National Energy Policy Development Group, 2001, "Reliable, Affordable."
85. Jordan Barab, deputy assistant secretary of labor for occupational safety and health, interview with author, February 14, 2011.
86. F.R.64, Part 1910, "Ergonomics Program; Proposed Rule," November 23, 1999, 65768.
87. Barab interview, 2011.
88. John Morall, OMB, interview with author, November 23, 2010.
89. Barab interview, 2011.
90. Jeffress, 2001, "Exit Interview."
91. Rossi, 2001, "Bargaining in the Shadow."
92. Prah, 2001, "Bush Will Take Aim."
93. George W. Bush, Statement of Administration Policy, S.J. Res.6: Joint Resolution of Disapproval of Ergonomics Regulation, March 6, 2001, *The American Presidency Project* (online).
94. Quoted in Espo, 2001, "Senate Votes to Repeal Ergonomics Rules."
95. Skrzycki, 2001, "Ergonomics Hearings Planned."
96. Loring and Roth, 2005, "After Midnight."
97. Marshall Whitenton, "A Rush to Regulate: The Congressional Review Act and Recent Federal Regulations" (testimony), Committee on Government Reform, Subcommittee on Energy Policy, Natural Resources and Public Affairs, U.S. House of Representatives, 107th Congress, *Congressional Record* 75-850 (March 27, 2001).
98. Jack, 2002, "Comment: Taking Care."
99. Loring and Roth, 2005, "After Midnight."
100. Rossi, 2001, "Bargaining in the Shadow."

Chapter 7

1. Robert F. Kennedy Jr., "Midnight Rulemaking: Shedding Some Light" (testimony), Committee of the Judiciary, Subcommittee on Commercial and Administrative Law, U.S. House of Representatives, 111th Congress, *Congressional Record* 47-33, February 4, 2009.
2. Smith, 2008, "A Last Push to Deregulate."
3. Warshaw, 2009, *Co-Presidency of Bush and Cheney*.
4. Daynes and Sussman, 2010, *White House Politics and the Environment*.
5. Abramowitz and Mufson, 2007, "Papers Detail Industry's Role."
6. "Uncertainty about future environmental controls is of particular concern for companies that operate existing coal power plants," the task force final report stated. "In addition, rules related to discharges to streams and coolingwater intake structures, possible regulation of large-volume wastes as hazardous wastes, uncertainty over rules requiring air permits for certain modifications to power plants. . . . This regulatory uncertainty discourages power

producers from building coal power plants." National Energy Policy Development Group. 2001. "Reliable, Affordable, and Environmentally Sound," chapter 5, 13–14.

7. Warshaw, 2009, *Co-Presidency of Bush and Cheney.*
8. Skrzycki, 2005, "OMB to Reconsider Some Rules."
9. West, 2004, "Formal Procedures, Informal Processes."
10. Andrews, 2006, "Risk-Based Decision-Making."
11. Rozell and Sollenberger, 2009, "Executive Privilege."
12. Henry Waxman, "Opening Statement, Business Meeting Regarding the Contempt Resolution," Committee on Oversight and Government Reform, U.S. House of Representatives (June 20, 2008), *http://oversight-archive.waxman.house.gov/documents/20080620121418.pdf*.
13. Goldenberg, 2008, "President for More than 60 Days," 3.
14. Tankersley, 2008, "Bush Angers Environmentalists."
15. Smith, 2008, "A Last Push to Deregulate."
16. Lovely and Grim, 2008, "Bush Fights to Loosen Fishery Rules."
17. The provision to block new species listings in FY 1995 was inserted into a supplemental spending bill (HR 889—PL 104–6). The takings bill (HR 9) failed to overcome a threatened filibuster in the Senate. See "Environmental Laws Face Revisions," 1995.
18. Union of Concerned Scientists, "Scientific Integrity in Policymaking," February 2004, http://www.ucsusa.org.
19. "More Sadness for Appalachia," 2008.
20. Tankersley, 2009, "Obama Overrides Bush."
21. "More Sadness for Appalachia," 2008.
22. Montrie, 2003, *To Save the Land and People*.
23. Ibid.
24. Surface Mining Control and Reclamation Act, 1977.
25. Cited in Office of Surface Mining, 2003, *25th Anniversary of the Surface Mining Law*. Others have placed the estimate closer to 2000 miles (Kennedy, 2009, "Hope in the Mountains.")
26. See Buffer Zone Rule, http://www.osmre.gov/resources/Ref/Pub/EIS/osm-eis-34.pdf.
27. See "More Sadness for Appalachia," 2008. The *Charleston Gazette* also published a series of reports on this important decision and its consequences: http://wvgazette.com/static/series/mining.
28. Dennis G. Rice, policy and regulatory analyst, US Department of Interior, Office of Surface Mining, Reclamation and Enforcement, interview with author, December 23, 2010.
29. Ibid.
30. Hughes, 2009, "Obama Seeks to Reverse."
31. By some estimates, oil shale development would require between two and five barrels of water for each barrel of oil produced. Nonetheless, the previous Congress passed the Oil Shale, Tar Sands, and Other Strategic Unconventional Fuels Act of 2005. Section 369 of the law encourages oil shale mining to meet increasing energy demands.
32. Quoted in Tankersley, 2008, "Bush Angers Environmentalists."

33. Riccardi and Tankersley, 2009, "Salazar Cancels Bush-Era Energy Leases."

34. A proposal to allow concealed weapons in national parks developed during his second term was controversial. Some interest groups considered this a way to improve the quality of the parks. The policy was later enacted into law in a compromise bill passed by Congress during the Obama Administration.

35. Clayton, 2008, "Why National Parks."

36. *North Carolina v. EPA US d*, D.C. Circuit, 05–1244, December 23, 2008.

37. Clayton, 2008, "Why National Parks."

38. Quoted in Eilperin, 2008a, "Clean-Air Rules."

39. Ibid.

40. Barringer, 2008, "Effort to Relax Pollution Limits."

41. Ibid.

42. The first published story regarding the "secret rule" appeared in the *Washington Post*: Leonnig, 2008, "U.S. Rushes to Change Workplace Toxin Rules."

43. Available at http://www.reginfo.gov.

44. Quoted in Leonnig, 2008, "U.S. Rushes to Change Workplace Toxin Rules."

45. Susan E. Dudley, director, Office of Information and Regulatory Affairs, interview with author, September 3, 2010./

46. Barab interview, 2011.

47. Margaret P. Seminario, "The Secret Rule: Impact of the Department of Labor's Worker Health Risk Assessment Proposal" (testimony). Committee on Education and Labor, U.S. House of Representatives, 110th Congress, *Congressional Record* 43-628 (September 17, 2008).

48. Miller and Kennedy, 2008, Letter to Elaine Chao.

49. In a blog entry titled "Secret Rule on OSHA Risk Assessment?" former MHSA official Celeste Monforton wrote, "I found the most curious item on OMB OIRA's webpage today, and my paranoia about end-of-the-term mischief by the Bush Administration kicked into high gear. The item is listed as a proposal rule submitted to OIRA for review on July 7. . . . Could this be OIRA's Susan Dudley teaming up with Labor Secretary Chao for a last-ditch effort to impose their anti-worker, anti-public health philosophy on OSHA and MSHA rulemaking on health hazards?" (Pump Handle Blog, July 8, 2008, http://www.thepumphandle.worpress.com).

50. Sapien, 2008, "Bush Forces Deregulation."

51. Seminario, "The Secret Rule."

52. Senator Barack Obama, Letter to Elaine Chao, Secretary of Labor, September 17, 2008, http://defendingscience.org/sites/default/files/upload/Obama-to-Chao-on-RS-Rule-Sept-17-2008.pdf.

53. Pear, 2008, "Bush Aides Rush to Enact a Rule."

54. 74 F.R. 44795–44797 (Aug. 31, 2009).

55. See *Building and Constr. Trades Dept., AFL-CIO v. Brock*, 838 F. 2d 1258, 1264–65 (D.C. Cir. 1987), cited in 74 F.R. 44795–44797 (Aug. 31, 2009).

56. Skrzycki, 2005, "OMB to Reconsider Some Rules."
57. Rahm Emmanuel, "Memorandum: Regulatory Review," 74 F.R. 4435–4436 (Jan. 20, 2009).

Chapter 8

1. Center for Progressive Reform, *Twelve Crucial Health, Safety, and Environmental Regulations: Will the Obama Administration Finish in Time?* (Washington, DC: Center for Progressive Reform, 2011), http://www.progressivereform.org/articles/12rules_1106.pdf.
2. Savage, 2012, "Shift on Executive Power."
3. Abramowitz, 2011, "Expect Confrontation."
4. Alter, 2010, *The Promise*.
5. Center for American Progress, 2012, "The Power of the President."
6. Ibid.
7. Ibid., 7.
8. Calmes, 2011, "Obama Announces Backing."
9. Eisner, 1993, *Regulatory Politics in Transition.*
10. President Barack Obama, Memorandum, "Establishing Policies for Addressing Workplace Violence Concerns in the Federal Workforce," April 18, 2012, http://www.whitehouse.gov/sites/default/files/docs/2012domesticviolence_mem_rel.pdf, accessed May 5, 2012.
11. White House Office of the Press Secretary, "We Can't Wait," April 18, 2012, *http://www.whitehouse.gov/the-press-office/2012/04/18/we-cant-wait-president-signs-memorandum-establishing-policies-addressing*, accessed May 5, 2012.
12. Johnson, 2010, "In the West."
13. Loring and Roth, 2005, "After Midnight."
14. Eisner, 1993, *Regulatory Politics in Transition*.
15. Cannon et al., 2001, "The Long Goodbye."
16. Quoted in Eilperin, 2001, "Republicans Target 45 Regulations."
17. Leshy, 2001, "Babbitt Legacy."
18. The only withdrawn NHTSA rule that was not revisited was a standard for rear-window visibility.
19. Cooper, 2002, *By Order of the President*.
20. Howell and Mayer, 2005, "Last One Hundred Days."
21. Morriss et al., 2003, "Between a Rock and a Hard Place."
22. Ibid.
23. Beermann, 2003, "Presidential Power in Transitions."
24. Lowi, 1987, "Two Roads to Serfdom."
25. Morriss et al., 2003, "Between a Rock and a Hard Place."
26. The term "free bird" has been applied to second-term presidents; see Cunion, 2005, "Second-Term Presidents."

References

Sources consulted at the Jimmy Carter Library, Atlanta, Georgia, are indicated as JCL, with folder, file, and/or box number.

Abramowitz, Alan I. 2011. "Expect Confrontation, Not Compromise: The 112th House of Representatives Is Likely to Be the Most Conservative and Polarized House in the Modern Era." *PS: Political Science and Politics* 44 (2): 293–96.

Abramowitz, Michael, and Steven Mufson. 2007. "Papers Detail Industry's Role in Cheney's Energy Report." *Washington Post,* July 18, A1.

Aderman, Gary. 1979. "Energy Standards for New Buildings—An Exercise in Futility?" *National Journal* 8 (June 30): 1083–85.

Alter, Jonathan. 2010. *The Promise: President Obama's First Year.* New York: Simon and Schuster.

Anderson, Martin. 1990. *Revolution: The Reagan Legacy,* 2nd ed. Stanford, Calif.: Hoover Institution.

Andrews, Richard N. L. 2006. "Risk-Based Decision-Making: Policy, Science and Politics." In *Environmental Policy: New Directions for the Twenty-First Century,* 6th ed., edited by Norman J. Vig and Michael E. Kraft, 215–38. Washington, DC: Congressional Quarterly Press.

Bailey, Christopher J. 1998. *Congress and Air Pollution.* Manchester, UK: Manchester University Press.

"Ban Is Urged on Cigarette Smoke in Public Places." 1992. *New York Times,* June 11, A20.

Barringer, Felicity. 1981. "Job Noise Rules Stretched to Cover More Ears" *Washington Post,* August 21, A27.

_____. 2008. "Effort to Relax Pollution Limits Is Dropped." *New York Times,* December 11, A34.

Beermann, Jack M. 2003. "Presidential Power in Transitions." *Boston University Law Review* 83 (5): 947–1017.

Bernick, Katherine. 1980. Memorandum to Stuart Eizenstat. "OSHA's Noise Standard." December 12. (JCL: FG 21–5.)

Berry, Jeffrey M. 1984. *The Interest Group Society.* Boston: Little, Brown and Company.

Berry, Jeffrey M., and Kent E. Portney. 1995. "Centralizing Regulatory Control and Interest Group Access: The Quayle Council on Competitiveness." In

Interest Group Politics, 4th ed., edited by Allan J. Cigler and Burdett A. Loomis. Washington, DC: Congressional Quarterly Press.

Blosser, Fred. 1992. *Primer on Occupational Safety and Health.* Washington, DC: Bureau of National Affairs.

Bolten, Joshua H. 2008. "Issuance of Agency Regulations at the End of the Administration." Memo to Heads of Executive Departments and Agencies. May 9. http://www.ombwatch.org/files/regs/PDFs/BoltenMem0050908.pdf.

Bosso, Christopher J. 1997. "Seizing Back the Day: The Challenge of Environmental Activism in the 1990s." In *Environmental Policy in the 1990s,* 3rd ed., edited by Norman J. Vig and Michael E. Kraft, 53–74. Washington, DC: Congressional Quarterly Press.

Brito, Jeremy, and Veronique de Rugy. 2008. "Midnight Regulations and Regulatory Review." Working Paper 08–34, Mercatus Center, George Mason University. Fairfax, Va.

Broder, John M. 2007. "A Legacy Bush Can Control." *New York Times,* September 9, A1.

Bryner, Gary C. 1995. *Blue Skies, Green Politics: The Clean Air Act of 1990 and Its Implementation,* 2nd ed. Washington, DC: Congressional Quarterly Press.

"Bush Administration Pushes their Final Environment and Energy Policies." 2008. *Washington Post,* December 19, A1.

Cahn, Matthew A. 1995. *Environmental Deceptions.* Albany: SUNY Press.

Calavita, Kitty. 1983. "The Demise of the Occupational Safety and Health Administration: A Case Study in Symbolic Action." *Social Problems* 30 (4): 437–48.

Calmes, Jackie. 2011. "Obama Announces Backing for Energy-Efficiency Initiative." *New York Times,* December 2, A1.

Cannon, Carl M., Chris Cillizza, and Margaret Kriz. 2001. "The Long Goodbye." *National Journal* 33 (January 27): 274.

Cannon, Lou. 1981. "U.S. Rules Frozen 60 Days." *Washington Post,* January 30, A1.

Carcasson, Martin. 2004. "Global Gridlock: The American Presidency and the Framing of International Environmentalism, 1988–2000. In *Green Talk in the White House,* edited by Tarla Rai Peterson. College Station: Texas A&M University Press.

Card, Andrew H. Jr. 2001. "Memorandum for the Heads and Acting Heads of Executive Departments and Agencies; Subject: Regulatory Review Plan." 66 F.R. 7702 (January 24).

Carnes, Sam A. 1982. "Confronting Complexity and Uncertainty: Implementation of Hazardous Waste Management Policy." In *Environmental Policy Implementation,* edited by Dean E. Mann. Lexington, Mass.: Lexington Books.

Carson, Rachel. 1962 (rev. 2002). *Silent Spring.* Boston: Houghton Mifflin.

Caudill, Harry M. 1962 (rev. 1963). *Night Comes to the Cumberlands.* Boston: Little, Brown.

Cawley, R. McGreggor. 1993. *Federal Land, Western Anger: The Sagebrush Rebellion and Environmental Politics.* Lawrence: University of Kansas Press.

Center for American Progress. 2010. "The Power of the President: Recommendations to Advance Progressive Change," by Sarah Rosen Wartell and John Podesta. November 15. http://www.americanprogress.org/issues/2010/11/executive_orders.html.

Clayton, Mark. 2008. "Why National Parks, Coal-Fired Power Plants May be Neighbors." *Christian Science Monitor,* April 24, 13.

Clinton,William J. 2001. "Remarks on Action to Preserve America's Forests." January 5. *Public Papers of the President.* Online at John T. Wooley and Gerhard Peters, *The American Presidency Project,* http://www.presidency.ucsb.edu/ws/?pid=62844. Santa Barbara, California.

Cloud, David S. 1993. "Clinton's Energy Tax Plan Hit by Blast of Cold Air." *Congressional Quarterly Weekly Report,* February 27, 450–51.

Cochran, Jay III. 2001. "The Cinderella Constraint: Why Regulations Increase Significantly during Post-Election Quarters." Working Paper. Arlington, Va.: Mercatus Center, George Mason University.

Cohen, Richard E. 1992. *Washington at Work: Back Rooms and Clean Air.* New York: Macmillan.

Cohn, Peter. 2001. "New Jersey Senators Mollified; Pipeline Safety Bill Approved." *Congressional Quarterly Daily Monitor,* February 8.

Coleman, Randy. 2001. "Gov. Bob Wise: Devastating Floods Could Have Been Much Worse." *Charleston Gazette,* August 5, 2A.

Cooper, Phillip J. 2002. *By Order of the President.* Lawrence: University Kansas Press.

Council on Wage and Price Stability. 1976. "Council Criticizes OSHA Approach to Reducing Occupational Noise Exposure." CWPS-187, September 22. (JCL: CEA-Schultze 59.)

_____. 1980. "Background Memorandum on the Department of Energy's Proposed Energy Efficiency Standards for Consumer Products." (JCL: Domestic Policy Staff-Government Reform, Bernick 1.)

Cunion, William. 2005. "Second-Term Presidents: Free Birds or Lame Ducks?" In *The Public Domain: Presidents and the Challenges of Leadership,* ed. Lori Cox and Diane Heith, 113–40. Albany: SUNY Press.

Cutler, Lloyd. 1981. Memorandum to President Carter, "Proposed Executive Order Re Export of Hazardous Substances." January 14. (JCL: Staff Offices-Cutler, box 74.)

Daynes, Byron W., and Glen Sussman. 2010. *White House Politics and the Environment.* College Station: Texas A&M University Press.

Davis, David H. 1993. *Energy Politics,* 4th edition. New York: St. Martin's Press.
Derthick, Martha, and Paul J. Quirk. 1985. *The Politics of Deregulation.* Washington, DC: Brookings.
Dickinson, Matthew J. 2011. "The Presidency and the Executive Branch." In *New Directions in the American Presidency,* edited by Lori Cox Han. New York: Routledge.
Dombeck, Michael P. 1999. Memorandum to Personnel of the US Forest Service. December 29. Available at USFS Roadless Area Document Archive, www.fs.usda.gov/Internet/FSE_DOCUMENTS/stelprdb5137329.pdf.
Dombeck, Michael P., Christopher A. Wood, and Jack E. Williams. 2003. *From Conquest to Conservation.* Washington, DC: Island Press.
Dudley, Susan E. 2001. "Reversing Midnight Regulations." *Regulation,* Spring, 9.
Duffy, Robert J. 1996. "Divided Government and Institutional Combat: The Case of the Quayle Council on Competitiveness." *Polity* 28 (3): 379–99.
Durant, Robert F. 1992. *The Administrative Presidency Revisited: Public Lands, the BLM, and the Reagan Revolution.* Albany: SUNY Press.
Eads, George C., and Michael Fix. 1984. *Relief or Reform: Reagan's Regulatory Dilemma.* Washington, DC: Urban Institute.
Edelman, Murray. 1964. *The Symbolic Uses of Politics.* Urbana: University of Illinois Press.
Edwards, George C. III, and Stephen J. Wayne. 1999. *Presidential Leadership,* 5th ed. New York: St. Martin's.
Eilperin, Juliet. 2001. "Republicans Target 45 Regulations to Overturn." *Washington Post,* April 8, A1.
_____. 2008a. "Clean-Air Rules Protecting Parks Set to Be Eased." *Washington Post,* May 16, A01.
_____. 2008b. "EPA Moves to Ease Air Rules for Parks; Regional Administrators Decry Decision." *Washington Post* November 19, A06.
Eisner, Marc Allen. 1993. *Regulatory Politics in Transition.* Baltimore: Johns Hopkins University Press.
Eisner, Marc Allen, Jeff Worsham, and Evan J. Ringquist. 2006. *Contemporary Regulatory Policy,* 2nd ed. Boulder, Colo.: Lynne Reinner.
"Environmental Laws Face Revisions." 1995. *Congressional Quarterly Weekly Report* 53 (24): 1698–1701 (June 17).
Epstein, Bruce A. 1993. "It's Ronald McDonald vs. Joe Camel in the Smoking Debate." *St. Petersburg Times,* April 24, D4.
Epstein, David, and Sharyn O'Halloran. 1999. *Delegating Powers.* Cambridge: Cambridge University Press.
Espo, David. 2001. "Senate Votes to Repeal Ergonomics Rules." *ABC News,* March 6. http://abcnews.go.com.

Fahrentold, David A. 2008. "Bush Administration Pushes Their Final Environment and Energy Policies." *Washington Post,* December 19, A1.

Fiorino, Daniel J. 2006. *The New Environmental Regulation.* Cambridge, Mass.: MIT Press.

Fix, Michael, and George C. Eads. 1985. "Regulatory Reform: The Legacy of Reagan's First Term." *Yale Journal on Regulation* 2: 293.

Fishel, Jeff. 1985. *Presidents and Promises: From Campaign Pledge to Presidential Performance.* Washington, DC: Congressional Quarterly Press.

Friedman, Barry D. 1995. *Regulation in the Reagan-Bush Era.* Pittsburgh: University of Pittsburgh Press.

Fuchs, Edward P. 1988. *Presidents, Management and Regulation.* Englewood Cliffs, N.J.: Prentice Hall.

Furlong, Scott R. 1995. "The 1992 Regulatory Moratorium: Did It Make a Difference?" *Public Administration Review* 55 (3): 254–62.

_____. 1997. "Interest Group Influence on Rule Making." *Administration and Society* 29 (3): 325–47.

_____. 2005. "Exploring Interest Group Participation in Executive Policymaking." In *The Interest Group Connection,* 2nd ed., edited by Paul S. Herrnson, Ronald G. Shaiko, and Clyde Wilcox. Washington, DC: Congressional Quarterly Press.

_____. 2007. "Business and the Environment." In *Business and Environmental Policy: Corporate Interests in the American Political System,* edited by Michael E. Kraft and Sheldon Kamieniecki, 155–84. Cambridge, Mass.: MIT Press.

Garrett, R. Sam, James A. Thurber, A. Lee Fritschler, and David H. Rosenbloom. 2006. "Assessing the Impact of Bureaucracy Bashing by Electoral Campaigns." *Public Administration Review* 66 (2): 228–40.

Germond, Jack W., and Jules Witcover. 1991. "Bush Resisting Domestic Policy Debate." *National Journal* 23 (August 31): 2109.

Golden, Marissa M. 1998. "Interest Groups in the Rule-Making Process: Who Participates? Whose Voices Get Heard?" *Journal of Public Administration Research and Theory* 8 (2): 245–70.

Goldenberg, Suzanne. 2008. "President for More than 60 Days, Bush Tearing Apart Protection for America's Wilderness." *Guardian,* November 20, 3.

Goldstein, Amy. 2001. "Last-Minute Spin on Regulatory Rite." *Washington Post,* June 9, A1.

Graham, John D. 2007. "The Evolving Regulatory Role of the U.S. Office of Management and Budget in Regulatory Policy." *Journal of Environmental Economics and Policy* 1 (2): 171–91.

Greider, William. 1982. *The Education of David Stockman and Other Americans.* New York: Dutton.

Hahn, Robert W., Sheila M. Olmstead, and Robert N. Stavins. 2003. "Environmental Regulation during the 1990s: A Retrospective Analysis." *Harvard Environmental Law Review* 27 (2): 377–415.

Hamilton, Alexander, James Madison, and John Jay. 2003. *The Federalist Papers,* edited by Charles Kesler. New York: Penguin.

Hamilton, Dane. 1992. "Hours of Service Proposal Divides Trucking Group." *Journal of Commerce,* October 27, 3B.

Havemann, Judith 1986. "How Prime Forces of Government Killed a Cutback." *Washington Post,* July 8, A7.

Hayes, Michael T. 1992. *Incrementalism and Public Policy.* New York: Longman.

Hays, Samuel P. 2009. *The American People, the National Forests.* Pittsburgh: University of Pittsburgh Press.

Heclo, Hugh. 1978. "Issue Networks and the Executive Establishment." In *The New American Political System,* edited by Anthony King. Washington, DC: American Enterprise Institute.

_____. 1983. "One Executive Branch or Many?" In *Both Ends of the Avenue,* edited by Anthony King, 26–58. Washington, DC: American Enterprise Institute.

Heinz, John P., Edward O. Laumann, Robert L. Nelson, and Robert H. Salisbury. 1993. *The Hollow Core: Private Interests in National Policymaking.* Cambridge, Mass.: Harvard University Press.

Hill, A. Allan. 1982. Letter to Natural Resources Defense Council. November 23. (JCL: Natural Resources-CEQ, box 1.)

Hockstader, Lee. 1988. "Judge Lifts Development Ban on Over 170 Million Acres." *Washington Post,* November 5, A2.

Holiday, Ede. 1991. Memo to John Sununu, September 13. George Bush Presidential Library, College Station, Texas, Domestic Policy and Council on Competitiveness, ID# 41304.

Holsendolph, Ernset. 1981. "Miss Claybrook Initiates 2 Rules Before Leaving Auto Safety Post." *New York Times,* January 26, A20.

Howell, William G. 2003. *Power without Persuasion: The Politics of Direct Presidential Action.* Princeton, N.J.: Princeton University Press.

Howell, William G., and Kenneth Mayer. 2005. "The Last One Hundred Days." *Presidential Studies Quarterly* 35 (3): 533–53.

Hughes, Siobhan. 2009. "Obama Seeks to Reverse Mountaintop-Mining Rule." *Wall Street Journal,* April 28, A1.

Hyatt, Deborah. 1980. Memo to Stuart Eizenstat, November 12. (JCL: Domestic Policy Staff, Hyatt 21.)

Jack, William M. 2002. "Comment: Taking Care that Presidential Oversight of the Regulatory Process Is Faithfully Executed." *Administrative Law Review* 54 (3): 1479–1517.

Janofsky, M. 2004. "Tougher Emission Rules Set for Big Diesel Vehicles." *New York Times.* May 10, A1.

Jeffress, Charles N. 2001. "Exit Interview." *Industrial Safety and Health News,* February 1. http://www.ishn.com/articles/charles-jeffress-8217-s-exit-interview.

Jehl, Douglas. 2001a. "EPA to Abandon New Limits for Arsenic in Water Supply." *New York Times,* March 21, A1.

_____ . 2001b. "Gold Miners Eager for Bush to Roll Back Clinton Rules." *New York Times,* August 16, A1.

Jennings, Veronica T. 1992. "Bridge Repaired after I-270 Crash." *Washington Post,* October 21, F1.

Johnson, Karen S. 1986. "The Portrayal of Lame-Duck Presidents by the National Print Media." *Presidential Studies Quarterly* 16 (1): 50–65.

Johnson, Kirk. 2010. "In the West, 'Monument' Is a Fighting Word." *New York Times,* February 20, A8.

"Justices Uphold Strip Mining Curbs Opposed by Watt." 1981. *New York Times,* June 16, B9.

Kagan, Elena. 2001. "Presidential Administration." *Harvard Law Review* 114: 2245–2385.

Kamen, Al, and Frank Swoboda. 1993. "Bush Angers Organized Labor by Naming Meat Company Official to Job-Safety Panel." *Washington Post,* January 18, A27.

Kamieniecki, Sheldon. 2006. *Corporate America and Environmental Policy.* Palo Alto, Calif.: Stanford University Press.

Kelley, Christopher S. 2010. "The Unitary Executive and the Clinton Administration." In *The Unitary Executive and the Modern Presidency,* edited by Ryan J. Barilleaux and Christopher S. Kelley, 107–22. College Station: Texas A&M Press.

Kennedy, Robert F. Jr. 2009. "Hope in the Mountains." *Washington Post,* March 25, A15.

Kenworthy, Tom. 1992. "Bush Air, Wetlands Proposals Likely to Die" *Washington Post* (Dec. 15): A10.

Kerwin, Cornelius M. 2003. *Rulemaking: How Government Agencies Write Law and Make Policy,* 3rd ed. Washington, DC: Congressional Quarterly Press.

Kingdon, John A. 1995. *Agendas, Alternatives and Public Policies.* Ann Arbor: University of Michigan Press.

Klotz, Robert J. 1997. "On the Way Out: Interregnum Presidential Activity." *Presidential Studies Quarterly* 27 (2): 320–32.

Klyza, Christopher McGrory, and David Sousa. 2008. *American Environmental Policy, 1990–2006.* Cambridge, Mass.: MIT Press.

Knight, Michael. 1980. "Toxic Wastes Hurriedly Dumped Before New Law Goes into Effect." *New York Times,* Nov. 15, A1.

Landers, Jim. 2001. "Sprint to the Finish." *Dallas Morning News,* January 6, 1A.

Landy, Marc K., Mark J. Roberts, and Stephen R. Thomas. 1990. *The Environmental Protection Agency: Asking the Wrong Questions.* New York: Oxford University Press.

Lee, J., and A. Revkin. 2003. "E.P.A. Plans Crackdown on Dirty Diesel Engines." *New York Times,* April 16, A1.

Leonnig, Carol D. 2008. "U.S. Rushes to Change Workplace Toxin Rules." *Washington Post,* July 23, A1.

Leshy, John. 2001. "The Babbitt Legacy at the Department of the Interior: A Preliminary View." *Environmental Law* 31 (2): 199–228.

Lewis, David E. 2003. *Presidents and the Politics of Agency Design.* Palo Alto, Calif.: Stanford University Press.

_____. 2008. *The Politics of Presidential Appointments.* Princeton, N.J.: Princeton University Press.

Light, Paul C. 1999. *The President's Agenda: Domestic Policy Choice from Kennedy to Reagan,* 3rd ed. Baltimore: Johns Hopkins University Press.

Lofgren, Don J. 1989. *Dangerous Premises.* Ithaca, N.Y.: ILR Press.

Loring, Jason M., and Liam R. Roth. 2005. "After Midnight: The Durability of the Midnight Regulations Passed by the Two Previous Outgoing Administrations." *Wake Forest Law Review* 40 (4): 1441–65.

Lovely, Erika, and Ryan Grim. 2008. "Bush Fights to Loosen Fishery Rules." *Politico,* December 9. http://www.politico.com/news/stories/1208/16321.html.

Lowi, Theodore. 1987. "Two Roads to Serfdom: Liberalism, Conservatism and Administrative Power." *American University Law Review* 36 (1): 295–322.

Lubbers, Jeffrey S. 2006. *A Guide to Federal Agency Rulemaking,* 4th ed. Chicago: American Bar Association.

MacKerron, Conrad B. 1989. "Has OMB Been Out of Bounds on EPA?" *Chemical Week,* March 22, 8.

Markey, Edward J. 1988. "Letters: Mr. Bush on the Environment." *Washington Post,* September 8, A20.

Mayer, Kenneth. 2001. *With the Stroke of a Pen.* Princeton, N.J.: Princeton University Press.

McAllister, Bill. 1988. "White House Rejects Request on Food Labeling." *Washington Post,* July 28, A12.

McCurdy, Howard E. 1986. "Environmental Protection and the New Federalism: The Sagebrush Rebellion and Beyond." In *Controversies in Environmental Policy,* edited by Sheldon Kamieniecki, Robert O'Brien, and Michael Clarke, 85–107. Albany: SUNY Press.

McDowell, Edwin. 1982. "Government Car Guide Is Published Secretly." *New York Times,* December 15, A15.

McElfish, James. M. Jr., and Anne E. Beier. 1990. *Environmental Regulation of Coal Mining: SMCRA's Second Decade.* Washington, DC: Environmental Law Institute.

McGarity, Thomas O., and Sidney A. Shapiro. 1993. *Workers at Risk: The Failed Promise of the Occupational Safety and Health Administration.* Westport, Conn.: Praeger.

McGinness, John O. 2001. "Regulatory Review as Constitutional Restoration." *Duke Law Journal* 51 (3): 901–61.

Meier, Kenneth J. 1985. *Regulation: Politics, Bureaucracy and Economics.* New York: St. Martin's.

______. 1987. *Politics and the Bureaucracy: Policymaking in the Fourth Branch of Government,* 2nd ed. Monterey, Calif.: Brooks-Cole.

Mendelson, Nina. 2003. "Agency Burrowing." *NYU Law Review* 78 (2): 557–675.

Menzel, Donald C. 1983. "Redirecting the Implementation of a Law: The Reagan Administration and Coal Surface Mining Regulation." *Public Administration Review* 43 (September–October): 411–20.

Miller, George, and Edward M. Kennedy. 2008. Letter to Elaine Chao, Secretary of Labor. July 10. http://edlabor.house.gov/letters/20080710GMChaoLetter.pdf.

Moe, Terry M. 1985. "The Politicized Presidency." In *New Directions in American Politics,* edited by John E. Chubb and Paul E. Peterson. Washington, DC: Brookings.

Montrie, Chad. 2003. *To Save the Land and People.* Chapel Hill: University of North Carolina Press.

"More Sadness for Appalachia" (editorial). 2008. *New York Times,* October 20, A28.

Morgan, Dan. 2001. "New Mining Regulations Overturn Late Clinton Rules." *Washington Post* (October 26): A33.

Morriss, Andrew P., Roger E. Meiners, and Andrew Dorchak. 2003. "Between a Rock and a Hard Place: Politics, Midnight Regulation, and Mining." *Administrative Law Review* 55 (2): 551–99.

Morrow, William S. Jr. 2001. "Midnight Regulations: Natural Order of Disorderly Governance." *Administrative and Regulatory Law News* 26 (3): 3–19.

Nash, Steve. 1988. "Rail Safety Proponents Dismayed over New Federal Drug Bill." *Christian Science Monitor,* October 25, A3.

Nathan, Richard P. 1983. *The Administrative Presidency.* New York: Wiley.

National Energy Policy Development Group. 2001. "Reliable, Affordable, and Environmentally Sound Energy for America's Future." http://www.pppl.gov/common_pages/national_energy_policy.html.

National Institute for Occupational Safety and Health. 1979. *Criteria for a Recommended Standard for Working in Confined Spaces.* Washington, DC: Department of Health, Education and Welfare Publication no. 80–106, December.

National Park Service. 2000. "Winter Use Plan: Record of Decision." F.R. 65 (November 22): 80, 908.

National Transportation Safety Board. 1998. Pipeline Accident Summary Report. Pipeline Rupture, Liquid Butane Release and Fire: Lively, Texas (November 6). NTSB/PAR-98/02/SUM: PB98–916503.

______. 2002. Pipeline Accident Summary Report. Pipeline Rupture and Subsequent Fire in Bellingham, Washington (October 8). NTSB/PAR-02/02: PB2002–916502.

______. 2003. Pipeline Accident Summary Report. Pipeline Rupture and Subsequent Fire in Carlsbad, New Mexico (February 11). NTSB/PAR-03/01: PB2003–916501.

Nesmith, Jeff, and Ralph K. Haurwitz. 2001. "Pipe Owners' Clout Imperils Land, Water." *Austin American-Statesman,* July 24, A1.

Neustadt, Richard E. 1991. *Presidential Power and the Modern Presidents: The Politics of Leadership from Roosevelt to Reagan,* 4th ed. New York: Free Press.

Nie, Martin 2008. *The Governance of Western Lands: Mapping Its Present and Future.* Lawrence: University of Kansas Press.

Nivola, Pietro S. 1986. *The Politics of Energy Conservation.* Washington, DC: Brookings.

Noah, Timothy. 1993a. "EPA Declares 'Passive' Smoke a Human Carcinogen." *Wall Street Journal,* January 6, B1.

_____. 1993b. "EPA Sets Rules, Some Independent of White House." *Wall Street Journal,* January 20, A14.

Noble, Charles. 1989. *Liberalism at Work: The Rise and Fall of OSHA.* Philadelphia, Penn.: Temple University Press.

O'Connell, Anne J. 2008. "Political Cycles of Rulemaking: An Empirical Portrait of the Modern Administrative State." *Virginia Law Review* 94 (4): 889–986.

Office of Surface Mining. 2003. *25th Anniversary of the Surface Mining Law.* Washington, D.C.: Office of Surface Mining.

Omang, Joanne, and Peter Behr. 1981. "Rules Freeze: Everyone Is Scrambling." *Washington Post,* January 31, A1.

"OSHA Issues Rules on Electrical Hazards and Noise in Workplace, Effective April." 1981. *Wall Street Journal,* January 14, A5.

Pear, Robert 2008. "Bush Aides Rush to Enact a Rule Obama Opposes." *New York Times,* November 30, A37.

Pew Research Center. 2001. "Tepid Opposition from Democrats, Little Fallout on Environment."(April 26). http://people-press.org/2001/04/26/bushs-base-backs-him-to-the-hilt.

Pfiffner, James P. 1983. "The Carter-Reagan Transition: Hitting the Ground Running." *Presidential Studies Quarterly* 13 (4): 623–45.

______. 1996. *The Strategic Presidency: Hitting the Ground Running,* 2nd ed. Lawrence: University Kansas Press.

______. 2005. *The Modern Presidency,* 4th ed. Belmont, Calif.: Thompson Wadsworth.

Powell, Mark R. 1999. *Science at EPA.* Washington, DC: Resources for the Future.

Power, Stephen, Elizabeth Williamson. and Christopher Conkey. 2008. "White House Pushes through a Flurry of Rule Changes Sought by Business." *Wall Street Journal,* November 20, A2.

Prah, Pamela M. 2001. "Bush Will Take Aim at Ergonomics Rule." *Kiplinger Business Forecast,* January 19.

Public Health Service. 1965. *Protecting the Health of 80 Million Americans.* Washington, DC: Government Printing Office.

Raines, Howell. 1981. "U.S. Begins Deregulation Review on Rights and Ecology Guidelines." *New York Times,* August 13, A1.

Ramsden, Todd. 1997. "Vehicle Inspection/Maintenance." In *Economic Analyses at EPA: Assessing Regulatory Impact,* edited by Richard Morgenstern, 333–63. Washington, DC: Resources for the Future.

Ranchod, Sanjay. 2001. "The Clinton National Monuments: Protecting Ecosystems with the Antiquities Act." *Harvard Law Review* 25: 535–89.

Rassmusen, Sara. 1997. "Managing Hazardous Waste." In *Economic Analysis at EPA,* edited by Richard A. Morgenstern, 233–66. Washington, DC: Resources for the Future.

Rattner, Steven. 1979. "Carter Announces Legislative Plan to Revise US Regulatory Process." *New York Times,* March 26, A1.

Rauch, Jonathan. 1991. "The Regulatory President." *National Journal* 23 (November 30): 2902–2906.

Riccardi, Nicholas, and Jim Tankersley. 2009. "Salazar Cancels Bush-Era Energy Leases in Utah." *Los Angeles Times,* February 5, A10.

Rogers, Paul, and Ron Hutcheson. 2001. "Clinton in Thick of Fight over Environmental Policy Transition." *San Jose Mercury-News,* January 6, A1.

Rose, Richard. 1991. *The Post-Modern President.* Chatham, N.J.: Chatham House.

Rosen, Yereth. 1992. "Bush Exempts Alaska from Policy to Stop Development on Wetlands." *Christian Science Monitor,* November 10, A7.

Rossi, Jim 2001. "Bargaining in the Shadow of Administrative Procedure: The Public Interest in Rulemaking Settlement." *Duke Law Journal* 51 (3): 1015–58.

Rosenbaum, Walter A. 1989. *Environmental Politics and Policy.* Washington, DC: Congressional Quarterly Press.

Rosenberg, Morton. 2008. *Congressional Review of Agency Rulemaking: An Update and Assessment of the Congressional Review Act after a Decade*. May 8. Washington, DC: Congressional Research Service Report for Congress.

Rothenberg, Lawrence. S. 2002. *Environmental Choices: Policy Responses to Green Demands*. Washington, DC: CQ Press.

Rozell, Mark J., and Mitchel A. Sollenberger. 2009. "Executive Privilege and the Unitary Executive Theory in the George W. Bush Administration." In *Rivals for Power: Presidential-Congressional Relations,* edited by James A. Thurber, 209–28. Lanham, Md.: Rowman and Littlefield.

Russakoff, Dale. 1982. "Watt Agrees to Postpone Relaxation of Strip-Mine Rules Pending Study." *Washington Post,* April 17, A7.

Sapien, Joaquin. 2008. "Bush Forces Deregulation in Waning Days of Administration." ProPublica, November 5, www.propublica.org/article/bush-foreces-deregulation-in-waning-days-of-administration.

Savage, Charlie. 2012. "Shift on Executive Power Lets Obama Bypass Rivals." *New York Times,* April 23, A1.

Scheberle, Denise 2004. *Federalism and Environmental Policy,* 2nd ed. Washington, DC: Georgetown University Press.

Schlozman, Kay Lehman, and John T. Tierney. 1986. *Organized Interests and American Democracy.* New York: Harper and Row.

Schneider, Greg. 2000. "Government Issues Guide on Contractors." *Washington Post,* December 20, A33.

Schneider, Keith 1992a. "Campaign Concerns Prompt White House to Drop Waste Plan." *New York Times,* September 30, A1.

_____. 1992b. "President's Strip-Mining Plan for National Parks Is Blocked." *New York Times,* October 3, A7.

_____. 1993. "U.S. Court Orders Gas-Vapor Traps for New Autos." *New York Times,* January 24, A24.

Schroeder, Patricia, and Andrea L. Nelson. 1986. "Drug Testing in the Federal Government." *Nova Law Review* 11: 685–91.

Shabecoff, Philip. 1980. "Andrus Prohibits Coal Strip Mining on 90,000 Acres Near Federal Park." *New York Times,* December 17, A20.

_____. 1988. "U.S. May Open Some Parklands to Coal Mining." *New York Times,* December 28, A1.

_____. 1989. "Interior Dept. Acts to Speed Sales of Public Lands for Development." *New York Times,* January 8, A1.

Shapiro, Stuart. 2007. "Why Do Agencies Change their Proposed Rules?" Paper presented at the Annual Meeting of the Association of Public Policy Analysis and Management. http://ssrn.com/abstract=1026066.

Shull, Steven. 2006. *Policy by Other Means.* College Station: Texas A&M University Press.

Skrzycki, Cindy. 2001. "Ergonomics Hearings Planned: Labor Dept. to Revisit Repetitive-Stress issue." *Washington Post,* June 7, E01.

_____. 2005. "OMB to Reconsider Some Rules." *Washington Post,* March 22, E01.

Smith, R. Jeffrey. 2008. "A Last Push to Deregulate." *Washington Post,* October 31, A1.

Soden, Dennis L., and Brent S. Steel. 1999. "Evaluating the Environmental Presidency." In *The Environmental Presidency,* edited by Dennis L. Soden. Albany: SUNY Press.

Speth, Gus. 1980. Memorandum, "Environmental Issues." (JCL: CEA-15.)

Stein, Diego. 2000. "Snowmobile Ban Set for '03 at 2 Parks." *Denver Post,* November 23, A1.

Stern, Gerald M. 1976. *The Buffalo Creek Disaster.* New York: Vintage.

Stockman, David. 1981. Memorandum for the President: Presidential Memorandum Postponing Federal Regulations. Fielding, 36F, WHORM: Subject File, Ronald Reagan Presidential Library.

Stockman, David, and Jack Kemp. 1980. "Avoiding a GOP Economic Dunkirk." *Washington Post,* December 14, C1.

Stone, Deborah. 2002. *Policy Paradox: The Art of Political Decisionmaking.* New York: Norton.

Sunstein, Cass R. 2002. "The Arithmetic of Arsenic." *Georgetown Law Journal* 90 (3): 2225–2304.

_____. "Is OSHA Unconstitutional?" *Virginia Law Review* 94 (September): 1407–49.

Sutton, Victoria. 2003. "The George W. Bush Administration and the Environment." *Western New England Law Review* 25 (1): 221–42.

Swoboda, Frank. 1988. "OSHA Rule Delays: Assessing Cost, Blame." *Washington Post,* April 41, A21.

_____. 1989. "U.S. Issues Safety Standards for Machinery." *Washington Post,*. September 2, C1.

Szasz, Andrew. 1984. "Industrial Resistance to Occupational Safety and Health Legislation: 1971–1981." *Social Problems* 32 (2): 103–16.

Tankersley, Jim. 2008. "Bush Angers Environmentalists with Last-Minute Rule Changes." *Los Angeles Times,* November 21, A1.

_____. 2009. "Obama Overrides Bush on Endangered Species Act." *Los Angeles Times,* March 4, A14.

Thaler, Richard H., and Cass R. Sunstein. 2008. *Nudge: Improving Decisions about Health, Wealth and Happiness.* New York: Penguin.

Thompson, Frank J., Norma M. Riccucci, and Carolyn Ban. 1991. "Drug Testing in the Federal Workplace: An Instrumental and Symbolic Assessment." *Public Administration Review* 51 (6): 515–25.

Tiefer, Charles. 1994. *The Semi-Sovereign Presidency: The Bush Administration's Strategy for Governing without Congress.* Boulder, Colo.: Westview Press.

Tolchin, Martin. 1983. "The Rush to Deregulate." *New York Times,* August 21, F34.

Triano, Christine, and Nancy Walzman. 1991. *All the Vice President's Men: How the Quayle Council on Competitiveness Secretly Undermines Health, Safety and Environmental Programs.* Washington, DC: OMB Watch–Public Citizen.

Turner, James M. 2006. "Conservation Science and Forest Service Policy for Roadless Areas." *Conservation Biology* 20 (3): 713–22.

Turner, Tom. 2009. *Roadless Rules: The Struggle for the Last Wild Forests.* Washington, DC: Island Press.

US Department of Agriculture. 2001. Press Conference on Roadless Areas Conservation Rule. May 4. USDA, Washington, DC.

US Environmental Protection Agency. 1993. *Respiratory Health Effect of Passive Smoking: Lung Cancer and Other Disorders.* Washington, DC: Environmental Protection Agency (January 6).

_____. 2001. Douglas M. Costle Oral History Interview, conducted August 4–5, 1996. EPA 202-K-01–002. http://www.epa.gov/history/publications/print/costle.htm.

US General Accounting Office. 2000. Report to the Ranking Minority Member of the House of Representatives, Committee on Commerce. "Pipeline Safety." GAO/RCED-00–128 (May).

Udall, Morris K. 1988. *Too Funny to Be President.* New York: Henry Holt.

Untermeyer, Chase. 1997. "Looking Forward: George Bush as Vice President." In *At the President's Side: The Vice President in the Twentieth Century,* edited by Timothy Walch, 157–75. Columbia: University of Missouri Press.

Victor, Kirk 1991. "Quayle's Quiet Coup." *National Journ*al 23 (July 6): 1676–80.

_____. 1992. "Is the Honeymoon Over?" *National Journal* 24 (January 25): 214–18.

Vig, Norman J. 2006. "Presidential Leadership and the Environment." In *Environmental Policy: New Directions for the Twenty-First Century,* 6th ed., edited by Norman J. Vig and Michael E. Kraft, 100–23. Washington, DC: Congressional Quarterly Press.

Warber, Adam. 2006. *Executive Orders and the Modern Presidency: Legislating from the Oval Office.* Boulder, Colo.: Lynne Rienner Publishers.

Ward, Ken III. 2001. "DEP Backs Off, Mine Citations." *Charleston Gazette,* July 13, 1A.

Warshaw, Shirley Anne. 1994. "The Carter Experience with Cabinet Government." In *The Presidency and Domestic Policies of Jimmy Carter,* edited by Herbert D. Rosenbaum and Alexej Ugrinsky, 375–86. Westport, Conn.: Greenwood.

______. 2009. *The Co-Presidency of Bush and Cheney.* Stanford, Calif.: Stanford University Press.

Webb Yackee, Susan. 2005. "Sweet-Talking the Fourth Branch: The Influence of Interest Group Comments on Federal Agency Rulemaking." *Journal of Public Administration Research and Theory* 16 (1):103–24.

Weinstein, Henry. 1981. "Disputed Work-Hazards Film to Air." *Los Angeles Times,* April 28, C1.

Weisskopf, Michael. 1992. "Administration Considers Weaker Protections for Unpolluted Air." *Washington Post,* October 29, A20.

Weisskopf, Michael, and Thomas W. Lippman 1992. "From Fumes to Water, Bush Is Flexing Regulatory Rules." *Washington Post,* March 7, A1.

West, William F. 1982. "The Politics of Administrative Rulemaking." *Public Administration Review* 42 (5): 420–26.

______. 2004. "Formal Procedures, Informal Processes, Accountability, and Responsiveness in Bureaucratic Policy Making: An Institutional Policy Analysis" *Public Administration Review* 64 (1): 66–80.

"White House Pushes Through a Flurry of Rule Changes Sought by Business." 2008. *Wall Street Journal,* November 20, A1.

Wicker, Tom. 1988. "Rescuing the Drug Bill." *New York Times,* October 25, A31.

Williss, Frank. 1985. *"Do Things Right the First Time": The National Park Service and the Alaska National Interest Lands Conservation Act of 1980.* Denver: NPS, September.

Woodward, Robert, and David S. Broder. 1992. "Quayle's Quest: Curb Rules, Leave 'No Fingerprints.'" *Washington Post,* January 9, A1.

Yates, Jeff, and Andrew Whitford. 2005. "Institutional Foundations of the President's Issue Agenda." *Political Research Quarterly* 58 (4): 577–85.

Index

Other Books in the Joseph V. Hughes Jr. and Holly O. Hughes Series on the Presidency and Leadership

The Politics of Shared Power: Congress and the Executive, Louis Fisher

Shaping and Signaling Presidential Policy: The National Security Decision Making of Eisenhower and Kennedy, Meena Bose

Games Advisors Play: Foreign Policy in the Nixon and Carter Administrations, Jean A. Garrison

The Managerial Presidency, James P. Pfiffner

Good Advice: Information and Policy Making in the White House, Daniel E. Ponder

Congressional Abdication on War and Spending, Louis Fisher

Vicious Cycle: Presidential Decision Making in the American Political Economy, Constantine J. Spiliotes

Presidents and the People: The Partisan Story of Going Public, Mel Laracey

The Opposition Presidency: Leadership and the Constraints of History, David A. Crockett

The Presidency, Congress, and Divided Government: A Postwar Assessment, R. S. Conley

The White House World: Transitions, Organization, and Office Operations, Martha Joynt Kumar and Terry Sullivan, eds.

Between Law and Politics: The Solicitor General and the Structuring of Race, Gender, and Reproductive Rights Litigation, Richard Pacelle Jr.

The Presidency and Women: Promise, Performance, and Illusion, Janet M. Martin

Out of Touch: The Presidency and Public Opinion, Michael J. Towle

Power and Prudence: The Presidency of George H. W. Bush, Ryan J. Barilleaux and Mark J. Rozell

The Character Factor: How We Judge America's Presidents, James P. Pfiffner

The Nerve Center: Lessons in Governing from the White House Chiefs of Staff, edited by Terry Sullivan; foreword by James A. Baker III

Nixon's Business: Authority and Power in Presidential Politics, Nigel Bowles

Saving the Reagan Presidency: Trust Is the Coin of the Realm, David M. Abshire

Policy by Other Means: Alternative Adoption by Presidents, Steven A. Shull

Institutionalizing Congress and the Presidency: The U.S. Bureau of Efficiency, 1916–1933, Mordecai Lee

Scripted for Change: The Institutionalization of the American Presidency, Victoria A. Farrar-Myers

The American Campaign: U.S. Presidential Campaigns and the National Vote, Second Edition, James E. Campbell

Running against the Grain: How Opposition Presidents Win the White House, David A. Crockett

Intelligence and National Security Policymaking on Iraq, James P. Pfiffner and Mark Phythian

Honest Broker? The National Security Advisor and Presidential Decision Making, John P. Burke

The Leadership of George Bush: An Insider's View of the Forty-first President, Roman Popadiuk

Bridging the Constitutional Divide: Inside the White House Office of Legislative Affairs, Russell L. Riley

The Unitary Executive and the Modern Presidency, Ryan J. Barilleaux and Christopher S. Kelley

The Provisional Pulpit: Modern Conditional Presidential Leadership of Public Opinion, Brandon Rottinghaus

White House Politics and the Environment: Franklin D. Roosevelt to George W. Bush, Byron W. Daynes and Glen Sussman

Nixon's Super-Secretaries: The Last Grand Presidential Reorganization Effort, Mordecai Lee

A Presidency Upstaged: The Public Leadership of George H. W. Bush, Lori Cox Han

Presidential Term Limits in American History: Power, Principles, and Politics, Michael J. Korzi

The Politics of the President's Wife, MaryAnne Borrelli

The Clinton Presidency and the Constitutional System, Rosanna Perotti

Prosecution among Friends: Presidents, Attorneys General, and Executive Branch Wrongdoing, David A. Yalof

Taking the Measure: The Presidency of George W. Bush, Kelley and Shields